中文
注释版

邂逅莎翁

莎士比亚阅读入门

莎士比亚美丽故事

Beautiful Stories from Shakespeare

Shakespeare

策　划　卞学华　刘慧敏　印　娜
主　编　居正华　强友芳　印　娜
副主编　王　芸　戚鸭玲　冯青韵
参　编　颜颖群　乔霖琳　孟瑞平　孙　娜
唐　淼　袁大梦　张　莎

华东理工大学出版社
EAST CHINA UNIVERSITY OF SCIENCE AND TECHNOLOGY PRESS
·上海·

图书在版编目(CIP)数据

邂逅莎翁：莎士比亚阅读入门：莎士比亚美丽故事：中文注释版：汉、英 / 居正华，强友芳，印娜主编. —上海：华东理工大学出版社，2023.5

ISBN 978-7-5628-7206-1

Ⅰ.①邂… Ⅱ.①居… ②强… ③印… Ⅲ.①英语-阅读教学-高中-教学参考资料 Ⅳ.①G634.413

中国国家版本馆 CIP 数据核字(2023)第 067588 号

策划编辑 / 舒欣如
责任编辑 / 梁 静
责任校对 / 金美玉
装帧设计 / 徐 蓉
出版发行 / 华东理工大学出版社有限公司
地址：上海市梅陇路 130 号，200237
电话：021-64250306
网址：www.ecustpress.cn
邮箱：zongbianban@ecustpress.cn
印　　刷 / 镇江恒华彩印包装有限责任公司
开　　本 / 787mm×1092mm 1/16
印　　张 / 15.5
字　　数 / 375 千字
版　　次 / 2023 年 5 月第 1 版
印　　次 / 2023 年 5 月第 1 次
定　　价 / 60.00 元

编者寄语
Introduction

莎士比亚是人类最伟大的天才之一，是人类文学奥林匹斯山上的宙斯。

——马克思

莎士比亚是时代的灵魂，他不只属于一个时代，而是属于千秋万代。

——本·琼森

关于莎士比亚，我们可以说，从他的作品里能够搜罗出一整套治国齐家的智慧。他为后来所有的作家所模仿；此外，从莎士比亚之后的所有作家身上搜集的理论知识或实用处世法则的总和，是否能够超过他一个人给予其国家的数量，至今依然是个疑问。

——塞缪尔·约翰逊

前事不忘，后事之师。众多英语专家学者都有这样一个共识：离开经典文学的英语学习路线是一种以实用主义为主导的路线，是近视而无远见的路线，是抄近路而反绕远的路线。这是他们在学习中受益于文学作品的真情实感，也充分体现出了经典文学在英语学习中的重要作用。著名翻译家梁实秋先生在推荐学生学英语时曾说，“先背诵莎士比亚的戏剧，再谈如何学习英语”。莎士比亚原著的语言对大多数读者来说可能较难理解，故编者选择了英国著名儿童文学作家伊迪丝·内斯比特(1858—1924)所改写的具有代表性的二十个故事，力求以浅显易懂的文字向读者展示莎士比亚戏剧的魅力。

要真正掌握一门语言，必须了解其所代表的文化，而要了解其文化，必须大量阅读以这种语言为载体的优秀文学作品。文学是语言的最高艺术形式，要学好语言，必须多读优秀的文学作品，这样无论是说话还是作文，才能有文采，才能有自己的风格，语言才不会索然无味。通过文学作品学习英语，容易从被动的接受状态转入主动欣赏的角色，而一旦进入欣赏的角色，也就自然进入了学习的角色。英语语言随着文学作品的思想情感和艺术形式直接印在脑海里，使人印象深刻，久久难以忘怀。

通过阅读英语经典文学名著学习英语，是掌握英语的绝佳方法，这已经是经过了数代英语学习者的实践检验而得出的真理。在阅读经典英语文学名著的过程中，既可以接触到原汁原味的英语，又能享受到文学阅读的愉悦，这对英语语感的形成大有裨益。一举多得，何乐而不为？你徜徉在英语文学的海洋中，英语也在不知不觉中提高了，无目的而达目的，正所谓“有意栽花花不开，无心插柳柳成荫”。

南宋诗论家严羽在《沧浪诗话》中说道：“学其上，仅得其中；学其中，斯为下矣。”可见，英语学习一定要放宽视野，定高标准，“入门须正，立志须高”，只有这样才能实现预期目标。莎士比亚作为欧洲文艺复兴时期人文主义的集大成者，作为西方文学史上一座不朽的丰碑，作为解读西方基本文化命题的精神源泉，他的作品在文学艺术等多个领域都产生了极其深远的影响，是全人类共同的宝贵精神财富。莎士比亚的语言精练优美、形式多样，笔下的人物及事理俱全、场景丰富，其语言的全面性和整体性优于其他形式的英文经典；同时，学习语言，“语”和“文”均不可偏废，莎翁剧作以人文对白为主，是“语”和“文”的高度融合，从莎翁剧作入手学习英语，“语”和“文”可以同时进步，这也是其他英文经典所不具备的。以此观之，英语学习从莎士比亚开始可谓绝妙途径。

明代著名思想家王阳明在回答"知识不长进,如何?"这一问题时曾经说道:"为学须有本原,须从本原上用力,渐渐盈科而进。"对于英语学习来说,其本原无非词汇和语法,而词汇的积累尤为重要,因为它往往是英语阅读的最大"拦路虎"。本书正是为了帮助读者扫除这一障碍,拿下"拦路虎"、啃下"硬骨头",实现无障碍阅读,最终能够进入英语阅读的"自由王国":详尽的词汇注解能帮助你扩充词汇量,从此轻松阅读原汁原味的英语;多样的英语同义词汇能丰富你的英语表达,从此写出纯正地道的英语;长难句语法分析能提升你的阅读理解能力,从此无惧冗长艰涩的英语。"求木之长者,必固其根本;欲流之远者,必浚其泉源",相信你经过努力最终可以走进莎士比亚的戏剧世界,领略其独一无二的丰富宝藏。

人对美的发掘是无穷的,人类对美的追求也是无止境的,所谓"爱美之心,人皆有之";相信只要能发现美,对英语的学习也就会变成对美的追求,这也应该是永无止境的。莎士比亚的戏剧情节生动丰富、跌宕起伏、扣人心弦,恩格斯也曾对其高度称赞。莎士比亚是英语语言的大师,他的语言珠辉玉润,其魅力夺魂摄魄,感染了你我、融化了观众,也改造了读者。莎士比亚的戏剧中刻画了几百个人物形象,个个栩栩如生;莎士比亚笔下的女性有的天生丽质,有的智慧超群,有的风姿绰约,一个个被刻画得生动细腻,仿佛就在眼前,美得超凡脱俗!

胸藏文墨虚若谷,腹有诗书气自华。多读经典名著能让人气质不凡,经典名著中的名言是书中的精华,莎士比亚的至理名言更是精华中的精华。莎士比亚富有人生哲理的经典语录,定能在你需要的时候为你指点迷津,给人以心灵的涤荡、精神的洗礼、情感的愉悦与升华和无穷无尽的人生启迪!

四百多年过去了,莎士比亚已然是神一般的存在,"人类文学奥林匹斯山上的宙斯"几乎是世界文学的共同信仰。莎士比亚是洞察人性与命运的大师,他的作品当中有历史的深刻、哲学的思辨、政治的机谋、心理学的洞察、诗人的浪漫。我相信,无论读者水平如何,都能从中发现引人入胜、令人不忍释卷的地方。希望读者能一遍遍地反复细读他的作品,你一定会领略到其中的无限精彩和无穷魅力!

人生苦短,譬如朝露;书海无涯,先读莎士比亚:一生一定要读一次莎士比亚!心灵若有他的灌溉,灵魂若有他的滋养,人生若有他的陪伴,他就一定会照亮你的生命,拓展心灵与生存的空间,同时让不可能的成为可能。读有些书,你或可跳着读;莎士比亚的美丽故事,你不必,也不舍:一行行、一句句、一篇篇,都是美的洗礼。

亲爱的读者朋友,值此莎士比亚诞辰459周年暨胡瑗(安定先生)诞辰1030周年之际,让我们一起跨越时空,步入英语经典文学的圣殿,走进《莎士比亚美丽故事》,邂逅莎翁,遇见更好的自己!读者服务与交流请关注微信公众号"邂逅莎翁",有声资源请在喜马拉雅搜索"邂逅莎翁:莎士比亚美丽故事"。

居正华

2023年4月23日

思源庭·安定书院·泰州(1226)

Ferdinand and Miranda：***THE TEMPEST***

腓迪南和米兰达：《暴风雨》

Titania and the Clown: ***A MIDSUMMER NIGHT'S DREAM***

提泰妮娅和小丑:《仲夏夜之梦》

Petruchio and Katharina: ***THE TAMING OF THE SHREW***

彼特鲁乔和凯瑟丽娜:《驯悍记》

Romeo and Juliet: ***ROMEO AND JULIET***

罗密欧和朱丽叶:《罗密欧与朱丽叶》

前言
Preface

The writings of Shakespeare have been justly① termed② "the richest, the purest, the fairest, that the genius uninspired③ ever penned④."[i]

Shakespeare instructed by delighting. His plays alone (leaving mere⑤ science out of the question), contain more actual wisdom than the whole body of English learning. He is the teacher of all good—pity, generosity, true courage, love. His bright wit is cut out "into little stars." His solid masses of knowledge are meted out⑥ in morsels⑦ and proverbs, and thus distributed⑧. There is scarcely⑨ a corner of the English-speaking world today which he does not illuminate⑩, or a cottage which he does not enrich.[ii] His bounty⑪ is like the sea, which, though often unacknowledged⑫, is everywhere felt. As his friend, Ben Jonson, wrote of him, "He was not of an age but for all time." He ever kept the high road of human life whereon⑬ all travel. He did not pick out bypaths⑭ of feeling and sentiment⑮. In his creations we have no moral highwaymen⑯, sentimental⑰ thieves, interesting villains⑱, and amiable⑲, elegant adventuresses⑳—no delicate㉑ entanglements㉒ of situation, in which the grossest㉓ images are presented to the mind disguised㉔ under the superficial㉕ attraction of style and sentiment.[iii] He flattered㉖ no bad passion, disguised

---

① justly [ˈdʒʌstli] *adv*. 理所应当地 rightly, correctly, properly
② term [tɜːm] *v*. 把……称为 name, label, describe as
③ uninspired [ˌʌnɪnˈspaɪəd] *adj*. 平凡的 ordinary, unimaginative
④ pen [pen] *v*. 写 write
⑤ mere [mɪə(r)] *adj*. 仅仅的 simple, pure
⑥ mete out: 分配 distribute, hand/share/deal out
⑦ morsel [ˈmɔːsl] *n*. 小部分,点滴 piece, part, bit, grain
⑧ distribute [dɪˈstrɪbjuːt] *v*. 分发 dispense, hand/give out
⑨ scarcely [ˈskeəsli] *adv*. 几乎不 hardly, barely, almost not
⑩ illuminate [ɪˈluːmɪneɪt] *v*. 照亮 light
⑪ bounty [ˈbaʊnti] *n*. 慷慨之举;大量给予之物 generous actions, abundance
⑫ unacknowledged [ˌʌnəkˈnɒlɪdʒd] *adj*. 未公开承认的 not publicly or officially recognized
⑬ whereon [weərˈɒn] *conj*. 在那上面 on which
⑭ bypath [ˈbaɪpɑːθ] *n*. 旁道;分支 indirect route, branch
⑮ sentiment [ˈsentɪmənt] *n*. 情绪 emotion
⑯ highwayman [ˈhaɪweɪmən] *n*. 拦路强盗 robber, bandit
⑰ sentimental [ˌsentɪˈmentl] *adj*. 多愁善感的 emotional
⑱ villain [ˈvɪlən] *n*. 恶棍 evildoer, rogue
⑲ amiable [ˈeɪmiəbl] *adj*. 和蔼可亲的 agreeable, lovable
⑳ adventuress [ədˈventʃəres] *n*. 女冒险家 female adventurer
㉑ delicate [ˈdelɪkət] *adj*. 微妙的 fine, subtle
㉒ entanglement [ɪnˈtæŋglmənt] *n*. 牵连 involvement
㉓ gross [grəʊs] *adj*. 令人不快的 nasty, offensive, disgusting
㉔ disguise [dɪsˈgaɪz] *v*. 伪装 camouflage
㉕ superficial [ˌsuːpəˈfɪʃl] *adj*. 肤浅的 shallow
㉖ flatter [ˈflætə(r)] *v*. 奉承 fawn, butter up

no vice① in the garb② of virtue, trifled with③ no just and generous principle.[iv] While causing us to laugh at folly④, and shudder⑤ at crime, he still preserves⑥ our love for our fellow-beings, and our reverence⑦ for ourselves.

Shakespeare was familiar with all beautiful forms and images, with all that is sweet or majestic⑧ in the simple aspects of nature, of that indestructible⑨ love of flowers and fragrance⑩, and dews, and clear waters—and soft airs and sounds, and bright skies and woodland solitudes⑪, and moonlight bowers⑫, which are the material elements of poetry—and with that fine sense of their indefinable⑬ relation to mental emotion, which is its essence⑭ and vivifying⑮ soul—and which, in the midst of⑯ his most busy and tragic⑰ scenes, falls like gleams⑱ of sunshine on rocks and ruins⑲—contrasting with all that is rugged⑳ or repulsive㉑, and reminding us of the existence of purer and brighter elements.[v]

These things considered, what wonder is it that the works of Shakespeare, next to the Bible, are the most highly esteemed㉒ of all the classics㉓ of English literature? "So extensively have the characters of Shakespeare been drawn upon㉔ by artists, poets, and writers of fiction㉕," says an American author—"So interwoven㉖ are these characters in the great body of English literature, that to be ignorant㉗ of the plot of these dramas is often a cause of embarrassment㉘."[vi]

But Shakespeare wrote for grown-up people, for men and women, and in words that little folks cannot understand.

---

① vice [vaɪs] *n*. 堕落，邪恶 evil, wickedness
② garb [gɑːb] *n*. 服装 clothes
③ trifle with: 戏弄；轻视 toy with
④ folly [ˈfɒli] *n*. 愚蠢 foolishness, stupidity, silliness, idiocy
⑤ shudder [ˈʃʌdə(r)] *v*. 发抖 shake, shiver, quiver, quake, tremble
⑥ preserve [prɪˈzɜːv] *v*. 维护；保持 keep, retain, maintain, conserve
⑦ reverence [ˈrevərəns] *n*. 尊敬 respect, honor, admiration
⑧ majestic [məˈdʒestɪk] *adj*. 壮丽的 grand, stately, magnificent
⑨ indestructible [ˌɪndɪˈstrʌktəbl] *adj*. 不可毁灭的 unbreakable
⑩ fragrance [ˈfreɪgrəns] *n*. 芳香 pleasant smell, scent, perfume
⑪ solitude [ˈsɒlɪtjuːd] *n*. 偏僻的地方 remote place
⑫ bower [ˈbaʊə(r)] *n*. 凉亭 summer house
⑬ indefinable [ˌɪndɪˈfaɪnəbl] *adj*. 难以解释的 inexpressible
⑭ essence [ˈesns] *n*. 本质 nature, core, substance
⑮ vivifying [ˈvɪvɪfaɪɪŋ] *adj*. 生机勃勃的 lively, spirited, dynamic
⑯ in the midst of: 当某事发生时 while sth. is happening or being done
⑰ tragic [ˈtrædʒɪk] *adj*. 悲惨的 sad, miserable, heartbreaking
⑱ gleam [gliːm] *n*. 一丝 ray, glimmer
⑲ ruins [ˈruːɪnz] *n*. 废墟 wreckage, debris
⑳ rugged [ˈrʌgɪd] *adj*. 崎岖的 rocky, rough, craggy, ragged
㉑ repulsive [rɪˈpʌlsɪv] *adj*. 令人厌恶的 foul, disgusting, offensive
㉒ esteemed [ɪˈstiːmd] *adj*. 受人尊敬的 respected, honored
㉓ classic [ˈklæsɪk] *n*. 经典作品，杰作 masterpiece
㉔ draw upon: 利用 use, apply, employ, utilize, make use of
㉕ fiction [ˈfɪkʃn] *n*. 小说 story, novel
㉖ interweave [ˌɪntəˈwiːv] *v*.（此处为过去分词用作形容词）交织 interlace, raddle
㉗ ignorant [ˈɪgnərənt] *adj*. 无知的 unaware, uninformed
㉘ embarrassment [ɪmˈbærəsmənt] *n*. 尴尬 awkwardness

Hence this volume①. To reproduce② the entertaining③ stories contained in the plays of Shakespeare, in a form so simple that children can understand and enjoy them, was the object had in view④ by the author of these Beautiful Stories from Shakespeare.

E. T. R.

ⅰ The writings of Shakespeare have been justly termed "the richest, the purest, the fairest, that the genius uninspired ever penned." 莎士比亚的著作一直被理所应当地称为"平凡天才写就的最丰富、最纯粹、最优美的作品"。

ⅱ His solid masses of knowledge are meted out in morsels and proverbs, and thus distributed. There is scarcely a corner of the English-speaking world today which he does not illuminate, or a cottage which he does not enrich. 他扎实渊博的知识也融入我们点点滴滴的日常生活和俗话谚语中,并因此广为流传。如今的英语世界中几乎没有一个角落不受到他的启发,没有一座茅屋村舍不因他而精彩。

ⅲ In his creations we have no moral highwaymen, sentimental thieves, interesting villains, and amiable, elegant adventuresses—no delicate entanglements of situation, in which the grossest images are presented to the mind disguised under the superficial attraction of style and sentiment. 在他的创作中,我们没有看到品行端正的拦路强盗、伤感的小偷、有趣的恶棍,以及和蔼而讲究的女冒险家——没有出现那种微妙纠结的场景,让最庸俗粗鲁的人出现在披着优雅伤感外衣、散发着肤浅魅力的聪明人面前。

ⅳ He flattered no bad passion, disguised no vice in the garb of virtue, trifled with no just and generous principle. 他没有吹捧不当的激情,不会以善的名义行恶,也不会戏讽正义而仁慈的原则。

ⅴ Shakespeare was familiar with all beautiful forms and images, with all that is sweet or majestic in the simple aspects of nature, of that indestructible love of flowers and fragrance, and dews, and clear waters—and soft airs and sounds, and bright skies and woodland solitudes, and moonlight bowers, which are the material elements of poetry—and with that fine sense of their indefinable relation to mental emotion, which is its essence and vivifying soul—and which, in the midst of his most busy and tragic scenes, falls like gleams of sunshine on rocks and ruins—contrasting with all that is rugged or repulsive, and reminding us of the existence of purer and brighter elements. 莎士比亚熟悉所有美丽的形式和意象,无论是甜美的还是宏伟的,全都存在于大自然的纯真面貌中,存在于对花草和芳香、露水、清泉等不可磨灭的爱中——除此之外,还有和风细语、晴朗的天空、寂寥的林地、月下的凉亭,这些都成了诗歌的素材。莎士比亚也熟悉它们与精神情感不可名状的微妙关系,而这正是他爱的本质和富有生机的灵魂。在他最混乱和悲剧性的场景中,它们的出现就像太阳的光芒洒在岩石和废墟上,与崎岖或可憎的一切形成鲜明的对比,提醒我们有更纯净和更明媚的事物存在。

ⅵ "So extensively have the characters of Shakespeare been drawn upon by artists, poets, and writers of fiction," says an American anthor—"So interwoven are these characters in the great body of English literature, that to be ignorant of the plot of these dramas is often a cause of embarrassment." 一名美国作家表示:"莎翁笔下的人物,被艺术家、诗人和小说家们广泛地引用。这些人物在英国文学作品中渗透得如此之深,以至于你如果不了解这些戏剧的情节,就往往会陷入窘境。"

---

① volume [ˈvɒljuːm] *n*. 书籍 book, work

② reproduce [ˌriːprəˈdjuːs] *v*. 再现 recreate

③ entertaining [ˌentəˈteɪnɪŋ] *adj*. 使人愉快的 interesting, amusing

④ have sth. in view: 心中有……目的(或打算等) have sth. in mind

写作由来
How the Stories Were Written

Anne Hathaway[1]'s Cottage

It was evening. The fire burned brightly in the inn[2] parlor[3]. We had been that day to see Shakespeare's house, and I had told the children all that I could about him and his work. Now they were sitting by the table, poring over[4] a big volume of the Master's plays, lent them by the landlord[5]. And I, with eyes fixed on[6] the fire, was wandering[7] happily in the immortal[8] dreamland peopled[9] by Rosalind[10] and Imogen[11], Lear[12] and Hamlet[13]. A small sigh roused[14] me —

"I can't understand a word of it," said Iris.

"And you said it was so beautiful," Rosamund added, reproachfully[15]. "What does it all mean?"

"Yes," Iris went on, "you said it was a fairy tale, and we've read three pages, and there's

---

① Anne Hathaway [æn ˈhæθəweɪ]：安妮·海瑟薇（莎翁之妻）
② inn [ɪn] *n*. 小旅馆 tavern
③ parlor [ˈpɑːlə(r)] *n*. 客厅 lounge, sitting/living room
④ pore over：认真研读 read sth. very carefully, examine
⑤ landlord [ˈlændlɔːd] *n*. 房东 house owner
⑥ fix on：盯住 focus/rivet on
⑦ wander [ˈwɒndə(r)] *v*. 漫游 roam, ramble, stroll
⑧ immortal [ɪˈmɔːtl] *adj*. 不朽的 eternal, perpetual
⑨ people [ˈpiːpl] *v*. 居住在 inhabit, occupy, populate
⑩ Rosalind [ˈrɒzəlɪnd]：罗瑟琳（莎士比亚《皆大欢喜》）
⑪ Imogen [ˈɪməʊdʒən]：伊摩琴（莎士比亚《辛白林》）
⑫ Lear [lɪə(r)]：李尔（莎士比亚《李尔王》）
⑬ Hamlet [ˈhæmlɪt]：哈姆莱特（莎士比亚《哈姆莱特》）
⑭ rouse [raʊz] *v*. 唤醒 arouse, awaken, wake up
⑮ reproachfully [rɪˈprəʊtʃfəli] *adv*. 责备地 rebukefully

nothing about fairies, nor even a dwarf, or a fairy godmother."

"And what does 'misgraffed①' mean?"

"And 'vantage②,' and 'austerity③,' and 'belike④,' and 'edict⑤,' and—"

"Stop, stop," I cried, "I will tell you the story."

In a moment they were nestling⑥ beside me, cooing⑦ with the pleasure that the promise of a story always brings them.

"But you must be quiet a moment, and let me think."

In truth it was not easy to arrange the story simply. Even with the collection of Lamb⑧'s tales to help me. I found it hard to tell *A Midsummer Night's Dream* in words that these little ones could understand. But presently⑨ I began the tale, and then the words came fast enough. When the story was ended, Iris drew a long breath⑩.

"It is a lovely story," she said, "but it doesn't look at all like that in the book."

"It is only put⑪ differently," I answered. "You will understand when you grow up that the stories are the least part of Shakespeare."

"But it's the stories we like," said Rosamund.

"You see he did not write for children."

"No, but you might," cried Iris, flushed⑫ with a sudden idea. "Why don't you write the stories for us so that we can understand them, just as you told us that, and then, when we are grown-up, we shall understand the plays so much better. Do! Do!"

"Ah, do! You will, won't you? You must!"

"Oh, well, if I must, I must," I said.

And so they settled⑬ it for me, and for them these tales were written.

---

① misgraffed [ˌmɪsˈgrɑːft] *adj*. 被误伤的 injured by mistake
② vantage [ˈvɑːntɪdʒ] *n*. 优势 advantage, superiority, edge
③ austerity [ɒˈsterəti] *n*. 苦行;禁欲 self-denial, abstinence
④ belike [bɪˈlaɪk] *adv*. 或许 perhaps, possibly, probably
⑤ edict [ˈiːdɪkt] *n*. 法令 law, act, decree
⑥ nestle [ˈnesl] *v*. 依偎 cuddle, snuggle, nuzzle
⑦ coo [kuː] *v*. 满足地轻哼;轻柔低语 murmur
⑧ Lamb [læm]: 兰姆(英国散文家,与人合写过《莎士比亚戏剧故事集》)
⑨ presently [ˈprezntli] *adv*. 随即 soon, shortly, before long
⑩ draw a long breath: 长叹一口气;深呼吸
⑪ put [pʊt] *v*. 表达 state, express, convey
⑫ flushed [flʌʃt] *adj*. 兴奋的 excited, thrilled
⑬ settle [ˈsetl] *v*. 决定 decide, determine

目录
Contents

米兰达《暴风雨》

O, wonder!
How many goodly creatures are there here!
How beauteous mankind is! O brave new world,
That has such people in 't!
真是奇迹!
这里有多少好看的人!
人类是多么美丽! 啊,新奇的世界,
有这么出色的人物!

暴风雨
The Tempest

主要人物

Prospero [ˈprɒspərəʊ] 普洛斯彼罗(旧米兰公爵)
Miranda [mɪˈrændə] 米兰达(普洛斯彼罗之女)
Ferdinand [ˈfɜːdɪnənd] 腓迪南(那不勒斯王子)
Antonio [ænˈtəʊnɪəʊ] 安东尼奥(普洛斯彼罗之弟)
Caliban [ˈkælɪbæn] 凯列班(野性而丑怪的奴隶)
Gonzalo [gənˈzɑːləʊ] 贡柴罗(正直的老大臣)
Alonso [əˈlɒnzəʊ] 阿隆佐(那不勒斯王)
Sebastian [sɪˈbæstjən] 西巴斯辛(阿隆佐之弟)
Ariel [ˈeərɪəl] 爱丽儿(缥缈的精灵)

Prospero, the Duke of Milan①, was a learned② and studious③ man, who lived among his books, leaving the management④ of his dukedom⑤ to his brother Antonio, in whom indeed he had complete trust.[i] But that trust was ill-rewarded⑥, for Antonio wanted to wear the duke's crown himself, and, to gain his ends, would have killed his brother but for the love the people bore⑦ him.[ii] However, with the help of Prospero's great enemy, Alonso, King of Naples⑧, he managed to get into his hands the dukedom with all its honor, power, and riches. For they took Prospero to sea, and when they were far away from land, forced him into a little boat with no tackle⑨, mast⑩, or sail⑪. In their cruelty⑫ and hatred they put his little daughter, Miranda (not yet three years old), into the boat with him, and sailed away,

---

① Milan [mɪˈlæn]：米兰(意大利北部城市)
② learned [ˈlɜːnɪd] *adj*. 有学问的 scholarly, well-read
③ studious [ˈstjuːdiəs] *adj*. 勤奋好学的 hard-working, diligent, scholarly
④ management [ˈmænɪdʒmənt] *n*. 治理 government
⑤ dukedom [ˈdjuːkdəm] *n*. 公爵领地 duchy
⑥ ill-rewarded [ɪl rɪˈwɔːdɪd] *adj*. 被辜负了的 betrayed, let down
⑦ bear [beə(r)] *v*. 心怀(感情等) entertain
⑧ Naples [ˈneɪplz]：那不勒斯(意大利南部城市)
⑨ tackle [ˈtækl] *n*. 索具
⑩ mast [mɑːst] *n*. 桅杆
⑪ sail [seɪl] *n*. 帆
⑫ cruelty [ˈkruːəlti] *n*. 残忍 ruthlessness, mercilessness

leaving them to their fate.

But one among the courtiers[1] with Antonio was true to his rightful[2] master, Prospero. To save the duke from his enemies was impossible, but much could be done to remind him of a subject[3]'s love. So this worthy[4] lord, whose name was Gonzalo, secretly placed in the boat some fresh water, provisions[5], and clothes, and what Prospero valued most of all, some of his precious books.

The boat was cast[6] on an island, and Prospero and his little one landed in safety[7]. Now this island was enchanted[8], and for years had lain under the spell[9] of a fell[10] witch, Sycorax, who had imprisoned[11] in the trunks[12] of trees all the good spirits she found there. She died shortly before Prospero was cast on those shores, but the spirits, of whom Ariel was the chief[13], still remained in their prisons.

Prospero was a great magician, for he had devoted[14] himself almost entirely to the study of magic during the years in which he allowed his brother to manage the affairs of Milan. By his art he set free the imprisoned spirits, yet kept them obedient[15] to his will, and they were more truly his subjects than his people in Milan had been. For he treated them kindly as long as they did his bidding[16], and he exercised[17] his power over them wisely and well. One creature[18] alone he found it necessary to treat with harshness[19]: this was Caliban, the son of the wicked[20] old witch, a hideous[21], deformed[22] monster, horrible to look on, and vicious[23] and brutal[24] in all his habits.[iii]

When Miranda was grown up into a maiden[25], sweet and fair to see, it chanced[26] that Antonio and Alonso, with Sebastian, his brother, and Ferdinand, his son, were at sea together with old Gonzalo, and their ship came near Prospero's island. Prospero, knowing they were there, raised

---

① courtier [ˈkɔːtiə(r)] *n*. 侍臣 attendant, follower, servant, assistant
② rightful [ˈraɪtfl] *adj*. 理应的 proper
③ subject [ˈsʌbdʒɪkt] *n*. 臣民 citizen, resident, inhabitant
④ worthy [ˈwɜːði] *adj*. 可敬的 respectable, honorable, admirable
⑤ provisions [prəˈvɪʒnz] *n*. 食物 food, nourishment
⑥ cast [kɑːst] *v*. 抛,扔 throw, toss, hurl, fling, sling
⑦ in safety: 安全地 safely
⑧ enchanted [ɪnˈtʃɑːntɪd] *adj*. 中魔法的 charmed, bewitched
⑨ spell [spel] *n*. 魔法 charm, magic
⑩ fell [fel] *adj*. 残暴的 cruel, savage, brutal
⑪ imprison [ɪmˈprɪzn] *v*. 囚禁 jail, detain, confine
⑫ trunk [trʌŋk] *n*. 树干 stem, bole
⑬ chief [tʃiːf] *n*. 首领 head, leader
⑭ devote [dɪˈvəʊt] *v*. 致力 dedicate, commit
⑮ obedient [əˈbiːdiənt] *adj*. 服从的 submissive, compliant
⑯ bidding [ˈbɪdɪŋ] *n*. 命令 order, command, demand
⑰ exercise [ˈeksəsaɪz] *v*. 行使 use, apply, exert, employ
⑱ creature [ˈkriːtʃə(r)] *n*. (具有某种特征的)人 man, person, individual
⑲ harshness [ˈhɑːʃnəs] *n*. 严厉;残酷 cruelty, severity, unkindness
⑳ wicked [ˈwɪkɪd] *adj*. 邪恶的 evil, vicious
㉑ hideous [ˈhɪdiəs] *adj*. 十分丑陋的 very ugly
㉒ deformed [dɪˈfɔːmd] *adj*. 畸形的 twisted
㉓ vicious [ˈvɪʃəs] *adj*. 恶毒的 cruel, malicious, spiteful, venomous
㉔ brutal [ˈbruːtl] *adj*. 残忍的 cruel, heartless, cold-blooded
㉕ maiden [ˈmeɪdn] *n*. 少女 girl, maid, damsel, lass
㉖ chance [tʃɑːns] *v*. 碰巧;偶然发生 happen to

by his art a great storm, so that even the sailors on board gave themselves up for lost, and first among them all Prince Ferdinand leaped[1] into the sea, and, as his father thought in his grief[2], was drowned[3]. But Ariel brought him safe ashore[4], and all the rest of the crew[5], although they were washed overboard[6], were landed unhurt in different parts of the island, and the good ship herself, which they all thought had been wrecked[7], lay at anchor[8] in the harbor whither[9] Ariel had brought her.[iv] Such wonders could Prospero and his spirits perform[10].

While yet the tempest[11] was raging[12], Prospero showed his daughter the brave ship laboring[13] in the trough[14] of the sea, and told her that it was filled with living human beings like themselves. She, in pity of their lives, prayed him who had raised this storm to quell[15] it. Then her father bade[16] her to have no fear, for he intended to save every one of them.

Then, for the first time, he told her the story of his life and hers, and that he had caused this storm to rise in order that his enemies, Antonio and Alonso, who were on board, might be delivered into his hands.

When he had made an end of his story he charmed[17] her into sleep, for Ariel was at hand, and he had work for him to do. Ariel, who longed for[18] his complete freedom, grumbled[19] to be kept in drudgery[20], but on being threateningly[21] reminded of all the sufferings he had undergone[22]

---

① leap [liːp] *v*. (leaped/leapt) 跳 jump
② grief [griːf] *n*. 悲痛 sadness, sorrow
③ drown [draʊn] *v*. 淹死 die under water, go to a watery grave
④ ashore [əˈʃɔː(r)] *adv*. 向(在)岸上 aground, on the shore
⑤ crew [kruː] *n*. 全体船员 all the people working on a ship
⑥ overboard [ˈəʊvəbɔːd] *adv*. 自船上落下 fall over the side of a boat into the water
⑦ wreck [rek] *v*. 破坏 break, destroy, devastate, demolish
⑧ at anchor:(船)抛锚,停泊
⑨ whither [ˈwɪðə(r)] *adv*. & *conj*. 〈古〉(= where)哪里,何处
⑩ perform [pəˈfɔːm] *v*. 执行 carry out
⑪ tempest [ˈtempɪst] *n*. 暴风雨 storm
⑫ rage [reɪdʒ] *v*. (暴风雨)肆虐 blow up
⑬ labor [ˈleɪbə(r)] *v*. 挣扎 struggle
⑭ trough [trɒf] *n*. 波谷 a low area between two waves
⑮ quell [kwel] *v*. 平息 squelch, pacify
⑯ bid [bɪd] *v*. 吩咐 order, direct, instruct, command
⑰ charm [tʃɑːm] *v*. 向……施魔法 enchant, bewitch
⑱ long for: 渴望 want, desire, crave, wish/hunger/yearn for
⑲ grumble [ˈgrʌmbl] *v*. 抱怨 complain
⑳ drudgery [ˈdrʌdʒəri] *n*. 苦差事 chore, toil
㉑ threateningly [ˈθretnɪŋli] *adv*. 威胁地 menacingly
㉒ undergo [ˌʌndəˈgəʊ] *v*. 经历 experience, go through

when Sycorax ruled in the land, and of the debt of gratitude he owed to the master① who had made those sufferings to end, he ceased② to complain, and promised faithfully to do whatever Prospero might command.[v]

"Do so," said Prospero, "and in two days I will discharge③ thee④."

Then he bade Ariel take the form of a water nymph⑤ and sent him in search of the young prince. And Ariel, invisible⑥ to Ferdinand, hovered⑦ near him, singing the while—

"Come unto these yellow sands,
And then take hands.
Courtesied⑧ when you have, and kiss'd
The wild waves whist⑨.
Foot it featly⑩ here and there,
And, sweet sprites, the burden⑪ bear."[vi]

And Ferdinand followed the magic singing, as the song changed to a solemn⑫ air⑬, and the words brought grief to his heart, and tears to his eyes, for thus they ran—

"Full fathom⑭ five thy⑮ father lies.
Of his bones are coral made.
Those are pearls that were his eyes.
Nothing of him that doth fade⑯,
But doth suffer a sea change
Into something rich and strange.
Sea nymphs hourly ring his knell⑰.
Hark⑱! Now I hear them—ding-dong, bell."[vii]

And so singing, Ariel led the spellbound⑲ prince into the presence of Prospero and Miranda.

---

① owe a debt of gratitude to sb.: 欠某人的情 owe sb. a favor
② cease [siːs] v. 停止 stop, end, finish
③ discharge [dɪsˈtʃɑːdʒ] v. 释放 free, release, liberate
④ thee [ðiː] *pron*. 〈古〉(第二人称单数的宾格)你,汝,尔
⑤ nymph [nɪmf] *n*. (古希腊、罗马神话中居于山林水泽的)仙女 naiad
⑥ invisible [ɪnˈvɪzəbl] *adj*. 看不见的 unseeable
⑦ hover [ˈhɒvə(r)] v. 盘旋 fly, float, drift
⑧ courtesy [ˈkɜːtəsi] v. 〈古〉行屈膝礼 curtsey, curtsy
⑨ whist [hwɪst] *v./adj*. 〈古〉(使)安静;安静的 quiet, hush/hushed
⑩ featly [ˈfiːtli] *adv*. 〈古〉优美地 skillfully
⑪ burden [ˈbɜːdn] *n*. 副歌 chorus, refrain
⑫ solemn [ˈsɒləm] *adj*. 庄严的 sincere, serious
⑬ air [eə(r)] *n*. 曲调,旋律 tune, melody
⑭ fathom [ˈfæðəm] *n*. 英寻(水深单位,合 6 英尺或 1.8 米)
⑮ thy [ðaɪ] *det*. 〈古〉(=your)你的
⑯ fade [feɪd] v. 褪色 discolor, lose color
⑰ knell [nel] *n*. 丧钟 death bell
⑱ hark [hɑːk] v. 听 listen
⑲ spellbound [ˈspelbaʊnd] *adj*. 入迷的 fascinated, captivated

Then, behold①! All happened as Prospero desired. For Miranda, who had never, since she could first remember, seen any human being save② her father, looked on the youthful prince with reverence in her eyes, and love in her secret heart.

"I might call him a thing divine③," she said, "for nothing natural I ever saw so noble."[viii]

And Ferdinand, beholding her beauty with wonder and delight, exclaimed④—

"Most sure the goddess on whom these airs attend⑤!"[ix]

Nor did he attempt to hide the passion⑥ which she inspired in him, for scarcely had they exchanged half a dozen sentences, before he vowed⑦ to make her his queen if she were willing.[x] But Prospero, though secretly delighted, pretended wrath⑧.

"You come here as a spy," he said to Ferdinand. "I will manacle⑨ your neck and feet together, and you shall feed on⑩ fresh water mussels⑪, withered⑫ roots and husk, and have sea water to drink. Follow."

"No," said Ferdinand, and drew his sword. But on the instant⑬ Prospero charmed him so that he stood there like a statue, still⑭ as stone; and Miranda in terror⑮ prayed her father to have mercy on her lover⑯. But he harshly⑰ refused her, and made Ferdinand follow him to his cell. There he set the prince to work, making him remove thousands of heavy logs⑱ of timber and pile them up. Ferdinand patiently obeyed, and thought his toil⑲ all too well repaid⑳ by the sympathy㉑ of the sweet Miranda.[xi]

She in very pity would have helped him in his hard work, but he would not let her, yet he could not keep from her the secret of his love, and she, hearing it, rejoiced㉒ and promised to be his wife.[xii]

Then Prospero released㉓ him from his servitude㉔, and glad at heart, he gave his consent to their marriage.

---

① behold [bɪˈhəʊld] *v*. 看 look, see
② save [seɪv] *prep*. 除……之外 except, apart/aside from
③ divine [dɪˈvaɪn] *adj*. 神圣的 holy
④ exclaim [ɪkˈskleɪm] *v*. 惊叫 cry, shout
⑤ attend [əˈtend] *v*. 侍候 serve, wait on
⑥ passion [ˈpæʃn] *n*. 强烈的爱 love, desire, affection
⑦ vow [vaʊ] *v*. 发誓 promise, pledge, swear
⑧ wrath [rɒθ] *n*. 盛怒 rage, fury
⑨ manacle [ˈmænəkl] *v*. 给……戴上镣铐 handcuff
⑩ feed on: 以……为食 live on
⑪ mussel [ˈmʌsl] *n*. 蚌;贻贝 shellfish
⑫ withered [ˈwɪðəd] *adj*. 干枯的 shriveled
⑬ on the instant: 立即 immediately, at once, right away
⑭ still [stɪl] *adj*. 静止的,不动的 motionless, stationary
⑮ terror [ˈterə(r)] *n*. 惊恐 fear, alarm, dread, fright, panic
⑯ have mercy on sb.: 对某人发慈悲 show mercy to sb.
⑰ harshly [ˈhɑːʃli] *adv*. 严厉地 strictly, severely
⑱ log [lɒg] *n*. 原木 timber
⑲ toil [tɔɪl] *n*. 苦活 drudgery
⑳ repay [rɪˈpeɪ] *v*. 回报 reward, reciprocate
㉑ sympathy [ˈsɪmpəθi] *n*. 同情 pity, compassion, empathy
㉒ rejoice [rɪˈdʒɔɪs] *v*. 非常高兴 exult
㉓ release [rɪˈliːs] *v*. 释放 free, discharge, liberate
㉔ servitude [ˈsɜːvɪtjuːd] *n*. 奴役 slavery, bondage, enslavement

"Take her," he said, "she is thine own."

In the meantime[1], Antonio and Sebastian in another part of the island were plotting[2] the murder of Alonso, the King of Naples, for Ferdinand being dead, as they thought, Sebastian would succeed to the throne[3] on Alonso's death. And they would have carried out their wicked purpose while their victim was asleep, but that Ariel woke him in good time[4].

Many tricks did Ariel play on them.[xiii]

Once he set a banquet[5] before them, and just as they were going to fall to[6], he appeared to them amid[7] thunder and lightning in the form of a harpy[8], and immediately the banquet disappeared. Then Ariel upbraided[9] them with their sins[10] and vanished[11] too.

Prospero by his enchantments[12] drew them all to the grove[13] without[14] his cell, where they waited, trembling[15] and afraid, and now at last bitterly repenting[16] them of their sins.

Prospero determined to make one last use of his magic power, and then, he said, "I'll break my staff and deeper than did ever plummet[17] sound[18] I'll drown[19] my book."[xiv]

So he made heavenly music to sound in the air, and appeared to them in his proper shape as the Duke of Milan. Because they repented, he forgave them and told them the story of his life since they had cruelly committed[20] him and his baby daughter to the mercy[21] of wind and waves.[xv] Alonso, who seemed sorriest of them all for his past crimes, lamented[22] the loss of his heir[23]. But Prospero drew back a curtain and showed them Ferdinand and Miranda playing at chess. Great was Alonso's joy to greet his loved son again, and when he heard that the fair maid with whom Ferdinand was playing was Prospero's daughter, and that the young folks had plighted their troth[24], he said—

"Give me your hands: let grief and sorrow still embrace[25] his heart that doth not wish

---

① in the meantime：与此同时 in the meanwhile
② plot [plɒt] v. 密谋 scheme, conspire, intrigue
③ succeed to the throne：登基 become a king or queen
④ in good time：及时；及早 in time, early
⑤ banquet ['bæŋkwɪt] n. 盛宴 feast
⑥ fall to：开始 begin, start, set about
⑦ amid [ə'mɪd] *prep*. 在……之中 among, in the middle of
⑧ harpy ['hɑːpi] n. 鸟身女妖，哈比（古希腊和罗马神话中的怪物）
⑨ upbraid [ʌp'breɪd] v. 责骂 scold, blame, rebuke, reproach
⑩ sin [sɪn] n. 罪过 evil, crime, misdeed
⑪ vanish ['vænɪʃ] v. 消失 disappear, dissolve, fade away
⑫ enchantment [ɪn'tʃɑːntmənt] n. 魔法 spell, magic, charm
⑬ grove [grəʊv] n. 树丛，小树林 wood, woodland
⑭ without [wɪ'ðaʊt] *prep*. (= outside of) 在……外面
⑮ tremble ['trembl] v. 颤抖 shake, shudder, shiver, quiver
⑯ repent [rɪ'pent] v. 后悔 regret
⑰ plummet ['plʌmɪt] n. 铅锤；测深锤 plumb
⑱ sound [saʊnd] v. 测量（水体深度）fathom, plumb, measure
⑲ drown [draʊn] v. 淹没 flood, soak, immerse, submerge
⑳ commit [kə'mɪt] v. 把……交给 give, deliver
㉑ mercy ['mɜːsi] n. 仁慈 humanity, forgiveness, kindness
㉒ lament [lə'ment] v. 对……感到悲痛 mourn, bemoan, grieve
㉓ heir [eə(r)] n. 继承人 successor, inheritor
㉔ plight one's troth：许婚，以身相许
㉕ embrace [ɪm'breɪs] v. 拥抱 hug, cuddle

you joy!"[xvi]

So all ended happily. The ship was safe in the harbor, and next day they all set sail for① Naples, where Ferdinand and Miranda were to be married. Ariel gave them calm seas and auspicious② gales③, and many were the rejoicings④ at the wedding.

Then Prospero, after many years of absence⑤, went back to his own dukedom, where he was welcomed with great joy by his faithful subjects. He practiced the arts of magic no more, but his life was happy, and not only because he had found his own again, but chiefly because, when his bitterest⑥ foes⑦ who had done him deadly⑧ wrong lay at his mercy⑨, he took no vengeance⑩ on them, but nobly forgave them.[xvii]

As for Ariel, Prospero made him free as air, so that he could wander where he would, and sing with a light heart his sweet song—

"Where the bee sucks⑪, there suck I.
In a cowslip⑫'s bell I lie.
There I couch⑬ when owls do cry.
On the bat's back I do fly
After summer merrily.
Merrily, merrily shall I live now
Under the blossom that hangs on the bough⑭."[xviii]

① set sail for：启航
② auspicious [ɔːˈspɪʃəs] *adj*. 吉利的 promising
③ gale [geɪl] *n*. 大风，狂风 extremely strong wind
④ rejoicing [rɪˈdʒɔɪsɪŋ] *n*. 欢庆 celebration
⑤ absence [ˈæbsəns] *n*. 缺席 leave
⑥ bitter [ˈbɪtə(r)] *adj*. 充满仇恨的 rancorous, revengeful
⑦ foe [fəʊ] *n*. 仇敌 enemy
⑧ deadly [ˈdedli] *adj*. 致命的 fatal, mortal, lethal
⑨ at one's mercy：任凭某人摆布 at one's discretion
⑩ vengeance [ˈvendʒəns] *n*. 报复 revenge, retaliation, reprisal
⑪ suck [sʌk] *v*. 吮吸 drink, draw
⑫ cowslip [ˈkaʊslɪp] *n*. 樱草
⑬ couch [kaʊtʃ] *v*. 躺下 lie, recline, lie down
⑭ bough [baʊ] *n*. 大树枝 branch

i Prospero, the Duke of Milan, was a learned and studious man, who lived among his books, leaving the management of his dukedom to his brother Antonio, in whom indeed he had complete trust. 米兰公爵普洛斯彼罗是一个知识渊博、勤奋好学的人,他整天跟他的书本打交道,把管理公国的事务全交给了弟弟安东尼奥,给予了安东尼奥百分之百的信任。(who..., in whom...:定语从句;leaving...:现在分词短语作结果状语)

ii But that trust was ill-rewarded, for Antonio wanted to wear the duke's crown himself, and, to gain his ends, would have killed his brother but for the love the people bore him. 但是安东尼奥却辜负了他的信任,想要把公爵的王冠戴到自己头上。为了达到这个目的,他恨不得杀死自己的哥哥,无奈老百姓们都太拥戴普洛斯彼罗了。(would have killed...:"本会杀死……",would have done...表示与过去事实相反的虚拟语气;but for...:"要不是……")

iii One creature alone he found it necessary to treat with harshness: this was Caliban, the son of the wicked old witch, a hideous, deformed monster, horrible to look on, and vicious and brutal in all his habits. 只有一个家伙他认为必须狠狠管教,那就是邪恶老女巫的儿子凯列班:一个面目狰狞的丑八怪,模样令人看了害怕,性情歹毒而残忍。(one creature 为 treat 的前置宾语)

iv But Ariel brought him safe ashore, and all the rest of the crew, although they were washed overboard, were landed unhurt in different parts of the island, and the good ship herself, which they all thought had been wrecked, lay at anchor in the harbor whither Ariel had brought her. 其实爱丽儿把腓迪南安全地带到了岸上。船上的其他人虽然都被冲到了海里,但都毫发无损地在荒岛的不同地方上了岸;而那艘气派的大船,大家都以为它肯定被冲毁了,其实已被爱丽儿送到海湾,正好好地停在那儿呢。[which..., whither(=where)...:定语从句;they all thought 为插入语]

v Ariel, who longed for his complete freedom, grumbled to be kept in drudgery, but on being threateningly reminded of all the sufferings he had undergone when Sycorax ruled in the land, and of the debt of gratitude he owed to the master who had made those sufferings to end, he ceased to complain, and promised faithfully to do whatever Prospero might command. 爱丽儿一心渴望获得完全的自由,不愿意继续做这些苦差事,但是普洛斯彼罗毫不客气地提醒他,让他别忘了西考拉克斯统治荒岛时他受到的种种折磨,也别忘了是现在的主人结束了他的痛苦以及他还欠着自己的恩情要还。爱丽儿便停止了抱怨,答应完全听从普洛斯彼罗的一切吩咐。[who..., sufferings (that)..., gratitude (that)..., who...:定语从句;on/upon doing...:"在……之后;一……就……"]

vi "Come unto these yellow sands, /And then take hands. /Courtesied when you have, and kiss'd/The wild waves whist. / Foot it featly here and there, /And, sweet sprites, the burden bear." "来吧,来到黄沙的海滨,把手儿牵得牢牢,深深地展拜细吻轻轻,叫海水莫起波涛——柔舞翩翩在水面飘扬;可爱的精灵,伴我歌唱。"(foot it featly=dance skillfully)

vii "Full fathom five thy father lies. / Of his bones are coral made. / Those are pearls that were his eyes. / Nothing of him that doth fade, / But doth suffer a sea change / Into something rich and strange. / Sea nymphs hourly ring his knell. / Hark! Now I hear them—ding-dong, bell." "五寻的水深处躺着你的父亲,他的骨骼已化成珊瑚;他眼睛是耀眼的明珠;他消失的全身没有一处不曾受到海水神奇的变幻,化成瑰宝,富丽而珍怪。海的女神时时摇起他的丧钟,叮!咚!听!我现在听到了叮咚的丧钟。"(doth=does)

viii "I might call him a thing divine," she said, "for nothing natural I ever saw so noble." "我简直要说他是个神,"她说,"因为我从来不曾见过宇宙中有这样出色的人物。"(nothing natural 为 saw 的前置宾语)

ix "Most sure the goddess on whom these airs attend!" "再不用疑惑,这一定是这些乐曲所敬奉的女神了!"

x Nor did he attempt to hide the passion which she inspired in him, for scarcely had they exchanged half a dozen sentences, before he vowed to make her his queen if she were willing. 米兰达在腓迪南内心激起了炽热的爱情,他对此没有加以掩饰,两人只短短地交流了几句,他就发下誓言,如果米兰达愿意的话,他要让她成为他的王后。

xi There he set the prince to work, making him remove thousands of heavy logs of timber and pile them up. Ferdinand patiently obeyed, and thought his toil all too well repaid by the sympathy of the sweet Miranda. 他在那里逼着腓迪南王子干活,让他把几千根沉重的大木头搬开,再重新堆放起来。腓迪南耐心地听从吩咐,他得到了美丽的米兰达的同情,他觉得这足以弥补自己的辛苦劳作。

xii She in very pity would have helped him in his hard work, but he would not let her, yet he could not keep from her the secret of his love, and she, hearing it, rejoiced and promised to be his wife. 米兰达心疼腓迪南,很想帮他分担一些艰苦的工作,可是他不让。他无法隐藏自己对米兰达的爱情,米兰达听了他的情话,欣喜若狂,答应做他的妻子。(would have done...:"本会……",与过去事实相反的虚拟语气)

xiii Many tricks did Ariel play on them. 爱丽儿跟他们玩了不少把戏。(部分倒装)

xiv “I’ll break my staff and deeper than did ever plummet sound I’ll drown my book.” “我会折断我的魔杖，把我的书投向深不可测的海心。”

xv Because they repented, he forgave them and told them the story of his life since they had cruelly committed him and his baby daughter to the mercy of wind and waves. 因为他们都已经忏悔了，所以普洛斯彼罗饶恕了他们，还对他们讲述了自己与幼女被残忍地遗弃在大海上任由风浪摆布的经历以及上岛后的生活。

xvi “Give me your hands: let grief and sorrow still embrace his heart that doth not wish you joy!” “让我握你们的手：谁不希望你们快乐的，就让忧伤和悲哀永远占据他的心灵！”(still = always)

xvii He practiced the arts of magic no more, but his life was happy, and not only because he had found his own again, but chiefly because, when his bitterest foes who had done him deadly wrong lay at his mercy, he took no vengeance on them, but nobly forgave them. 他不再使用魔法，但生活得非常幸福，这不仅是因为他重新夺回了自己所拥有的，更主要的是因为曾经置他于死地的仇敌落在他手里时，他并没有报复他们，而是高贵地选择了原谅。

xviii “Where the bee sucks, there suck I. / In a cowslip’s bell I lie. / There I couch when owls do cry. / On the bat’s back I do fly / After summer merrily. / Merrily, merrily shall I live now / Under the blossom that hangs on the bough.” “蜂儿吮啜的地方，我也在那儿吮啜；在一朵莲香花的冠中我躺着休息；我安然睡去，当夜枭开始它的呜咽。骑在蝙蝠背上我快活地飞舞翩翩，快活地快活地追随着逝去的夏天；快活地快活地我要如今向垂在枝头的花底安身。”

提泰妮娅《仲夏夜之梦》

I am a spirit of no common rate.
The summer still doth tend upon my state.
And I do love thee; therefore, go with me.
I'll give thee fairies to attend on thee;
And they shall fetch thee jewels from the deep,
And sing, while thou on pressed flowers dost sleep.
And I will purge thy mortal grossness so
That thou shalt like an airy spirit go.
Peaseblossom! Cobweb! Moth! And Mustardseed!

我不是一个平常的精灵，
夏天永远听从我的命令；
我真是爱你，因此跟我去吧。
我将使神仙们侍候你，
他们会从海底里捞起珍宝献给你；
当你在花茵上睡去的时候，他们会给你歌唱；
而且我要给你洗涤去俗体的污垢，
使你身轻得像个精灵一样。
豆花！蛛网！飞蛾！芥子！

仲夏夜之梦
A Midsummer Night's Dream

主要人物

Hermia [ˈhɜːmɪə] 赫米娅(恋拉山德)

Helena [ˈhelɪnə] 海丽娜(恋狄米特律斯)

Lysander [laɪˈsændə(r)] 拉山德(恋赫米娅)

Demetrius [dɪˈmiːtrɪəs] 狄米特律斯(恋赫米娅)

Oberon [ˈəʊbərən] 奥布朗(仙王)

Titania [tɪˈtɑːnɪə] 提泰妮娅(仙后)

Puck [pʌk] 迫克(又名好人儿罗宾)

Duke [djuːk] of Athens [ˈæθənz] 雅典公爵

Hermia and Lysander were lovers, but Hermia's father wished her to marry another man, named Demetrius.

Now, in Athens①, where they lived, there was a wicked law, by which any girl who refused to marry according to her father's wishes, might be put to death②.[i] Hermia's father was so angry with her for refusing to do as he wished, that he actually brought her before the Duke of Athens to ask that she might be killed, if she still refused to obey him. The Duke gave her four days to think about it, and, at the end of that time, if she still refused to marry Demetrius, she would have to die.

Lysander of course was nearly mad with grief, and the best thing to do seemed to him for Hermia to run away to his aunt's house at a place beyond the reach③ of that cruel④ law; and there he would come to her and marry her. But before she started, she told her friend, Helena, what she was going to do.

Helena had been Demetrius' sweetheart long before his marriage with Hermia had been thought of, and being very silly, like all jealous people, she could not see that it was not poor Hermia's fault that Demetrius wished to marry her instead of his own lady, Helena.[ii] She knew that if she told Demetrius that Hermia was going, as she was, to the wood outside Athens, he would follow her. "And I can follow him, and at least I shall see him," she said to herself. So she went to him, and betrayed⑤ her friend's secret.

Now this wood where Lysander was to meet Hermia, and where the other two had decided to follow them, was full of fairies, as most woods are, if one only had the eyes to see them, and in

---

① Athens [ˈæθənz]: 雅典(希腊首都)

② put sb. to death: 处死某人 kill/hang/execute/behead sb.

③ reach [riːtʃ] *n*. 影响范围 range, scope, limit

④ cruel [ˈkruːəl] *adj*. 残酷的 brutal, heartless, inhumane

⑤ betray [bɪˈtreɪ] *v*. 泄露 disclose, reveal, expose, give away

this wood on this night were the King and Queen of the fairies, Oberon and Titania.[iii] Now fairies are very wise people, but now and then they can be quite as foolish as mortal[1] folk. Oberon and Titania, who might have been as happy as the days were long[2], had thrown away all their joy in a foolish quarrel[3].[iv] They never met without saying disagreeable[4] things to each other, and scolded[5] each other so dreadfully[6] that all their little fairy followers, for fear, would creep[7] into acorn cups[8] and hide them there.[v]

So, instead of keeping one happy Court[9] and dancing all night through in the moonlight as is fairies' use[10], the King with his attendants[11] wandered through one part of the wood, while the Queen with hers kept state in another. And the cause of all this trouble was a little Indian boy whom Titania had taken to be one of her followers. Oberon wanted the child to follow him and be one of his fairy knights, but the Queen would not give him up.

On this night, in a mossy[12] moonlit glade[13], the King and Queen of the fairies met.

"Ill[14] met by moonlight, proud Titania," said the King.

"What! Jealous, Oberon?" answered the Queen. "You spoil[15] everything with your quarreling. Come, fairies, let us leave him. I am not friends with him now."

"It rests with you[16] to make up[17] the quarrel," said the King.

"Give me that little Indian boy, and I will again be your humble[18] servant and suitor[19]."

"Set your mind at rest," said the Queen. "Your whole fairy kingdom buys not that boy from me. Come, fairies."

And she and her train[20] rode off down the moonbeams.

"Well, go your ways," said Oberon. "But I'll be even with you[21] before you leave this wood."

Then Oberon called his favorite fairy, Puck. Puck was the spirit of mischief[22]. He used to slip[23] into the dairies and take the cream away, and get into the churn[24] so that the butter would

---

① mortal ['mɔːtl] *adj*. 凡人的 human, ordinary
② as happy as the days is long: 非常快乐
③ quarrel ['kwɒrəl] *n*./*v*. 争吵 row, argument/argue, dispute
④ disagreeable [ˌdɪsə'griːəbl] *adj*. 不愉快的 nasty, unpleasant
⑤ scold [skəʊld] *v*. 责骂 blame, reproach, rebuke, condemn
⑥ dreadfully ['dredfəli] *adv*. 糟糕地 terribly, horribly
⑦ creep [kriːp] *v*. 爬行 crawl
⑧ acorn cup: 橡碗(橡果的壳斗)
⑨ court [kɔːt] *n*. 宫廷 palace
⑩ use [juːs] *n*. 习惯 way, practice, custom, habit, mannerism
⑪ attendant [ə'tendənt] *n*. 侍者 assistant, servant
⑫ mossy ['mɒsi] *adj*. 长满苔藓的 moss-grown
⑬ glade [gleɪd] *n*. 林中空地 clearing
⑭ ill [ɪl] *adv*. 讨厌地 unpleasantly, unfortunately
⑮ spoil [spɔɪl] *v*. 糟蹋 damage, destroy, ruin, wreck, impair
⑯ rest with sb. (to do sth.): (做某事)是某人的责任(或分内的事) it is sb.'s responsibility (to do sth.)
⑰ make up: 和解 settle, reconcile, patch up
⑱ humble ['hʌmbl] *adj*. 卑微的 modest, lowly
⑲ suitor ['suːtə(r)] *n*. 随从 follower, attendant
⑳ train [treɪn] *n*. 队列 queue, rank, entourage
㉑ be even (with sb.): (跟某人)算账
㉒ mischief ['mɪstʃɪf] *n*. 恶作剧 hoax, naughtiness, prank
㉓ slip [slɪp] *v*. 悄悄溜入 sneak, creep
㉔ churn [tʃɜːn] *n*. 搅乳器

not come, and turn the beer sour, and lead people out of their way on dark nights and then laugh at them, and tumble① people's stools from under them when they were going to sit down, and upset② their hot ale③ over their chins when they were going to drink.[vi]

"Now," said Oberon to this little sprite④, "fetch me the flower called love-in-idleness⑤. The juice of that little purple flower laid on the eyes of those who sleep will make them, when they wake, to love the first thing they see. I will put some of the juice of that flower on my Titania's eyes, and when she wakes she will love the first thing she sees, were it lion, bear, or wolf, or bull, or meddling⑥ monkey, or busy ape.[vii]"

While Puck was gone, Demetrius passed through the glade followed by poor Helena, and still she told him how she loved him and reminded him of all his promises, and still he told her that he did not and could not love her, and that his promises were nothing. Oberon was sorry for poor Helena, and when Puck returned with the flower, he bade him follow Demetrius and put some of the juice on his eyes, so that he might love Helena when he woke and looked on her, as much as she loved him. So Puck set off, and wandering through the wood found, not Demetrius, but Lysander, on whose eyes he put the juice; but when Lysander woke, he saw not his own Hermia, but Helena, who was walking through the wood looking for the cruel Demetrius; and directly⑦ he saw her he loved her and left his own lady, under the spell of the purple flower.[viii]

When Hermia woke she found Lysander gone, and wandered about the wood trying to find him. Puck went back and told Oberon what he had done, and Oberon soon found that he had made a mistake, and set about looking for Demetrius, and having found him, put some of the juice on his eyes. And the first thing Demetrius saw when he woke was also Helena. So now Demetrius and Lysander were both following her through the wood, and it was Hermia's turn to follow her lover as Helena had done before. The end of it was that Helena and Hermia began to quarrel, and Demetrius and Lysander went off to fight. Oberon was very sorry to see his kind scheme⑧ to help these lovers turn out⑨ so badly. So he said to Puck—

"These two young men are going to fight. You must overhang⑩ the night with drooping⑪ fog,

---

① tumble [ˈtʌmbl] *v*. 使跌倒 fall, topple
② upset [ʌpˈset] *v*. 打翻 overturn, topple, tip over
③ ale [eɪl] *n*. 麦芽啤酒 beer, brew
④ sprite [spraɪt] *n*. 小精灵 spirit, fairy, elf
⑤ love-in-idleness [ˈlʌv ɪn ˈaɪdlnəs] *n*. 三色堇(朱生豪译本中译为"爱懒花")
⑥ meddling [ˈmedlɪŋ] *adj*. 好管闲事的 officious, meddlesome
⑦ directly [dəˈrektli] *conj*. 一……就…… immediately
⑧ scheme [skiːm] *n*. 计划 plan, project
⑨ turn out: 结果 end up
⑩ overhang [ˌəʊvəˈhæŋ] *v*. 悬于……之上 hang, dangle
⑪ drooping [ˈdruːpɪŋ] *adj*. 低垂的 droopy, sagging

and lead them so astray① that one will never find the other. When they are tired out, they will fall asleep. Then drop this other herb② on Lysander's eyes. That will give him his old sight and his old love. Then each man will have the lady who loves him, and they will all think that this has been only a Midsummer Night's Dream. Then when this is done, all will be well with them."

So Puck went and did as he was told, and when the two had fallen asleep without meeting each other, Puck poured the juice on Lysander's eyes, and said—

"When thou wak'st,
Thou tak'st
True delight
In③ the sight
Of thy former lady's eye:
Jack shall have Jill;
Nought④ shall go ill."[ix]

Meanwhile Oberon found Titania asleep on a bank where grew wild thyme⑤, oxlips⑥, and violets⑦, and woodbine⑧, musk roses⑨ and eglantine⑩. There Titania always slept a part of the night, wrapped in the enameled⑪ skin of a snake. Oberon stooped⑫ over her and laid the juice on her eyes, saying—

"What thou seest when thou dost wake,
Do it for thy true love take."[x]

Now, it happened that when Titania woke the first thing she saw was a stupid clown, one of a party of players who had come out into the wood to rehearse⑬ their play. This clown had met with Puck, who had clapped⑭ an ass's head on his shoulders so that it looked as if it grew there. Directly Titania woke and saw this dreadful monster, she said, "What angel is this? Are you as wise as you are beautiful?"

"If I am wise enough to find my way out of this wood, that's enough for me," said the foolish clown.

"Do not desire to go out of the wood," said Titania. The spell of the love juice was on her,

① lead sb. astray：使某人迷路；把某人引入歧途 make sb. go in the wrong direction or do things that are wrong
② herb [hɜːb] *n*. 药草 a plant used in medicines
③ take delight in：以……为乐 enjoy, take pleasure in
④ nought [nɔːt] (=naught) *n*. 没有什么 nothing
⑤ thyme [taɪm] *n*. 百里香
⑥ oxlip [ˈɒkslɪp] *n*. 高报春
⑦ violet [ˈvaɪələt] *n*. 紫罗兰
⑧ woodbine [ˈwuːdbaɪn] *n*. 忍冬
⑨ musk rose：麝香蔷薇
⑩ eglantine [ˈegləntaɪn] *n*. 多花蔷薇
⑪ enameled [ɪˈnæmld] *adj*. 涂了瓷釉的；坚硬而发亮的
⑫ stoop [stuːp] *v*. 俯身 bend, crouch
⑬ rehearse [rɪˈhɜːs] *v*. 排练 practise, prepare, run through
⑭ clap [klæp] *v*. 快速（或用力）放置 put quickly or firmly

and to her the clown seemed the most beautiful and delightful creature on all the earth. "I love you," she went on. "Come with me, and I will give you fairies to attend on you."

So she called four fairies, whose names were Peaseblossom①, Cobweb②, Moth③, and Mustardseed④.

"You must attend this gentleman," said the Queen. "Feed him with apricots⑤ and dewberries⑥, purple grapes, green figs⑦, and mulberries⑧. Steal honey bags for him from the bumblebees⑨, and with the wings of painted butterflies fan the moonbeams⑩ from his sleeping eyes."

"I will," said one of the fairies. And all the others said, "I will."

"Now, sit down with me," said the Queen to the clown, "and let me stroke⑪ your dear cheeks, and stick⑫ musk roses in your smooth, sleek⑬ head, and kiss your fair large ears, my gentle joy.[xi]"

"Where's Peaseblossom?" asked the clown with the ass's head. He did not care much about the Queen's affection⑭, but he was very proud of having fairies to wait on him⑮. "Ready," said Peaseblossom.

"Scratch⑯ my head, Peaseblossom," said the clown. "Where's Cobweb?"

"Ready," said Cobweb.

"Kill me," said the clown, "the red bumblebee on the top of the thistle⑰ yonder⑱, and bring me the honey bag. Where's Mustardseed?"

"Ready," said Mustardseed.

"Oh, I want nothing," said the clown. "Only just help Cobweb to scratch. I must go to the barber's, for methinks⑲ I am marvelous⑳ hairy㉑ about the face."

"Would you like anything to eat?" said the fairy Queen.

"I should like some good dry oats," said the clown—for his donkey's head made him desire donkey's food—"and some hay to follow."

"Shall some of my fairies fetch you new nuts from the squirrel's house?" asked the Queen.

---

① pease blossom：豌豆花(这里合在一起并且首字母大写特指精灵名)
② cobweb [ˈkɒbweb] *n*. 蜘蛛网(这里首字母大写特指精灵名)
③ moth [mɒθ] *n*. 飞蛾(这里首字母大写特指精灵名)
④ mustard seed：芥菜籽(这里合在一起并且首字母大写特指精灵名)
⑤ apricot [ˈeɪprɪkɒt] *n*. 杏子
⑥ dewberry [ˈdjuːbəri] *n*. 露莓
⑦ fig [fɪg] *n*. 无花果
⑧ mulberry [ˈmʌlbəri] *n*. 桑葚
⑨ bumblebee [ˈbʌmblbiː] *n*. 大黄蜂
⑩ moonbeam [ˈmuːnbiːm] *n*. (一道)月光 a ray of moonlight
⑪ stroke [strəʊk] *v*. 抚摸 caress, fondle, pet
⑫ stick [stɪk] *v*. 插入 insert
⑬ sleek [sliːk] *adj*. 光亮的 shiny, glossy, lustrous
⑭ affection [əˈfekʃn] *n*. 喜爱 love, fondness, attachment
⑮ wait on/upon sb.：服侍某人 serve, tend, attend, minister to
⑯ scratch [skrætʃ] *v*. 挠，搔 rub
⑰ thistle [ˈθɪsl] *n*. 蓟(野生植物)
⑱ yonder [ˈjɒndə(r)] *adv*. 〈古〉在那边 yon/yond, over there
⑲ methinks [mɪˈθɪŋks] *v*. 我想 meseems, I think
⑳ marvelous [ˈmɑːvələs] *adj*. 令人惊奇的(这里相当于 marvelously) wondrous, remarkable
㉑ hairy [ˈheəri] *adj*. 多毛的 hirsute, comate

“I'd rather have a handful or two of good dried peas,” said the clown. “But please don't let any of your people disturb me. I am going to sleep.”

Then said the Queen, “And I will wind① thee in my arms.”

And so when Oberon came along he found his beautiful Queen lavishing② kisses and endearments③ on a clown with a donkey's head.

And before he released her from the enchantment, he persuaded her to give him the little Indian boy he so much desired to have. Then he took pity on④ her, and threw some juice of the disenchanting⑤ flower on her pretty eyes; and then in a moment she saw plainly⑥ the donkey-headed clown she had been loving, and knew how foolish she had been.

Oberon took off the ass's head from the clown, and left him to finish his sleep with his own silly head lying on the thyme and violets.

Thus all was made plain⑦ and straight⑧ again. Oberon and Titania loved each other more than ever. Demetrius thought of no one but Helena, and Helena had never had any thought of anyone but Demetrius.

As for Hermia and Lysander, they were as loving a couple as you could meet in a day's march, even through a fairy wood.[xii]

So the four mortal lovers went back to Athens and were married, and the fairy King and Queen live happily together in that very wood at this very day.

ⅰ Now, in Athens, where they lived, there was a wicked law, by which any girl who refused to marry according to her father's wishes, might be put to death. 当时，在他们生活的雅典，有一条严酷的法律：凡是不听从父亲意愿结婚的女孩子，都会被处以死刑。（where..., by which..., who...：定语从句）

ⅱ Helena had been Demetrius' sweetheart long before his marriage with Hermia had been thought of, and being very silly,

---

① wind [waɪnd] *v*. 缠绕 coil, twine

② lavish [ˈlævɪʃ] *v*. 滥施 shower

③ endearment [ɪnˈdɪəmənt] *n*. 情话；亲热的表示 love, affection

④ take pity on：怜悯 pity, sympathize with, have mercy on

⑤ disenchanting [ˌdɪsɪnˈtʃɑːntɪŋ] *adj*. 使不再着迷的 disenthralling

⑥ plainly [ˈpleɪnli] *adv*. 清楚地 clearly, obviously

⑦ plain [pleɪn] *adj*. 清楚的 clear, obvious, evident, apparent

⑧ straight [streɪt] *adj*. 简单明了的 clear, simple

like all jealous people, she could not see that it was not poor Hermia's fault that Demetrius wished to marry her instead of his own lady, Helena. 早在狄米特律斯考虑要跟赫米娅结婚之前,海丽娜曾是他的恋人,她像所有嫉妒心重的人一样,表现得非常愚蠢;她不明白狄米特律斯要娶赫米娅而不是自己这件事,并不能怪可怜的赫米娅。

iii Now this wood where Lysander was to meet Hermia, and where the other two had decided to follow them, was full of fairies, as most woods are, if one only had the eyes to see them, and in this wood on this night were the King and Queen of the fairies, Oberon and Titania. 拉山德要去树林里跟赫米娅见面,另一对男女决定跟踪他们。这座树林里居住着许多神仙,就像大多数的树林那样,只是凡人的眼睛不会轻易看见神仙。这天夜里,树林里出现了仙王奥布朗和仙后提泰妮娅。

iv Oberon and Titania, who might have been as happy as the days were long, had thrown away all their joy in a foolish quarrel. 奥布朗和提泰妮娅本来可以高高兴兴的,如今却因为一场荒唐的争吵,所有的欢乐都不复存在。(might have done...:"本可能会是……",与过去事实相反的虚拟语气)

v They never met without saying disagreeable things to each other, and scolded each other so dreadfully that all their little fairy followers, for fear, would creep into acorn cups and hide them there. 两人一见面就互相说些难听的话,恶狠狠地咒骂对方;他们身边的小神仙们都吓坏了,一个个躲进了橡果的壳里。(never...without...:"从没有一次……不……,每一次……必会……";so...that...:"如此……以至于……")

vi He used to slip into the dairies and take the cream away, and get into the churn so that the butter would not come, and turn the beer sour, and lead people out of their way on dark nights and then laugh at them, and tumble people's stools from under them when they were going to sit down, and upset their hot ale over their chins when they were going to drink. 他过去经常溜进牛奶场,把奶油偷走;也钻进过搅拌桶,让黄油做不成功;他还把啤酒变得发酸。人们在黑暗的夜间赶路时,他把他们引到岔路上去,然后大声嘲笑;人们刚要往凳子上坐时,他突然从下方把凳子打翻;人们正要喝热腾腾的麦芽酒时,他故意让酒泼洒在他们的下巴上。

vii I will put some of the juice of that flower on my Titania's eyes, and when she wakes she will love the first thing she sees, were it lion, bear, or wolf, or bull, or meddling monkey, or busy ape. 我要把那种花的汁液挤在我的提泰妮娅的眼睛上,等她醒来,她就会爱上第一眼看见的东西,无论是狮子也好,熊也好,狼也好,公牛也好,或者好事的猕猴、忙碌的无尾猿也好。(were it... or... = whether it were... or...:"无论……还是……,不管……还是……",表示让步的虚拟语气)

viii So Puck set off, and wandering through the wood found, not Demetrius, but Lysander, on whose eyes he put the juice; but when Lysander woke, he saw not his own Hermia, but Helena, who was walking through the wood looking for the cruel Demetrius; and directly he saw her he loved her and left his own lady, under the spell of the purple flower. 于是迫克动身了,他在树林里寻寻觅觅,结果找到的不是狄米特律斯,而是拉山德。他往拉山德的眼睛里滴了花汁。可是拉山德醒来时,看见的不是他的心上人赫米娅,而是海丽娜——她正在树林里到处寻找那个狠心郎狄米特律斯。在紫红色鲜花魔力的作用下,拉山德立刻就爱上了海丽娜,离开了自己的恋人赫米娅。

ix "When thou wak'st, / Thou tak'st / True delight / In the sight / Of thy former lady's eye: / Jack shall have Jill; / Nought shall go ill." "醒眼见,旧人脸,乐满心,情不禁,从此欢爱复深深。哥儿爱姐儿,两两无参差。"(thou=you;wak'st=wake;thy=your;nought=nothing)

x "What thou seest when thou dost wake, / Do it for thy true love take." "等你眼睛一睁开,你就看见你的爱。"(thou=you;seest=see;dost=do;thy=your)

xi ...let me stroke your dear cheeks, and stick musk roses in your smooth, sleek head, and kiss your fair large ears, my gentle joy. ……我要爱抚你可爱的脸颊,我要把麝香蔷薇插在你柔软光滑的头颅上,我要吻你美丽的大耳朵,我的温柔的宝贝。

xii As for Hermia and Lysander, they were as loving a couple as you could meet in a day's march, even through a fairy wood. 至于赫米娅和拉山德,他们是如此相爱,即使在仙树林里行走一天,也很难遇到这样相爱的一对儿。

罗瑟琳《皆大欢喜》

From the east to western Inde,
No jewel is like Rosalind.
Her worth being mounted on the wind,
Through all the world bears Rosalind.
All the pictures fairest lin'd
Are but black to Rosalind.
Let no fair be kept in mind
But the fair of Rosalind.

从东印度到西印度找遍奇珍，
没有一颗珠玉比得上罗瑟琳。
她的名声随着好风播满诸城，
整个世界都在仰慕着罗瑟琳。
画工描摹下一幅幅倩影真真，
都要黯然无色一见了罗瑟琳。
任何的脸貌都不用铭记在心，
单单牢记住了美丽的罗瑟琳。

西莉娅《皆大欢喜》

I was too young that time to value her,
But now I know her. If she be a traitor,
Why so am I: we still have slept together,
Rose at an instant, learn'd, play'd, eat together;
And wheresoe'er we went, like Juno's swans,
Still we went coupled and inseparable.

那时我还太小,不曾知道她的好处;
但现在我知道她了。要是她是个叛逆,
那么我也是。我们一直都睡在一起,
同时起床,一块儿读书,同游同食,
无论到什么地方去,都像朱诺的一双天鹅,
永远成着对,拆不开来。

皆大欢喜
As You Like It

主要人物

Duke [djuːk] 长公爵（在流亡放逐中）

Frederick [ˈfredrɪk] 弗莱德里克公爵（长公爵之弟，篡位者）

Rosalind [ˈrɒzəlɪnd] 罗瑟琳（流亡公爵之女）

Celia [ˈsiːljə] 西莉娅（弗莱德里克之女）

Orlando [ɔːˈlændəʊ] 奥兰多（罗兰·德·鲍埃爵士的幼子）

Sir Rowland [ˈrəʊlənd] de Boys 罗兰·德·鲍埃爵士

Oliver [ˈɒlɪvə(r)] 奥列佛（罗兰·德·鲍埃爵士的长子）

Ganymede [ˈgænɪmiːd] 盖尼米德（罗瑟琳化名）

Aliena [ˌælɪˈiːnə] 爱莲娜（西莉娅化名）

There was once a wicked Duke named Frederick, who took the dukedom that should have belonged to his brother, sending him into exile①. His brother went into the Forest of Arden②, where he lived the life of a bold forester, as Robin Hood③ did in merry England.

The banished④ Duke's daughter, Rosalind, remained with Celia, Frederick's daughter, and the two loved each other more than Sherwood Forest⑤ most sisters. One day there was a wrestling⑥ match at Court, and Rosalind and Celia went to see it. Charles, a celebrated⑦ wrestler⑧, was there, who had killed many men in contests of this kind. Orlando, the young man

---

① exile [ˈeksaɪl] *n*. 流放 banishment, deportation, expulsion
② Forest of Arden [ˈɑːdən]：亚登森林
③ Robin Hood [ˌrɒbɪn ˈhʊd]：罗宾汉（英格兰民间传说中劫富济贫的绿林好汉）
④ banish [ˈbænɪʃ] *v*. 驱逐 expel, exile, deport, drive away
⑤ Sherwood [ˈʃɜːwʊd] Forest：舍伍德森林（又名侠盗林，因罗宾汉而闻名）
⑥ wrestling [ˈreslɪŋ] *n*. 摔跤运动
⑦ celebrated [ˈselɪbreɪtɪd] *adj*. 著名的 famous, renowned
⑧ wrestler [ˈreslə(r)] *n*. 摔跤运动员

he was to wrestle[1] with, was so slender[2] and youthful[3], that Rosalind and Celia thought he would surely be killed, as others had been; so they spoke to him, and asked him not to attempt so dangerous an adventure; but the only effect of their words was to make him wish more to come off[4] well in the encounter[5], so as to win praise from such sweet ladies.[ii]

Orlando, like Rosalind's father, was being kept out of his inheritance[6] by his brother, and was so sad at his brother's unkindness that, until he saw Rosalind, he did not care much whether he lived or died. But now the sight of the fair Rosalind gave him strength and courage, so that he did marvelously[7], and at last, threw Charles to such a tune[8] that the wrestler had to be carried off the ground.[iii] Duke Frederick was pleased with his courage, and asked his name.

"My name is Orlando, and I am the youngest son of Sir Rowland de Boys," said the young man.

Now Sir Rowland de Boys, when he was alive, had been a good friend to the banished Duke, so that Frederick heard with regret whose son Orlando was, and would not befriend[9] him. But Rosalind was delighted to hear that this handsome young stranger was the son of her father's old friend, and as they were going away, she turned back more than once to say another kind word to the brave young man.

"Gentleman," she said, giving him a chain from her neck, "wear this for me. I could give more, but that my hand lacks means[10][iv]."

Rosalind and Celia, when they were alone, began to talk about the handsome wrestler, and Rosalind confessed[11] that she loved him at first sight.

---

① wrestle ['resl] *v*. 摔跤
② slender ['slendə(r)] *adj*. 修长的 slim, lean, svelte, willowy
③ youthful ['juːθfl] *adj*. 年轻的 young
④ come off: 成功 succeed, make it, work out, be successful
⑤ encounter [ɪn'kaʊntə(r)] *n*. (体育)比赛,交锋 match, contest
⑥ inheritance [ɪn'herɪtəns] *n*. 遗产 heritage
⑦ marvelously ['mɑːvələsli] *adv*. 奇迹般地 miraculously
⑧ tune [tjuːn] *n*. 数量;程度 amount, degree
⑨ befriend [bɪ'frend] *v*. 友善对待 make friends with
⑩ means [miːnz] *n*. 钱财 money, capital, riches, resources
⑪ confess [kən'fes] *v*. 承认 admit, acknowledge

"Come, come," said Celia, "wrestle with[1] thy affections."

"Oh," answered Rosalind, "they take the part of a better wrestler than myself. Look, here comes the Duke."

"With his eyes full of anger," said Celia.

"You must leave the Court at once," he said to Rosalind.

"Why?" she asked.

"Never mind why," answered the Duke. "You are banished. If within ten days you are found within twenty miles of my Court, you die."

So Rosalind set out[2] to seek her father, the banished Duke, in the Forest of Arden. Celia loved her too much to let her go alone, and as it was rather a dangerous journey, Rosalind, being the taller, dressed up[3] as a young countryman, and her cousin as a country girl, and Rosalind said that she would be called Ganymede, and Celia, Aliena.[v] They were very tired when at last they came to the Forest of Arden, and as they were sitting on the grass a countryman passed that way, and Ganymede asked him if he could get them food. He did so, and told them that a shepherd[4]'s flocks[5] and house were to be sold. They bought these and settled down[6] as shepherd and shepherdess[7] in the forest.

In the meantime, Oliver having sought to take his brother Orlando's life, Orlando also wandered into the forest, and there met with the rightful Duke, and being kindly received, stayed with him.[vi] Now, Orlando could think of nothing but Rosalind, and he went about the forest carving her name on trees, and writing love sonnets[8] and hanging them on the bushes, and there Rosalind and Celia found them. One day Orlando met them, but he did not know Rosalind in her boy's clothes, though he liked the pretty shepherd youth, because he fancied[9] a likeness[10] in him to her he loved.

"There is a foolish lover," said Rosalind, "who haunts[11] these woods and hangs sonnets on the trees. If I could find him, I would soon cure him of his folly.[vii]"

Orlando confessed that he was the foolish lover, and Rosalind said—

"If you will come and see me every day, I will pretend to be Rosalind, and I will take her part, and be wayward[12] and contrary[13], as is the way of women, till I make you ashamed of your folly in loving her."[viii]

And so every day he went to her house, and took a pleasure in saying to her all the pretty

---

① wrestle with：全力解决，努力处理 grapple with
② set out：出发 set off
③ dress up：打扮；伪装 trick out, disguise oneself
④ shepherd [ˈʃepəd] *n*. 牧羊人 herder, herdsman, stockman
⑤ flock [flɒk] *n*. 羊群 herd, group
⑥ settle down：定居 take up residence
⑦ shepherdess [ˌʃepəˈdes] *n*. 牧羊女 a woman shepherd
⑧ sonnet [ˈsɒnɪt] *n*. 十四行诗
⑨ fancy [ˈfænsi] *v*. 认为 think, believe
⑩ likeness [ˈlaɪknəs] *n*. 相似 similarity, resemblance
⑪ haunt [hɔːnt] *v*. 出没 frequent
⑫ wayward [ˈweɪwəd] *adj*. 任性的 wilful, unruly, headstrong
⑬ contrary [ˈkɒntrəri] *adj*. 乖戾的 perverse, obstinate

things he would have said to Rosalind; and she had the fine and secret joy of knowing that all his love words came to the right ears.[ix] Thus many days passed pleasantly away.

One morning, as Orlando was going to visit Ganymede, he saw a man asleep on the ground, and that there was a lioness① crouching② near, waiting for the man who was asleep to wake: for they say that lions will not prey on③ anything that is dead or sleeping. Then Orlando looked at the man, and saw that it was his wicked brother, Oliver, who had tried to take his life. He fought with the lioness and killed her, and saved his brother's life.

While Orlando was fighting the lioness, Oliver woke to see his brother, whom he had treated so badly, saving him from a wild beast at the risk of④ his own life. This made him repent of his wickedness⑤, and he begged Orlando's pardon, and from thenceforth⑥ they were dear brothers. The lioness had wounded Orlando's arm so much that he could not go on to see the shepherd, so he sent his brother to ask Ganymede to come to him.

Oliver went and told the whole story to Ganymede and Aliena, and Aliena was so charmed with his manly⑦ way of confessing his faults, that she fell in love with him⑧ at once. But when Ganymede heard of the danger Orlando had been in she fainted⑨, and when she came to herself⑩, said truly enough, "I should have been a woman by right."[x]

Oliver went back to his brother and told him all this, saying, "I love Aliena so well that I will give up my estates⑪ to you and marry her, and live here as a shepherd."

"Let your wedding be tomorrow," said Orlando, "and I will ask the Duke and his friends."

When Orlando told Ganymede how his brother was to be married on the morrow⑫, he added: "Oh, how bitter a thing it is to look into happiness through another man's eyes."[xi]

Then answered Rosalind, still in Ganymede's dress and speaking with his voice—"If you do love Rosalind so near the heart, then when your brother marries Aliena, shall you marry her."[xii]

---

① lioness [ˈlaɪənes] *n*. 母狮

② crouch [kraʊtʃ] *v*. 蹲伏 squat

③ prey on: 捕食 hunt

④ at the risk of: 冒着……的危险 run a risk of

⑤ wickedness [ˈwɪkɪdnəs] *n*. 邪恶 evil

⑥ thenceforth [ˌðensˈfɔːθ] *adv*. 从那时起 from then on

⑦ manly [ˈmænli] *adj*. 有男子汉气概的 masculine

⑧ fall in love with sb.: 与某人坠入爱河;爱上某人

⑨ faint [feɪnt] *v*. 昏厥 swoon, pass out, lose consciousness

⑩ come to oneself: 苏醒,恢复知觉 come around

⑪ estate [ɪˈsteɪt] *n*. 地产 lands, property

⑫ morrow [ˈmɒrəʊ] *n*. 次日 tomorrow, the next day

Now the next day the Duke and his followers, and Orlando, and Oliver, and Aliena, were all gathered together for the wedding.

Then Ganymede came in and said to the Duke, "If I bring in your daughter Rosalind, will you give her to Orlando here?"

"That would I," said the Duke, "had I kingdoms to give with her."[xiii]

"And you say you will have her when I bring her?" she said to Orlando. "That would I," he answered, "were I of all kingdoms king."[xiv]

Then Rosalind and Celia went out, and Rosalind put on her pretty woman's clothes again, and after a while came back.

She turned to her father—

"I give myself to you, for I am yours."

"If there be truth in sight," he said, "you are my daughter."

Then she said to Orlando, "I give myself to you, for I am yours." "If there be truth in sight," he said, "you are my Rosalind."

"I will have no father if you be not he," she said to the Duke, and to Orlando. "I will have no husband if you be not he."

So Orlando and Rosalind were married, and Oliver and Celia, and they lived happy ever after, returning with the Duke to the kingdom. For Frederick had been shown by a holy hermit[①] the wickedness of his ways, and so gave back the dukedom of his brother, and himself went into a monastery[②] to pray for forgiveness[③].

The wedding was a merry one, in the mossy glades of the forest. A shepherd and shepherdess who had been friends with Rosalind, when she was herself disguised as a shepherd, were married on the same day, and all with such pretty feasting[④] and merrymaking[⑤] as could be nowhere within four walls, but only in the beautiful green wood.[xv]

① hermit [ˈhɜːmɪt] *n*. 隐士 recluse, anchorite

② monastery [ˈmɒnəstri] *n*. 修道院 abbey

③ forgiveness [fəˈɡɪvnəs] *n*. 原谅 pardon

④ feasting [ˈfiːstɪŋ] *n*. 盛宴 banquet

⑤ merrymaking [ˈmerimeɪkɪŋ] *n*. 狂欢 festivity, jollification, revelry

i His brother went into the Forest of Arden, where he lived the life of a bold forester, as Robin Hood did in Sherwood Forest in merry England. 他哥哥来到亚登森林，过着勇敢无畏的护林人的生活，就像罗宾汉当年在欢乐英格兰的舍伍德森林里那样。（“罗宾汉”是英国民间传说中的英雄人物，以他为首的一帮绿林好汉在舍伍德森林占林为王、劫富济贫，留下了一连串的传奇故事，至今仍为世人所津津乐道；“欢乐英格兰”指的是一种理想化、田园牧歌式的生活方式和乌托邦观念）

ii ...but the only effect of their words was to make him wish more to come off well in the encounter, so as to win praise from such sweet ladies. ……可是，她们的话只起到了一个效果——让奥兰多更加渴望在比赛中取得好成绩，只为了得到这两位漂亮姑娘的夸奖。

iii But now the sight of the fair Rosalind gave him strength and courage, so that he did marvelously, and at last, threw Charles to such a tune that the wrestler had to be carried off the ground. 但是，看到姣美的罗瑟琳，他又获得了力量和勇气，在比赛中表现得非常出色，竟然把查尔斯重重摞倒在地，最后查尔斯不得不被人抬出了赛场。

iv I could give more, but that my hand lacks means. 我心有余而力不足，只能略表诚意。

v Celia loved her too much to let her go alone, and as it was rather a dangerous journey, Rosalind, being the taller, dressed up as a young countryman, and her cousin as a country girl, and Rosalind said that she would be called Ganymede, and Celia, Aliena. 西莉娅深爱着她，不忍心让她独自上路。由于旅途中充满了危险，个头较高的罗瑟琳就打扮成一个乡下小伙子，她的堂妹扮作一个村姑。罗瑟琳给自己起名叫盖尼米德，给西莉娅起名叫爱莲娜。

vi In the meantime, Oliver having sought to take his brother Orlando's life, Orlando also wandered into the forest, and there met with the rightful Duke, and being kindly received, stayed with him. 这个时候，奥列佛想要谋害他哥哥奥兰多的性命，奥兰多也逃进了森林。他在那里碰到了真正的长公爵，受到了热情的款待，便留在了长公爵身边。（Oliver having...：独立主格结构）

vii If I could find him, I would soon cure him of his folly. 如果我能找到他，很快就能治好他的相思病。

viii “If you will come and see me every day, I will pretend to be Rosalind, and I will take her part, and be wayward and contrary, as is the way of women, till I make you ashamed of your folly in loving her.” “要是你每天都来看我，我就会假扮罗瑟琳，模仿她，任性善变、刁钻古怪，就像其他女人那样，直到我让你为自己傻傻地爱上她而害臊。”

ix And so every day he went to her house, and took a pleasure in saying to her all the pretty things he would have said to Rosalind; and she had the fine and secret joy of knowing that all his love words came to the right ears. 从那以后，奥兰多每天都来到她家，高高兴兴地把自己想对罗瑟琳说的甜言蜜语，都说给她听。她私下里感到美滋滋的，因为她知道他的这些情话，本来就是要说给她听的。

x “I should have been a woman by right.” “我理应是个女人。”（should have been：“本该是……”，与过去事实相反的虚拟语气）

xi “Oh, how bitter a thing it is to look into happiness through another man's eyes.” “唉！看到别人的眼中闪烁着幸福的光芒，自己真有说不出的酸楚！”

xii “If you do love Rosalind so near the heart, then when your brother marries Aliena, shall you marry her.” “要是你爱罗瑟琳真是爱得那么深，那么你哥哥和爱莲娜结婚的时候，你就可以和她结婚。”（shall you marry...：部分倒装）

xiii “That would I,” said the Duke, “had I kingdoms to give with her.” 长公爵说：“即使再要我把几个王国作为陪嫁，我也愿意。”（had I...＝if I had...：与现在事实相反的非真实条件句省略 if 时的部分倒装）

xiv “That would I,” he answered, “were I of all kingdoms king.” 他回应道：“即使我是统治万国的君王，我也愿意。”（were I...＝if I were...：与现在事实相反的非真实条件句省略 if 时的部分倒装）

xv A shepherd and shepherdess who had been friends with Rosalind, when she was herself disguised as a shepherd, were married on the same day, and all with such pretty feasting and merrymaking as could be nowhere within four walls, but only in the beautiful green wood. 当罗瑟琳扮成一个放牧的小伙子时，跟一对牧羊的男女青年成了朋友，他们俩也在这一天结婚了。所有的一切，都何其美好，何其欢乐啊！这样热闹的氛围，只会出现在那片郁郁葱葱的美丽树林里，在室内是不会有的。（such...as...：定语从句中 as 作主语）

潘狄塔《冬天的故事》

What you do
Still betters what is done.
When you do dance, I wish you
A wave o' the sea, that you might ever do
Nothing but that; move still, still so,
And own no other function: each your doing,
So singular in each particular,
Crowns what you are doing in the present deeds,
That all your acts are queens.

无论你做什么事,
总比已经做过的更为美妙。
当你跳舞的时候,我希望你是
海中的一朵浪花,永远那么波动着,
再不做别的事。你的每一个动作,
在无论哪一点上都是那么特殊的美妙;
每看到一件眼前的事,
都会令人以为不会有更胜于此的了;
在每项事情上你都是个女王。

冬天的故事
The Winter's Tale

主要人物

Leontes [liːˈɒntiːz] 里昂提斯（西西里国王）
Polixenes [pɒˈlɪksəniːz] 波力克希尼斯（波希米亚国王）
Hermione [hɜːˈmaɪəni] 赫米温妮（里昂提斯之后）
Camillo [kəˈmɪləʊ] 卡密罗（西西里大臣）
Paulina [pɔːˈlaɪnə] 宝丽娜（安提哥纳斯之妻）
Perdita [ˈpɜːdɪtə] 潘狄塔（里昂提斯及赫米温妮之女）
Florizel [ˈflɒrɪzel] 弗罗利泽（波希米亚王子）
Doricles [ˈdɒrɪkliːz] 道里克尔斯（弗罗利泽化名）
Shepherd [ˈʃepəd] 牧人（潘狄塔的假父）

Leontes was the King of Sicily[1], and his dearest friend was Polixenes, King of Bohemia[2]. They had been brought up[3] together, and only separated when they reached man's estate[4] and each had to go and rule over his kingdom. After many years, when each was married and had a son, Polixenes came to stay with Leontes in Sicily.

Leontes was a violent-tempered[5] man and rather silly, and he took it into his stupid head that his wife, Hermione, liked Polixenes better than she did him, her own husband.[i] When once he had got this into his head, nothing could put it out; and he ordered one of his lords, Camillo, to put a poison[6] in Polixenes' wine. Camillo tried to dissuade[7] him from this wicked action, but finding he was not to be moved[8], pretended to consent. He then told Polixenes what was proposed against him, and they fled[9] from the Court of Sicily that night, and returned to Bohemia, where Camillo lived on as Polixenes' friend and counselor[10].

Leontes threw the Queen into prison and her son, the heir to the throne, died of sorrow to see his mother so unjustly[11] and cruelly treated.

While the Queen was in prison she had a little baby, and a friend of hers, named Paulina, had

---

① Sicily [ˈsɪsɪli]：西西里岛（位于意大利南部）
② Bohemia [bəʊˈhiːmɪə]：波希米亚（位于今捷克境内）
③ bring up：抚养 rear, raise, care for
④ reach man's estate：达到成年男子期 be grown-up, be adult
⑤ violent-tempered [ˌvaɪələnt ˈtempəd] *adj*. 脾气暴躁的 bad-tempered
⑥ poison [ˈpɔɪzn] *n*. 毒药 toxicant
⑦ dissuade [dɪˈsweɪd] *v*. 劝阻 persuade not to
⑧ move [muːv] *v*. 使改变观点 change, shift, convert, alter
⑨ flee [fliː] *v*. 逃离 escape, fly, run away, take flight
⑩ counselor [ˈkaʊnsələ(r)] *n*. 参事 adviser, counsel
⑪ unjustly [ˌʌnˈdʒʌstli] *adv*. 不公正地 unfairly, wrongfully

the baby dressed in its best, and took it to show the King, thinking that the sight of his helpless little daughter would soften[1] his heart towards his dear Queen, who had never done him any wrong, and who loved him a great deal more than he deserved[ii]; but the King would not look at the baby, and ordered Paulina's husband to take it away in a ship, and leave it in the most desert[2] and dreadful[3] place he could find, which Paulina's husband, very much against his will, was obliged[4] to do.

Then the poor Queen was brought up to be tried[5] for treason[6] in preferring Polixenes to her King, but really she had never thought of anyone except Leontes, her husband. Leontes had sent some messengers to ask the god, Apollo[7], whether he was not right in his cruel thoughts of the Queen. But he had no patience to wait till they came back, and so it happened that they arrived in the middle of the trial[8]. The Oracle[9] said—

"Hermione is innocent, Polixenes blameless[10], Camillo a true subject, Leontes a jealous tyrant[11], and the King shall live without an heir, if that which is lost be not found."

Then a man came and told them that the little Prince was dead. The poor Queen, hearing this, fell down in a fit[12], and then the King saw how wicked and wrong he had been. He ordered Paulina and the ladies who were with the Queen to take her away, and try to restore[13] her. But Paulina came back in a few moments, and told the King that Hermione was dead.

Now Leontes' eyes were at last opened to his folly. His Queen was dead, and the little daughter who might have been a comfort to him he had sent away to be the prey[14] of wolves and kites[15].[iii] Life had nothing left for him now. He gave himself up to his grief, and passed in many

① soften [ˈsɒfn] *v*. 使软化 melt
② desert [ˈdezət] *adj*. 荒凉的 wild, bare, barren, desolate
③ dreadful [ˈdredfl] *adj*. 可怕的 terrible, horrible, frightful
④ oblige [əˈblaɪdʒ] *v*. 被迫 force, compel
⑤ try [traɪ] *v*. 审判 judge, examine
⑥ treason [ˈtriːzn] *n*. 叛国 treachery, betrayal
⑦ Apollo [əˈpɒləʊ]：阿波罗（古希腊神话中的太阳神）
⑧ trial [ˈtraɪəl] *n*. 审判 examination, judgement
⑨ oracle [ˈɒrəkl] *n*. 祭司 priest, priestess
⑩ blameless [ˈbleɪmləs] *adj*. 清白的 faultless, innocent
⑪ tyrant [ˈtaɪrənt] *n*. 暴君 dictator, oppressor, despot
⑫ fit [fɪt] *n*. 昏厥 convulsion
⑬ restore [rɪˈstɔː(r)] *v*. 使苏醒 revive, revitalize, reanimate
⑭ prey [preɪ] *n*. 猎物 quarry, game, target
⑮ kite [kaɪt] *n*. 鸢（猛禽） a bird of prey of the hawk family

sad years in prayer① and remorse②.

The baby Princess was left on the seacoast of Bohemia, the very kingdom where Polixenes reigned③. Paulina's husband never went home to tell Leontes where he had left the baby, for as he was going back to the ship, he met a bear and was torn to pieces. So there was an end of him.

But the poor deserted④ little baby was found by a shepherd. She was richly dressed, and had with her some jewels, and a paper was pinned⑤ to her cloak⑥, saying that her name was Perdita, and that she came of noble⑦ parents.

The shepherd, being a kind-hearted man, took home the little baby to his wife, and they brought it up as their own child. She had no more teaching than a shepherd's child generally has, but she inherited⑧ from her royal⑨ mother many graces and charms, so that she was quite different from the other maidens in the village where she lived.[iv]

One day Prince Florizel, the son of the good King of Bohemia, was hunting near the shepherd's house and saw Perdita, now grown up to a charming woman. He made friends with the shepherd, not telling him that he was the Prince, but saying that his name was Doricles, and that he was a private⑩ gentleman; and then, being deeply in love with the pretty Perdita, he came almost daily to see her.[v]

The King could not understand what it was that took his son nearly every day from home, so he set people to watch him, and then found out that the heir of the King of Bohemia was in love with Perdita, the pretty shepherd girl.[vi] Polixenes, wishing to see whether this was true, disguised himself, and went with the

① prayer [preə(r)] *n*. 祈祷 orison, invocation
② remorse [rɪˈmɔːs] *n*. 懊悔 regret, contrition, self-reproach
③ reign [reɪn] *v*. 统治 rule, govern, administer, be in power
④ deserted [dɪˈzɜːtɪd] *adj*. 被遗弃的 abandoned, forsaken
⑤ pin [pɪn] *v*. (用别针)别住 fasten, attach
⑥ cloak [kləʊk] *n*. 披风 coat, cape, mantle
⑦ noble [ˈnəʊbl] *adj*. 贵族的 aristocratic
⑧ inherit [ɪnˈherɪt] *v*. 继承 succeed to, fall heir to
⑨ royal [ˈrɔɪəl] *adj*. 皇家的;高贵的 kingly, regal, grand, majestic
⑩ private [ˈpraɪvət] *adj*. 〈古〉隐居的 reclusive, cloistered

faithful① Camillo, in disguise② too, to the old shepherd's house. They arrived at the feast③ of sheepshearing④, and, though strangers, they were made very welcome. There was dancing going on, and a peddler⑤ was selling ribbons and laces and gloves, which the young men bought for their sweethearts⑥.

Florizel and Perdita, however, were taking no part in this gay⑦ scene, but sat quietly together talking. The King noticed the charming manners and great beauty of Perdita, never guessing that she was the daughter of his old friend, Leontes. He said to Camillo—

"This is the prettiest low-born⑧ lass⑨ that ever ran on the green sward⑩. Nothing she does or seems but smacks of⑪ something greater than herself—too noble for this place."[vii]

And Camillo answered, "In truth she is the Queen of curds⑫ and cream."[viii]

But when Florizel, who did not recognize his father, called upon the strangers to witness his betrothal⑬ with the pretty shepherdess, the King made himself known and forbade the marriage, adding that if ever she saw Florizel again, he would kill her and her old father, the shepherd; and with that he left them. But Camillo remained behind, for he was charmed with Perdita, and wished to befriend her.

Camillo had long known how sorry Leontes was for that foolish madness of his, and he longed to go back to Sicily to see his old master. He now proposed that the young people should go there and claim the protection of Leontes. So they went, and the shepherd went with them, taking Perdita's jewels, her baby clothes, and the paper he had found pinned to her cloak.

Leontes received them with great kindness. He was very polite to Prince Florizel, but all his looks were for Perdita. He saw how much she was like the Queen Hermione, and said again and again—

"Such a sweet creature my daughter might have been, if I had not cruelly sent her from me."[ix]

When the old shepherd heard that the King had lost a baby daughter, who had been left upon the coast of Bohemia, he felt sure that Perdita, the child he had reared⑭, must be the King's daughter, and when he told his tale and showed the jewels and the paper, the King perceived⑮ that Perdita was indeed his long-lost child.[x] He welcomed her with joy, and rewarded the good shepherd.

① faithful [ˈfeɪθfl] *adj*. 忠诚的 trusty, loyal, devoted,
② in disguise: 伪装,乔装
③ feast [fiːst] *n*. 宴会 banquet
④ sheepshearing [ˈʃiːpˌʃɪərɪŋ] *n*. 剪羊毛 the act or process of shearing sheep
⑤ peddler [ˈpedlə(r)] *n*. 小贩 vendor, hawker, huckster
⑥ sweetheart [ˈswiːthɑːt] *n*. 心上人 dearest, beloved
⑦ gay [geɪ] *adj*. 快乐的 joyful, happy
⑧ low-born [ˌləʊ ˈbɔːn] *adj*. 出身低微的 humble
⑨ lass [læs] *n*. 少女 girl, maid, maiden, damsel
⑩ sward [swɔːd] *n*. 草地 grassland, lawn, pasture
⑪ smack of: 含有……的意味 echo, mirror, reflect
⑫ curd [kɜːd] *n*. 凝乳 a thick soft substance that is formed when milk turns sour
⑬ betrothal [bɪˈtrəʊðl] *n*. 订婚 engagement, plight, troth
⑭ rear [rɪə(r)] *v*. 养育 raise, nurture, care for, bring up
⑮ perceive [pəˈsiːv] *v*. 察觉 notice, discover, be aware of

Polixenes had hastened[1] after his son to prevent his marriage with Perdita, but when he found that she was the daughter of his old friend, he was only too glad to give his consent.

Yet Leontes could not be happy. He remembered how his fair Queen, who should have been at his side to share his joy in his daughter's happiness, was dead through his unkindness, and he could say nothing for a long time but—

"Oh, thy mother! Thy mother!" and ask forgiveness of the King of Bohemia, and then kiss his daughter again, and then the Prince Florizel, and then thank the old shepherd for all his goodness.

Then Paulina, who had been high all these years in the King's favor, because of her kindness to the dead Queen Hermione, said—"I have a statue made in the likeness of the dead Queen, a piece many years in doing, and performed by the rare[2] Italian master, Giulio Romano[3]. I keep it in a private house apart[4], and there, ever since you lost your Queen, I have gone twice or thrice a day. Will it please Your Majesty[5] to go and see the statue?"

So Leontes and Polixenes, and Florizel and Perdita, with Camillo and their attendants, went to Paulina's house where there was a heavy purple curtain screening off[6] an alcove[7]; and Paulina, with her hand on the curtain, said—

"She was peerless[8] when she was alive, and I do believe that her dead likeness excels[9] whatever yet you have looked upon, or that the hand of man hath[10] done.[xi] Therefore I keep it lonely, apart. But here it is—behold, and say, 'tis well."

And with that she drew back[11] the curtain and showed them the statue. The King gazed[12] and gazed on the beautiful statue of his dead wife, but said nothing.

"I like your silence," said Paulina. "It the more shows off[13] your wonder.[xii] But speak, is it not like her?"

---

① hasten [ˈheɪsn] *v*. 赶往 rush, run, race, hurry, make haste
② rare [reə(r)] *adj*. 杰出的 excellent, outstanding, incomparable
③ Giulio Romano [ˈdʒuːljɔː rɔːˈmɑːnɔː]：裘里奥·罗曼诺(现译朱里奥·罗马诺,意大利画家和建筑师)
④ apart [əˈpɑːt] *adv*. 分开地 separately, independently
⑤ Your Majesty：(对国王或女王的尊称)陛下 a title given to a sovereign or a sovereign's wife or widow
⑥ screen off：(用屏风等)隔开 separate
⑦ alcove [ˈælkəʊv] *n*. 凹室;壁龛 recess, niche
⑧ peerless [ˈpɪələs] *adj*. 无与伦比的 matchless, incomparable
⑨ excel [ɪkˈsel] *v*. 超过,胜过 beat, exceed, surpass, outdo
⑩ hath：has 的古体形式,即 have 的第三人称单数形式
⑪ draw back：移开 move away from
⑫ gaze [geɪz] *v*. 凝视 stare, look fixedly
⑬ show off：表现;炫耀

"It is almost herself," said the King, "and yet, Paulina, Hermione was not so much wrinkled①, nothing so old as this seems.[xiii]"

"Oh, not by much," said Polixenes.

"Ah," said Paulina, "that is the cleverness of the carver②, who shows her to us as she would have been had she lived till now."[xiv]

And still Leontes looked at the statue and could not take his eyes away.

"If I had known," said Paulina, "that this poor image③ would so have stirred④ your grief, and love, I would not have shown it to you."[xv]

But he only answered, "Do not draw the curtain."

"No, you must not look any longer," said Paulina, "or you will think it moves."

"Let be! Let be!" said the King. "Would you not think it breathed?"

"I will draw the curtain," said Paulina. "You will think it lives presently."

"Ah, sweet Paulina," said Leontes, "make me to think so twenty years together."[xvi]

"If you can bear it," said Paulina, "I can make the statue move, make it come down and take you by the hand. Only you would think it was by wicked magic."

"Whatever you can make her do, I am content to look on," said the King.

And then, all folks there admiring and beholding, the statue moved from its pedestal⑤ and came down the steps and put its arms round the King's neck, and he held her face and kissed her many times, for this was no statue, but the real living Queen Hermione herself. She had lived hidden⑥, by Paulina's kindness, all these years, and would not discover herself⑦ to her husband, though she knew he had repented, because she could not quite forgive him till she knew what had become of her little baby.[xvii]

Now that Perdita was found, she forgave her husband everything, and it was like a new and beautiful marriage to them, to be together once more.

Florizel and Perdita were married and lived long and happily.

To Leontes his many years of suffering were well paid for in the moment when, after long grief and pain, he felt the arms of his true love around him once again.

① wrinkled [ˈrɪŋkld] *adj*. 有皱纹的 lined
② carver [ˈkɑːvə(r)] *n*. 雕刻师 engraver, sculptor
③ image [ˈɪmɪdʒ] *n*. 雕像 statue, figure
④ stir [stɜː(r)] *v*. 激起 cause, generate, bring about
⑤ pedestal [ˈpedɪstl] *n*. 基座 base, support
⑥ hidden [ˈhɪdn] *adj*. 隐藏的 secret, covered, unseen
⑦ discover oneself：显露真容

ⅰ Leontes was a violent-tempered man and rather silly, and he took it into his stupid head that his wife, Hermione, liked Polixenes better than she did him, her own husband. 里昂提斯是一个脾气非常暴躁的男人，而且品性愚蠢。他不知怎么搞的脑子发昏，竟然以为他的妻子赫米温妮喜欢波力克希尼斯，超过了喜欢他——她自己的丈夫。

ⅱ While the Queen was in prison she had a little baby, and a friend of hers, named Paulina, had the baby dressed in its best, and took it to show the King, thinking that the sight of his helpless little daughter would soften his heart towards his dear Queen, who had never done him any wrong, and who loved him a great deal more than he deserved... 王后在牢里生下一个孩子。她的一个名叫宝丽娜的朋友给小宝宝穿上最漂亮的衣服，抱去给国王看。她以为国王看到这个柔弱无助的小女儿，心就会变软，就不会那样对待他亲爱的王后了。毕竟王后并没有做任何对不起他的事，她一直都那么忠诚地爱着他，而他根本就不配得到这份爱……

ⅲ His Queen was dead, and the little daughter who might have been a comfort to him he had sent away to be the prey of wolves and kites. 他的王后死了，而本可以给他带来安慰的小女儿，却被他送到荒郊野外，喂了野兽。(the little daughter who...为 sent 的前置宾语)

ⅳ She had no more teaching than a shepherd's child generally has, but she inherited from her royal mother many graces and charms, so that she was quite different from the other maidens in the village where she lived. 作为牧人的孩子，她没有受到多少教育，但是她从王后母亲那里继承了许多优雅的风度和魅力，使她跟村子里的其他姑娘完全不一样。

ⅴ He made friends with the shepherd, not telling him that he was the Prince, but saying that his name was Doricles, and that he was a private gentleman; and then, being deeply in love with the pretty Perdita, he came almost daily to see her. 弗罗利泽跟牧人交上了朋友，但他没有说自己是王子，只说他叫道里克尔斯，是一位隐居的绅士。后来，弗罗利泽深深地爱上了美丽的潘狄塔，几乎每天都来看她。

ⅵ The King could not understand what it was that took his son nearly every day from home, so he set people to watch him, and then found out that the heir of the King of Bohemia was in love with Perdita, the pretty shepherd girl. 国王不明白他的儿子为何几乎天天外出，于是派人监视他，结果发现波希米亚国王的继承人爱上了牧人的漂亮女儿潘狄塔。(what it was that...:宾语从句中的强调句型)

ⅶ "This is the prettiest low-born lass that ever ran on the green sward. Nothing she does or seems but smacks of something greater than herself—too noble for this place." "这是牧场上最美的小家碧玉。她的每一个动作、每一个姿态，都有一种比她自身更为高贵的品质，这地方似乎屈辱了她。"

ⅷ "In truth she is the Queen of curds and cream." "真的，她可以说是牛奶场的女王。"(借代修辞：凝乳和奶油从牛奶中提取，牛奶关联牛奶场和牧人)

ix "Such a sweet creature my daughter might have been, if I had not cruelly sent her from me." "我的女儿,如果我没有残忍地把她打发走,也会长成这样一个美丽动人的姑娘。"(such a sweet creature 是前置表语;might have done..., if...had done...:与过去事实相反的虚拟语气)

x When the old shepherd heard that the King had lost a baby daughter, who had been left upon the coast of Bohemia, he felt sure that Perdita, the child he had reared, must be the King's daughter, and when he told his tale and showed the jewels and the paper, the King perceived that Perdita was indeed his long-lost child. 老牧人听说国王丢失过一个小女婴,而且那孩子是被遗弃在波希米亚的海滩上的,他相信自己抚养长大的潘狄塔就是国王的女儿。当他讲了这个故事,并把珠宝和那张纸拿出来时,国王发现潘狄塔真的就是他失散多年的孩子。

xi She was peerless when she was alive, and I do believe that her dead likeness excels whatever yet you have looked upon, or that the hand of man hath done. 她活着的时候是绝世无双的,她的遗像,我相信一定远胜于你们眼中所曾见到的,或者人手所曾制作的一切。

xii "I like your silence," said Paulina. "It the more shows off your wonder." "我喜欢你们的静默,"宝丽娜说,"因为它更能表示出你们的惊奇。"

xiii Hermione was not so much wrinkled, nothing so old as this seems. 赫米温妮脸上没有这么多皱纹,模样也不像这样衰老呀。

xiv "Ah," said Paulina, "that is the cleverness of the carver, who shows her to us as she would have been had she lived till now." "啊,"宝丽娜说,"这就是雕刻家的高明之处,让我们看到了如果她现在还活着,会是一副什么模样。"(had she lived =if she had lived:与过去事实相反的非真实条件句省略 if 时的部分倒装)

xv "If I had known," said Paulina, "that this poor image would so have stirred your grief, and love, I would not have shown it to you." 宝丽娜说:"如果我知道这座小小的雕像会这样触动您的悲伤和爱意,我一定不给您看。"(if...had done..., ...would have done...:与过去事实相反的虚拟语气)

xvi "Ah, sweet Paulina," said Leontes, "make me to think so twenty years together." 里昂提斯说:"啊,亲爱的宝丽娜!让我把这种思想保持二十年吧。"(make me to think=make me think)

xvii She had lived hidden, by Paulina's kindness, all these years, and would not discover herself to her husband, though she knew he had repented, because she could not quite forgive him till she knew what had become of her little baby. 好心的宝丽娜把她藏了起来,她瞒着丈夫偷偷活了这么些年。她虽然知道丈夫已经悔悟,但不愿意原谅他,直至得知小宝宝的下落为止。(what becomes of sb.:某人的结果是怎样,某人遭遇了什么事)

考狄利娅《李尔王》

Good My Lord,	父亲，您生下我来，
You have begot me, bred me, loved me;	把我教养成人，爱惜我、厚待我；
I return those duties back as are right fit—	我受到您这样的恩德，只有恪尽我的责任，
Obey you, love you, and most honor you.	服从您、爱您、敬重您。
Why have my sisters husbands if they say They love you all?	我的姐姐们要是用她们整个的心来爱您， 那么她们为什么要嫁人呢？
Haply when I shall wed,	要是我有一天出嫁了，
That lord whose hand must take my plight shall carry	那接受我的忠诚誓约的丈夫，将要得到
Half my love with him, half my care and duty.	我的一半的爱、我的一半的关心和责任；
Sure, I shall never marry like my sisters,	我只爱我的父亲，
To love my father all.	我一定不会像我的两个姐姐一样再去嫁人的。

李尔王
King Lear

主要人物

Lear [lɪə(r)] 李尔（不列颠国王）

Goneril [ˈgɒnərɪl] 高纳里尔（李尔的长女）

Regan [ˈriːgən] 里根（李尔的次女）

Cordelia [kɔːˈdiːljə] 考狄利娅（李尔的三女）

Earl [ɜːl] of Kent [kent] 肯特伯爵

Duke [djuːk] of Albany [ˈɔːlbəni] 奥本尼公爵（高纳里尔的丈夫）

Duke of Cornwall [ˈkɔːnwɔːl] 康华尔公爵（里根的丈夫）

Duke of Burgundy [ˈbɜːgəndi] 勃艮第公爵

King of France　法兰西国王（考狄利娅的求婚者）

Fool　弄人

King Lear was old and tired. He was weary of[1] the business of his kingdom, and wished only to end his days quietly near his three daughters. Two of his daughters were married to the Dukes of Albany and Cornwall, and the Duke of Burgundy and the King of France were both suitors[2] for the hand of Cordelia, his youngest daughter.

Lear called his three daughters together, and told them that he proposed to divide[3] his kingdom among them. "But first," he said, "I should like to know how much you love me."

Goneril, who was really a very wicked woman, and did not love her father at all, said she loved him more than words could say; she loved him dearer than eyesight, space or liberty[4], more than life, grace, health, beauty, and honor.

"I love you as much as my sister and more," professed[5] Regan, "since I care for nothing but my father's love."

Lear was very much pleased with Regan's professions[6], and turned to his youngest daughter, Cordelia. "Now, our joy, though last not least," he said, "the best part of my kingdom have I kept for you. What can you say?"

"Nothing, My Lord," answered Cordelia.

---

① weary of：对……感到厌倦 tired of, bored of

② suitor [ˈsuːtə(r)] *n*. 求婚者 admirer, wooer, courter

③ divide [dɪˈvaɪd] *v*. 分配 share, distribute, allocate, deal out

④ liberty [ˈlɪbəti] *n*. 自由 freedom

⑤ profess [prəˈfes] *v*. 表白 claim, state, declare

⑥ profession [prəˈfeʃn] *n*. 表白 claim, statement, declaration

"Nothing can come of nothing. Speak again," said the King.

And Cordelia answered, "I love Your Majesty according to my duty—no more, no less."

And this she said, because she was disgusted① with the way in which her sisters professed love, when really they had not even a right sense of duty② to their old father.

"I am your daughter," she went on, "and you have brought me up and loved me, and I return you those duties back as are right and fit, obey you, love you, and most honor you."

Lear, who loved Cordelia best, had wished her to make more extravagant③ professions of love than her sisters. "Go," he said, "be forever a stranger to my heart and me."

The Earl of Kent, one of Lear's favorite courtiers and captains, tried to say a word for Cordelia's sake④, but Lear would not listen. He divided the kingdom between Goneril and Regan, and told them that he should only keep a hundred knights at arms, and would live with his daughters by turns⑤.

When the Duke of Burgundy knew that Cordelia would have no share of the kingdom, he gave up his courtship⑥ of her. But the King of France was wiser, and said, "Thy dowerless⑦ daughter, King, is Queen of us—of ours, and our fair France."

"Take her, take her," said the King, "for I will never see that face of hers again."

So Cordelia became Queen of France, and the Earl of Kent, for having ventured⑧ to take her part⑨, was banished from the kingdom. The King now went to stay with his daughter Goneril, who had got everything from her father that he had to give, and now began to grudge⑩ even the hundred knights that he had reserved for himself. She was harsh⑪ and undutiful⑫ to him, and her servants either refused to obey his orders or pretended that they did not hear them.

Now the Earl of Kent, when he was banished, made as though he would go into another

---

① disgusted [dɪsˈgʌstɪd] *adj*. 厌恶的 sickened, repelled, repulsed
② a sense of duty: 责任感 a sense of responsibility
③ extravagant [ɪkˈstrævəgənt] *adj*. 过度的 excessive
④ for sb.'s sake: 为某人起见 in sb.'s interests
⑤ by turns: 轮流 alternately, in succession, one after another
⑥ courtship [ˈkɔːtʃɪp] *n*. 求婚 wooing, courting, suit, pursuit
⑦ dowerless [ˈdaʊələs] *adj*. 无嫁妆的 lacking a dowry
⑧ venture [ˈventʃə(r)] *v*. 冒险 risk
⑨ take one's part: 支持某人 support, side with, stand by
⑩ grudge [grʌdʒ] *v*. 吝惜 begrudge
⑪ harsh [hɑːʃ] *adj*. 严厉的 severe, cruel, unkind
⑫ undutiful [ˌʌnˈdjuːtɪfʊl] *adj*. 不孝的 disobedient, unfilial

country, but instead he came back in the disguise[1] of a servingman[2] and took service with[3] the King. The King had now two friends—the Earl of Kent, whom he only knew as his servant, and his Fool, who was faithful to him. Goneril told her father plainly that his knights only served to fill her Court with riot[4] and feasting, and so she begged him only to keep a few old men about him such as himself.

"My train are men who know all parts of duty," said Lear. "Goneril, I will not trouble you further—yet I have left another daughter."

And his horses being saddled[5], he set out with his followers for the castle of Regan. But she, who had formerly outdone[6] her sister in professions of attachment[7] to the King, now seemed to outdo her in undutiful conduct, saying that fifty knights were too many to wait on him, and Goneril (who had hurried thither[8] to prevent Regan showing any kindness to the old King) said five were too many, since her servants could wait on him.[i]

Then when Lear saw that what they really wanted was to drive him away, he left them. It was a wild and stormy night, and he wandered about the heath[9] half mad with misery[10], and with no companion but the poor Fool. But presently his servant, the good Earl of Kent, met him, and at last persuaded him to lie down in a wretched[11] little hovel[12]. At daybreak the Earl of Kent removed his royal master to Dover[13], and hurried to the Court of France to tell Cordelia what had happened.

Cordelia's husband gave her an army and with it she landed at Dover. Here she found poor King Lear, wandering about the fields, wearing a crown of nettles[14] and weeds. They brought him back and fed and clothed[15] him, and Cordelia came to him and kissed him.

"You must bear with me," said Lear. "Pray you now, forget and forgive. I am old and foolish."

And now he knew at last which of his children it was that had loved him best, and who was worthy of his love.[ii]

Goneril and Regan joined their armies to fight Cordelia's army, and were successful; and Cordelia and her father were thrown into prison. Then Goneril's husband, the Duke of Albany, who was a good man, and had not known how wicked his wife was, heard the truth of the whole story; and when Goneril found that her husband knew her for the wicked woman she was, she

---

① disguise [dɪsˈɡaɪz] *n*. 伪装 false appearance
② servingman [ˈsɜːvɪŋmæn] *n*. 〈古〉男仆,男用人
③ take service with: 帮佣,服侍
④ riot [ˈraɪət] *n*. 喧闹,狂欢 bustle, hilarity
⑤ saddle [ˈsædl] *v*. 给(马)装鞍 put a saddle on a horse
⑥ outdo [ˌaʊtˈduː] *v*. 超过 beat, exceed, surpass
⑦ attachment [əˈtætʃmənt] *n*. 喜欢 love, fondness, affection
⑧ thither [ˈðɪðə(r)] *adv*. 〈古〉(= there) 向那边
⑨ heath [hiːθ] *n*. 荒地 moor, wasteland
⑩ misery [ˈmɪzəri] *n*. 苦难 suffering, distress, hardship
⑪ wretched [ˈretʃɪd] *adj*. 极差的 awful, woeful, miserable
⑫ hovel [ˈhɒvl] *n*. 小屋,茅舍 hut, cabin, shack
⑬ Dover [ˈdəʊvə(r)]: 多佛(英国东南部港口)
⑭ nettle [ˈnetl] *n*. 荨麻
⑮ clothe [kləʊð] *v*. 给……穿衣 dress

killed herself, having a little time before giving a deadly poison to her sister, Regan, out of a spirit of jealousy.[iii]

But they had arranged that Cordelia should be hanged in prison, and though the Duke of Albany sent messengers at once, it was too late. The old King came staggering① into the tent of the Duke of Albany, carrying the body of his dear daughter Cordelia, in his arms.

And soon after, with words of love for her upon his lips, he fell with her still in his arms, and died.

ⅰ But she, who had formerly outdone her sister in professions of attachment to the King, now seemed to outdo her in undutiful conduct, saying that fifty knights were too many to wait on him, and Goneril (who had hurried thither to prevent Regan showing any kindness to the old King) said five were too many, since her servants could wait on him. 当初，在向李尔王表达爱意的时候，里根超过了她姐姐；如今在不孝顺方面，她也是有过之而无不及——她说五十个骑士伺候李尔王一个人太浪费。高纳里尔（她匆匆赶来，想阻止里根对老国王发善心）说五个也太多了，因为她手下的仆人就可以伺候老父亲。

ⅱ And now he knew at last which of his children it was that had loved him best, and who was worthy of his love. 事到如今，他总算明白哪个孩子最爱他，哪个孩子最值得被他爱。（which...it was that...：宾语从句中的强调结构）

ⅲ Then Goneril's husband, the Duke of Albany, who was a good man, and had not known how wicked his wife was, heard the truth of the whole story; and when Goneril found that her husband knew her for the wicked woman she was, she killed herself, having a little time before giving a deadly poison to her sister, Regan, out of a spirit of jealousy. 后来，高纳里尔的丈夫——奥本尼公爵，一个好心肠的人，从不知道他的妻子有多歹毒——听说了整个故事。高纳里尔发现她的丈夫认清她是个邪恶的妇人之后，她便自杀了。出于嫉妒，在临死前，她用致命的毒药毒死了她的妹妹里根。

---

① stagger ['stægə(r)] *v.* 踉跄 reel, falter, totter, teeter, wobble

薇奥拉《第十二夜》

She never told her love,
But let concealment, like a worm in the bud,
Feed on her damask cheek. She pined in thought,
And with a green and yellow melancholy
She sat like patience on a monument,
Smiling at grief. Was not this love indeed?
We men may say more, swear more, but indeed
Our shows are more than will, for still we prove
Much in our vows, but little in our love.

她从来不向人诉说她的爱情，
让隐藏在内心中的抑郁像蓓蕾中的蛀虫一样，
侵蚀着她的绯红的脸颊；她因相思而憔悴，
疾病和忧愁折磨着她，像是墓碑上刻着的
"忍耐"的化身，默坐着向着悲哀微笑。
这不是真的爱情吗？我们男人也许更多话，
更会发誓，可是我们所表示的，总多于
我们所决心实行的；不论我们怎样
山盟海誓，我们的爱情总不过如此。

奥丽维娅《第十二夜》

Is 't not well done?
Excellently done, if God did all.
'Tis in grain, sir. 'Twill endure wind and weather.
'Tis beauty truly blent, whose red and white
Nature's own sweet and cunning hand laid on.
Lady, you are the cruel'st she alive,
If you will lead these graces to the grave
And leave the world no copy.

它不是画得很好吗?
要是一切都出于上帝的手,那真是绝妙之笔。
它的色彩很耐久,先生,受得起风霜的侵蚀。
那真是各种色彩精妙地调和而成的美貌;
那红红的白白的都是造化亲自用他的
可爱的巧手敷上去的。小姐,您是世上
最忍心的女人,要是您甘心让这种美
埋没在坟墓里,不给世间留下一份副本。

第十二夜
Twelfth Night

主要人物

Orsino [ɔːˈsiːnəʊ] 奥西诺（伊利里亚公爵）

Sebastian [sɪˈbæstjən] 西巴斯辛（薇奥拉之兄）

Olivia [əˈlɪvɪə] 奥丽维娅（富有的伯爵小姐）

Viola [ˈvaɪələ] 薇奥拉（热恋公爵者）

Cesario [siːˈzɑːrɪəʊ] 西萨里奥（薇奥拉化名）

Malvolio [mælˈvəʊljəʊ] 马伏里奥（奥丽维娅的管家）

Sir Toby [ˈtəʊbi] 托比爵士（奥丽维娅的叔父）

Sir Andrew [ˈændruː] Aguecheek [ˈeɪgjuːtʃiːk] 安德鲁·艾古契克爵士（奥丽维娅的追求者）

Orsino, the Duke of Illyria①, was deeply in love with a beautiful Countess② named Olivia. Yet was all his love in vain③, for she disdained④ his suit⑤; and when her brother died, she sent back a messenger from the Duke, bidding him tell his master that for seven years she would not let the very air behold her face, but that, like a nun⑥, she would walk veiled⑦; and all this for the sake of⑧ a dead brother's love, which she would keep fresh and lasting in her sad remembrance⑨.[i]

The Duke longed for someone to whom he could tell his sorrow, and repeat over and over again the story of his love. And chance brought him such a companion. For about this time a goodly⑩ ship was wrecked on the Illyrian coast, and among those who reached land in safety were the captain and a fair young maid, named Viola. But she was little grateful for being rescued from the perils⑪ of the sea, since she feared that her twin brother Sebastian was drowned. Sebastian was as dear to her as the heart in her bosom⑫, and so like her that, but for the difference in their manner of dress, one could hardly be told from the other.[ii] The captain, for her comfort, told her that he had seen her brother bind⑬ himself "to a strong mast that lived upon the sea", and that

---

① Illyria [ɪˈlɪrɪə]：伊利里亚（欧洲古地区名，位于今巴尔干半岛西北部）
② countess [ˈkaʊntəs] *n*. 女伯爵 a woman who has the rank of a count or an earl
③ in vain：徒然 vainly, to no avail, without success
④ disdain [dɪsˈdeɪn] *v*. 鄙视 scorn, despise
⑤ suit [suːt] *n*. 求婚 courtship, courting, wooing
⑥ nun [nʌn] *n*. 修女，尼姑 sister
⑦ veiled [veɪld] *adj*. 蒙上面纱的 wearing a veil
⑧ for the sake of：为了…… in order to
⑨ remembrance [rɪˈmembrəns] *n*. 回忆 memory, recollection
⑩ goodly [ˈgʊdli] *adj*. 好看的 good, wonderful, beautiful
⑪ peril [ˈperɪl] *n*. 危险 danger, risk, threat, hazard, jeopardy
⑫ bosom [ˈbʊzəm] *n*. 胸部 breast, chest
⑬ bind [baɪnd] *v*. 捆绑 tie (up) fasten

thus there was hope that he might be saved.

Viola now asked in whose country she was, and learning that the young Duke Orsino ruled there, and was as noble in his nature as in his name, she decided to disguise herself in male attire[1], and seek for employment with him as a page[2].

In this she succeeded, and now from day to day she had to listen to the story of Orsino's love. At first she sympathized[3] very truly with him, but soon her sympathy grew to love. At last it occurred to Orsino that his hopeless love-suit might prosper[4] better if he sent this pretty lad[5] to woo[6] Olivia for him. Viola unwillingly went on this errand[7], but when she came to the house, Malvolio, Olivia's steward[8], a vain[9], officious[10] man, sick, as his mistress told him, of self-love, forbade the messenger admittance[11].[iii]

Viola, however (who was now called Cesario), refused to take any denial[12], and vowed to have speech with the Countess. Olivia, hearing how her instructions were defied[13] and curious to see this daring[14] youth, said, "We'll once more hear Orsino's embassy[15]."

When Viola was admitted to her presence and the servants had been sent away, she listened patiently to the reproaches[16] which this bold messenger from the Duke poured upon her, and listening she fell in love with the supposed[17] Cesario; and when Cesario had gone, Olivia longed to send some love token[18] after him. So, calling Malvolio, she bade him follow the boy.

"He left this ring behind him," she said, taking one from her finger. "Tell him I will none of it."

Malvolio did as he was bid, and then Viola, who of course knew perfectly well that she had left no ring behind her, saw with a woman's quickness that Olivia loved her. Then she went back

---

① attire [ə'taɪə(r)] *n*. 服装 clothes, clothing
② page [peɪdʒ] *n*. 男侍从 attendant, pageboy, footboy, servant
③ sympathize ['sɪmpəθaɪz] *v*. 同情 pity, commiserate
④ prosper ['prɒspə(r)] *v*. 蓬勃发展 advance, progress
⑤ lad [læd] *n*. 小伙子 boy, young man
⑥ woo [wuː] *v*. 求爱 court, chase, pursue
⑦ errand ['erənd] *n*. 差事 job, commission, task, mission
⑧ steward ['stjuːəd] *n*. 管家 butler, housekeeper
⑨ vain [veɪn] *adj*. 自负的 proud, arrogant, conceited
⑩ officious [ə'fɪʃəs] *adj*. 爱指手画脚的，好管闲事的 self-important, bossy, meddlesome
⑪ admittance [əd'mɪtns] *n*. 进入(权) access, entry, entrance
⑫ denial [dɪ'naɪəl] *n*. 拒绝 refusal, rejection, rebuff
⑬ defy [dɪ'faɪ] *v*. 反抗 resist, oppose, confront, stand up to
⑭ daring ['deərɪŋ] *adj*. 大胆的 brave, bold, fearless
⑮ embassy ['embəsi] *n*. 使者 messenger, go-between
⑯ reproach [rɪ'prəʊtʃ] *n*. 指责 denunciation, reprimand, rebuke
⑰ supposed [sə'pəʊzd] *adj*. 所谓的 so-called, alleged
⑱ love token：爱情信物 keepsake, souvenir, memento

to the Duke, very sad at heart for her lover, and for Olivia, and for herself.

It was but cold comfort① she could give Orsino, who now sought to ease the pangs② of despised③ love by listening to sweet music, while Cesario stood by his side.[iv]

"Ah," said the Duke to his page that night, "you too have been in love."

"A little," answered Viola.

"What kind of woman is it?" he asked.

"Of your complexion④," she answered.

"What years, in faith⑤?" was his next question.

To this came the pretty answer, "About your years, My Lord."

"Too old, by Heaven!" cried the Duke. "Let still the woman take an elder than herself."

And Viola very meekly⑥ said, "I think it well, My Lord."

By and by Orsino begged Cesario once more to visit Olivia and to plead⑦ his love suit. But she, thinking to dissuade him, said—

"If some lady loved you as you love Olivia?"

"Ah! That cannot be," said the Duke.

"But I know," Viola went on, "what love a woman may have for a man. My father had a daughter loved a man, as it might be," she added blushing⑧, "perhaps, were I a woman, I should love Your Lordship."[v]

"And what is her history?" he asked.

"A blank, My Lord," Viola answered. "She never told her love, but let concealment⑨, like a worm in the bud, feed on her damask⑩ cheek. She pined⑪ in thought, and with a green and yellow melancholy⑫ she sat like patience on a monument, smiling at grief. Was not this love indeed?"

"But died thy sister of her love, my boy?" the Duke asked. And Viola, who had all the time been telling her own love for him in this pretty fashion, said—

"I am all the daughters my father has and all the brothers, too[vi]—Sir, shall I go to the lady?"

① cold comfort: 于事无补的安慰 little or no comfort
② pang [pæŋ] *n*. 剧痛 pain, stab, twinge
③ despise [dɪ'spaɪz] *v*.(此处为过去分词用作形容词)轻视 scorn, disdain, look down on
④ complexion [kəm'plekʃn] *n*. 肤色 skin color, skin tone
⑤ in faith: 老实说 honestly, frankly
⑥ meekly ['miːkli] *adv*. 温顺地 mildly, tenderly
⑦ plead [pliːd] *v*. 恳求 beg, appeal, petition
⑧ blush [blʌʃ] *v*. 脸红 redden, flush, turn red, go scarlet
⑨ concealment [kən'siːlmənt] *n*. 隐藏 cover, hiding
⑩ damask ['dæməsk] *adj*. 淡红色的,粉红色的 pink, reddish
⑪ pine [paɪn] *v*.(因悲伤、病痛等)消瘦,憔悴 waste away, decline, weaken, wither
⑫ melancholy ['melənkəli] *n*. 忧郁 sadness, sorrow

"To her in haste[①]," said the Duke, at once forgetting all about the story, "and give her this jewel."

So Viola went, and this time poor Olivia was unable to hide her love, and openly confessed it with such passionate[②] truth, that Viola left her hastily, saying—

"Nevermore[③] will I deplore[④] my master's tears to you."

But in vowing this, Viola did not know the tender[⑤] pity she would feel for other's suffering. So when Olivia, in the violence of her love, sent a messenger, praying Cesario to visit her once more, Cesario had no heart to refuse the request.

But the favors which Olivia bestowed[⑥] upon this mere page aroused[⑦] the jealousy of Sir Andrew Aguecheek, a foolish, rejected lover of hers, who at that time was staying at her house with her merry old uncle Sir Toby. This same Sir Toby dearly loved a practical joke, and knowing Sir Andrew to be an arrant[⑧] coward, he thought that if he could bring off a duel[⑨] between him and Cesario, there would be rare sport[⑩] indeed. So he induced[⑪] Sir Andrew to send a challenge, which he himself took to Cesario. The poor page, in great terror, said—

"I will return again to the house. I am no fighter."

"Back you shall not to the house," said Sir Toby, "unless you fight me first."

And as he looked a very fierce old gentleman, Viola thought it best to await[⑫] Sir Andrew's coming; and when he at last made his appearance[⑬], in a great fright[⑭], if the truth had been known, she tremblingly drew her sword, and Sir Andrew in like fear followed her example.[vii] Happily for them both, at this moment some officers of the Court came on the scene[⑮], and stopped the intended[⑯] duel. Viola gladly made off[⑰] with what speed she might, while Sir Toby called after her—

"A very paltry[⑱] boy, and more a coward than a hare!"

Now, while these things were happening, Sebastian had escaped all the dangers of the deep, and had landed safely in Illyria, where he determined to make his way to the Duke's Court. On his way thither he passed Olivia's house just as Viola had left it in such a hurry, and whom should he

---

① in haste：快速地 quickly, rapidly, hastily
② passionate [ˈpæʃənət] *adj*. 狂热的 wild, enthusiastic
③ nevermore [ˌnevəˈmɔː(r)] *adv*. 不再 never again
④ deplore [dɪˈplɔː(r)] *v*. 悲叹 regret, lament, grieve
⑤ tender [ˈtendə(r)] *adj*. 温柔的 gentle
⑥ bestow [bɪˈstəʊ] *v*. 给予 give, present, award, grant, confer
⑦ arouse [əˈraʊz] *v*. 激起 inspire, stimulate, stir up
⑧ arrant [ˈærənt] *adj*. 彻头彻尾的 total, complete, utter, thorough
⑨ duel [ˈdjuːəl] *n*. 决斗 fight, battle
⑩ sport [spɔːt] *n*. 乐趣 fun, amusement, entertainment
⑪ induce [ɪnˈdjuːs] *v*. 劝说 persuade, influence
⑫ await [əˈweɪt] *v*. 等待 expect, wait for, look forward to
⑬ make one's appearance：公开露面，出现 emerge, turn up
⑭ fright [fraɪt] *n*. 惊恐 fear, alarm, horror, terror
⑮ come on the scene：出场，出现 arrive, appear, turn up
⑯ intended [ɪnˈtendɪd] *adj*. 蓄意的 planned, intentional
⑰ make off：逃走 fly, flee, run away, take to one's heels
⑱ paltry [ˈpɔːltri] *adj*. 微不足道的 unimportant, insignificant

meet but Sir Andrew and Sir Toby. Sir Andrew, mistaking Sebastian for the cowardly① Cesario, took his courage in both hands, and walking up to him struck him, saying, "There's for you."

"Why, there's for you, and there, and there!" said Sebastian, hitting back a great deal harder, and again and again, till Sir Toby came to the rescue of his friend. Sebastian, however, tore himself free from Sir Toby's clutches②, and drawing his sword would have fought them both, but that Olivia herself, having heard of the quarrel, came running in, and with many reproaches sent Sir Toby and his friend away.[viii] Then turning to Sebastian, whom she too thought to be Cesario, she besought③ him with many a pretty speech to come into the house with her.

Sebastian, half dazed④ and all delighted with her beauty and grace, readily consented, and that very day, so great was Olivia's haste, they were married before she had discovered that he was not Cesario, or Sebastian was quite certain whether or not he was in a dream.[ix]

Meanwhile Orsino, hearing how ill Cesario sped with Olivia, visited her himself, taking Cesario with him. Olivia met them both before her door, and seeing, as she thought, her husband there, reproached⑤ him for leaving her, while to the Duke she said that his suit was as fat and fulsome⑥ to her as howling⑦ after music.[x]

"Still so cruel?" said Orsino.

"Still so constant⑧," she answered.

Then Orsino's anger growing to cruelty, he vowed that, to be revenged⑨ on her, he would kill Cesario, whom he knew she loved. "Come, boy," he said to the page.

And Viola, following him as he moved away, said, "I, to do you rest, a thousand deaths would die."[xi]

A great fear took hold on Olivia, and she cried aloud, "Cesario, husband, stay!"

"Her husband?" asked the Duke angrily.

"No, My Lord, not I," said Viola.

"Call forth the Holy Father⑩," cried Olivia.

And the priest⑪ who had married Sebastian and Olivia, coming in, declared Cesario to be the bridegroom⑫.

"O thou dissembling⑬ cub⑭!" the Duke exclaimed. "Farewell⑮, and take her, but go where

---

① cowardly [ˈkauədli] *adj*. 怯懦的 spineless, faint-hearted, timid
② clutch [klʌtʃ] *n*. 控制 power, control
③ beseech [bɪˈsiːtʃ] *v*. 恳求 beg, implore, petition
④ dazed [deɪzd] *adj*. 茫然的 confused
⑤ reproach [rɪˈprəutʃ] *v*. 指责 blame, scold, find fault with
⑥ fulsome [ˈfulsəm] *adj*. 过分恭维的 oily, smarmy
⑦ howling [ˈhaulɪŋ] *n*. 啸鸣 cry, scream
⑧ constant [ˈkɒnstənt] *adj*. 坚定的 firm, unswerving, steadfast
⑨ revenge [rɪˈvendʒ] *v*. 报仇 avenge, retaliate
⑩ Holy Father: 教皇 the Pope
⑪ priest [priːst] *n*. 神父 pastor, churchman, clergyman
⑫ bridegroom [ˈbraɪdgruːm] *n*. 新郎 husband, newly-wed
⑬ dissembling [dɪˈsemblɪŋ] *adj*. 骗人的 cheating, pretending
⑭ cub [kʌb] *n*. 〈古〉(尤指笨拙或举止粗鲁的)毛头小伙子
⑮ farewell [ˌfeəˈwel] *n*. & *int*. 告别 goodbye, so long, adieu

thou and I henceforth① may never meet."

At this moment Sir Andrew came up with bleeding crown②, complaining that Cesario had broken his head, and Sir Toby's as well.

"I never hurt you," said Viola, very positively. "You drew your sword on me, but I bespoke③ you fair, and hurt you not."[xii]

Yet, for all her protesting, no one there believed her, but all their thoughts were on a sudden④ changed to wonder, when Sebastian came in.

"I am sorry, madam," he said to his wife. "I have hurt your kinsman⑤. Pardon me, sweet, even for the vows we made each other so late ago."

"One face, one voice, one habit⑥, and two persons!" cried the Duke, looking first at Viola, and then at Sebastian.

"An apple cleft⑦ in two," said one who knew Sebastian, "is not more twin than these two creatures. Which is Sebastian?"

"I never had a brother," said Sebastian. "I had a sister, whom the blind waves and surges have devoured⑧." "Were you a woman," he said to Viola, "I should let my tears fall upon your cheek, and say, 'Thrice⑨ welcome, drowned Viola!'"[xiii]

Then Viola, rejoicing to see her dear brother alive, confessed that she was indeed his sister, Viola. As she spoke, Orsino felt the pity that is akin to⑩ love.

"Boy," he said, "thou hast said to me a thousand times thou never shouldst love woman like to me."[xiv]

"And all those sayings will I overswear," Viola replied, "and all those swearings keep true."[xv]

"Give me thy hand," Orsino cried in gladness. "Thou shalt be my wife, and my fancy's queen."[xvi]

Thus was the gentle Viola made happy, while Olivia found in Sebastian a constant⑪ lover, and a good husband, and he in her a true and loving wife.[xvii]

---

① henceforth [ˌhensˈfɔːθ] *adv*. 从今以后 from now on, hereafter
② crown [kraʊn] *n*. 头顶 head, pate
③ bespeak [bɪˈspiːk] *v*. 〈古〉对……说 address
④ on a sudden: 突然间 suddenly, all of a sudden
⑤ kinsman [ˈkɪnzmən] *n*. 亲戚 relative, relation
⑥ habit [ˈhæbɪt] *n*. 衣服 clothing, garment, outfit
⑦ cleave [kliːv] *v*. 切开 cut, split, slice, divide
⑧ devour [dɪˈvaʊə(r)] *v*. 吞噬 swallow, engulf
⑨ thrice [θraɪs] *adv*. 三次;三倍 three times
⑩ akin to: 类似的 similar/related/comparable to
⑪ constant [ˈkɒnstənt] *adj*. 忠诚的 true, loyal, faithful

ⅰ ...bidding him tell his master that for seven years she would not let the very air behold her face, but that, like a nun, she would walk veiled; and all this for the sake of a dead brother's love, which she would keep fresh and lasting in her sad remembrance. ……让他告诉主人，以后整整七年，就连空气也无法窥见她的面容。她要像一位修女一样，蒙着面纱而行。这都是为了纪念她对死去的哥哥的爱，她要让这份爱永远鲜活地保留在她悲伤的记忆里。（bid sb. do...：bid 的宾语补足语为不带 to 的动词不定式；that..., but that...：并列宾语从句；which...：非限制性定语从句）

ⅱ But she was little grateful for being rescued from the perils of the sea, since she feared that her twin brother Sebastian was drowned. Sebastian was as dear to her as the heart in her bosom, and so like her that, but for the difference in their manner of dress, one could hardly be told from the other. 但是，薇奥拉对于从大海中死里逃生并不感到庆幸，因为她担心自己的孪生哥哥西巴斯辛已经淹死。她把西巴斯辛看得像胸腔中的心脏一样珍贵，而且兄妹俩长得非常相像，如果不是穿着不同的衣服，几乎谁也无法区分他们。（so...that...："如此……以至于……"，that 引导结果状语从句；but for...："要不是……"）

ⅲ Viola unwillingly went on this errand, but when she came to the house, Malvolio, Olivia's steward, a vain, officious man, sick, as his mistress told him, of self-love, forbade the messenger admittance. 薇奥拉不情愿地去办这件差事，可是到了伯爵小姐府上，奥丽维娅的管家马伏里奥，一个虚荣的、喜欢多管闲事的男人，厌倦了公爵的这种自作多情——这是女主人告诉他的——不让这位使者进门。

ⅳ It was but cold comfort she could give Orsino, who now sought to ease the pangs of despised love by listening to sweet music, while Cesario stood by his side. 她能给予奥西诺的，只是一些无用的安慰。奥西诺通过听柔美的音乐来缓解失恋的痛苦，西萨里奥默默地站在一旁陪伴他。

ⅴ "But I know," Viola went on, "what love a woman may have for a man. My father had a daughter loved a man, as it might be," she added blushing, "perhaps, were I a woman, I should love Your Lordship." "但我很清楚地知道女人对于男人会怀着怎样的爱。"薇奥拉继续说。"我父亲有一个女儿，她爱上了一个男人，"她红着脸往下说道，"正像假如我是个女人，也许会爱上殿下您一样。"（daughter 后省略了关系代词 who/that，关系代词引导定语从句并在定语从句中作主语，现代英语的定语从句中作主语的关系代词通常不能省略）

ⅵ I am all the daughters my father has and all the brothers, too... 我父亲的女儿只有我一个，儿子也只有我一个……（薇奥拉认定哥哥已经淹死，这样说的言外之意是：我父亲只剩我一个女儿，也只有我一个不得不女扮男装的儿子。公爵当然听不懂她话里的意思。）

ⅶ ...when he at last made his appearance, in a great fright, if the truth had been known, she tremblingly drew her sword, and Sir Andrew in like fear followed her example. 安德鲁爵士终于露面了，薇奥拉陷入了极度恐惧之中，生怕自己的身份露馅儿。她颤颤巍巍地拔出了剑，安德鲁爵士也是在恐惧中拔剑自卫。

ⅷ Sebastian, however, tore himself free from Sir Toby's clutches, and drawing his sword would have fought them both, but that Olivia herself, having heard of the quarrel, came running in, and with many reproaches sent Sir Toby and his friend away. 西巴斯辛挣脱了托比爵士的纠缠，拔出剑来要跟他们俩较量。这时，奥丽维娅听见争吵声跑了过来，她把托比爵士和他的朋友狠狠训斥了一番，把他们打发走了。

ⅸ Sebastian, half dazed and all delighted with her beauty and grace, readily consented, and that very day, so great was Olivia's haste, they were married before she had discovered that he was not Cesario, or Sebastian was quite certain whether or not he was in a dream. 西巴斯辛一头雾水，但他非常喜欢奥丽维娅的美丽和典雅，就欣然答应了。奥丽维娅太迫不及待了，当天两个人就结婚了。奥丽维娅都没发现新郎不是西萨里奥；而西巴斯辛呢，他一直没弄清自己是不是在做梦。[so..., (that) they...:"如此……以至于……"，此处省略了引导结果状语从句的连词 that; before:"还没有……就……"]

ⅹ Olivia met them both before her door, and seeing, as she thought, her husband there, reproached him for leaving her, while to the Duke she said that his suit was as fat and fulsome to her as howling after music. 奥丽维娅在门口见到他们，以为看见了她的丈夫，就责怪他不该离开自己。她还对公爵说，他的求爱实在令人生腻，就像奏过音乐以后的啸鸣一样令人不耐。

ⅺ "I, to do you rest, a thousand deaths would die." "我甘愿受死一千次，只要您心里得到安慰。"

ⅻ "I never hurt you," said Viola, very positively. "You drew your sword on me, but I bespoke you fair, and hurt you not." "我没有伤害过你。"薇奥拉一口否认，"你向我拔出剑来，但是我对你很客气，并没有伤害你。"(hurt you not＝did not hurt you)

xiii "Were you a woman," he said to Viola, "I should let my tears fall upon your cheek, and say, 'Thrice welcome, drowned Viola!'" "如果你是个女人，"他对薇奥拉说，"我会让我的眼泪滴在你的脸上，说一声'热烈地欢迎你，被海水吞没的薇奥拉！'"(were you...＝if you were...：与现在事实相反的非真实条件句省略 if 时的部分倒装）

xiv "Boy," he said, "thou hast said to me a thousand times thou never shouldst love woman like to me." "孩子，"他说，"你曾经对我说过一千次，绝不会爱一个女人像爱我一样。"(thou＝you; hast＝have; shouldst＝should; like to me＝like me)

xv "And all those sayings will I overswear," Viola replied, "and all those swearings keep true." 薇奥拉答道："我愿意再次发誓说一遍所有的话，那一切的誓言我都坚守在心。"

xvi "Give me thy hand," Orsino cried in gladness. "Thou shalt be my wife, and my fancy's queen." 奥西诺喜极而泣："把你的手给我，你要做我的妻子，我梦寐以求的王后。"(thy＝your; thou＝you; shalt＝shall)

xvii Thus was the gentle Viola made happy, while Olivia found in Sebastian a constant lover, and a good husband, and he in her a true and loving wife. 就这样，温柔的薇奥拉获得了幸福。奥丽维娅发现西巴斯辛是忠贞的爱人和理想的丈夫，西巴斯辛也发现奥丽维娅是真诚而温情脉脉的妻子。(and he in her...＝and he found in her...：省略结构）

希罗《无事生非》

O god of love! I know he doth deserve
As much as may be yielded to a man;
But Nature never framed a woman's heart
Of prouder stuff than that of Beatrice;
Disdain and scorn ride sparkling in her eyes,
Misprizing what they look on, and her wit
Values itself so highly that to her
All matter else seems weak. She cannot love,
Nor take no shape nor project of affection
She is so self-endeared.

爱神在上，我也知道像他这样的人品
是值得享受世间一切至美至好的事物的；
可是造物造下的女人的心，
没有一颗比得上像贝特丽丝那样骄傲冷酷的；
轻蔑和讥嘲在她的眼睛里闪耀着，
把她所看见的一切贬得一文不值，
她因为自恃才情，
所以什么都不放在她的眼里。她不会恋爱，
也从来不想到有恋爱这件事；
她是太自命不凡了。

贝特丽丝《无事生非》

But Nature never framed a woman's heart
Of prouder stuff than that of Beatrice.
Disdain and scorn ride sparkling in her eyes,
Misprizing what they look on, and her wit
Values itself so highly that to her
All matter else seems weak. She cannot love
Nor take no shape nor project of affection
She is so self-endeared.

可是造物造下的女人的心，
没有一颗比得上像贝特丽丝那样骄傲冷酷的；
轻蔑和讥嘲在她的眼睛里闪耀着，
把她所看见的一切贬得一文不值，
她因为自恃才情，
所以什么都不放在她的眼里。她不会恋爱，
也从来不想到有恋爱这件事；
她是太自命不凡了。

无事生非
Much Ado About Nothing

主要人物

Leonato [liːəˈnɑːtəʊ] 里奥那托(墨西拿总督)
Hero [ˈhɪərəʊ] 希罗(里奥那托的女儿)
Beatrice [ˈbɪətrɪs] 贝特丽丝(里奥那托的侄女)
Don Pedro [dɒn ˈpeɪdrəʊ] 唐·彼德罗(阿拉贡亲王)
Don John [dɒn dʒɒn] 唐·约翰(唐·彼德罗的庶弟)
Claudio [ˈklɔːdɪəʊ] 克劳狄奥(佛罗伦萨的少年贵族)
Benedick [ˈbenɪdɪk] 培尼狄克(帕多瓦的少年贵族)
Ursula [ˈɜːsjʊlə] 欧苏拉(希罗的侍女)
Margaret [ˈmɑːgərɪt] 玛格莱特(希罗的侍女)
Borachio [bəʊˈrɑːtʃɪəʊ] 波拉契奥(唐·约翰的侍从)
Friar [ˈfraɪə(r)] Francis [ˈfrɑːnsɪs] 法兰西斯神父

In Sicily there is a town called Messina①, which is the scene of a curious② storm in a teacup that raged several hundred years ago.ⁱ

It began with sunshine. Don Pedro, Prince of Arragon③, in Spain, had gained so complete a victory over his foes that the very land whence they came is forgotten.ⁱⁱ Feeling happy and playful after the fatigues④ of war, Don Pedro came for a holiday to Messina, and in his suite⑤ were his stepbrother Don John and two young Italian lords, Benedick and Claudio.

Benedick was a merry chatterbox⑥, who had determined to live a bachelor⑦. Claudio, on the other hand, had no sooner arrived at Messina than he fell in love with Hero, the daughter of Leonato, Governor of Messina.ⁱⁱⁱ

One July day, a perfumer⑧ called Borachio was burning dried lavender⑨ in a musty⑩ room in Leonato's house, when the sound of conversation floated through the open window.

"Give me your candid⑪ opinion of Hero," Claudio, asked, and Borachio settled⑫ himself for

---

① Messina [meˈsiːnə]: 墨西拿(西西里岛东北部城市)
② curious [ˈkjʊəriəs] *adj*. 不寻常的 strange, unusual, bizarre
③ Arragon[ˈærəgən]: 阿拉贡自治区(位于西班牙东北部)
④ fatigue [fəˈtiːg] *n*. 疲乏 tiredness, weariness
⑤ suite [swiːt] *n*. (一批)随员 train, follower, entourage
⑥ chatterbox [ˈtʃætəbɒks] *n*. 话多的人 chatterer
⑦ bachelor [ˈbætʃələ(r)] *n*. 单身汉 a man who has never been married
⑧ perfumer [pəˈfjuːmə(r)] *n*. 调香师 one who makes perfumes
⑨ lavender [ˈlævəndə(r)] *n*. 薰衣草;干薰衣草花
⑩ musty [ˈmʌsti] *adj*. 发霉的 stale, smelly, mouldy
⑪ candid [ˈkændɪd] *adj*. 坦率的 open, honest, frank
⑫ settle [ˈsetl] *v*. 使处于舒适的位置 install, make comfortable

comfortable listening.

"Too short and brown for praise," was Benedick's reply. "But alter[1] her color or height, and you spoil[2] her."[iv]

"In my eyes she is the sweetest of women," said Claudio.

"Not in mine," retorted[3] Benedick, "and I have no need for glasses. She is like the last day of December compared with[4] the first of May if you set her beside her cousin.[v] Unfortunately, the Lady Beatrice is a fury[5]. "

Beatrice was Leonato's niece. She amused[6] herself by saying witty[7] and severe[8] things about Benedick, who called her dear Lady Disdain. She was wont[9] to say that she was born under a dancing star, and could not therefore be dull.[vi]

Claudio and Benedick were still talking when Don Pedro came up and said good-humoredly[10], "Well, gentlemen, what's the secret?"

"I am longing," answered Benedick, "for Your Grace[11] to command me to tell."

"I charge[12] you, then, on your allegiance[13] to tell me," said Don Pedro, falling in with[14] his humor.

"I can be as dumb as a mute[15]," apologized Benedick to Claudio, "but His Grace commands my speech." To Don Pedro he said, "Claudio is in love with Hero, Leonato's short daughter."

Don Pedro was pleased, for he admired Hero and was fond of Claudio. When Benedick had departed[16], he said to Claudio, "Be steadfast[17] in your love for Hero, and I will help you to win her. Tonight her father gives a masquerade[18], and I will pretend I am Claudio, and tell her how Claudio loves her, and if she be pleased, I will go to her father and ask his consent to your union[19]."

Most men like to do their own wooing[20], but if you fall in love with a Governor's only daughter, you are fortunate if you can trust a prince to plead for you.

Claudio then was fortunate, but he was unfortunate as well, for he had an enemy who was

---

① alter [ˈɔːltə(r)] *v*. 改变 change, transform, adjust, modify
② spoil [spɔɪl] *v*. 破坏，糟蹋 damage, destroy, ruin
③ retort [rɪˈtɔːt] *v*. 反驳 refute, contradict, counter
④ compare with：与……相比
⑤ fury [ˈfjʊəri] *n*. 泼妇 shrew
⑥ amuse [əˈmjuːz] *v*.（使）娱乐 delight, entertain
⑦ witty [ˈwɪti] *adj*. 诙谐机智的 clever, brilliant, funny, humorous
⑧ severe [sɪˈvɪə(r)] *adj*. 严厉的 strict, hard, harsh, cruel, rigid
⑨ wont [wəʊnt] *adj*. 习惯的 used, accustomed, given
⑩ good-humoredly [ˌgʊdˈhjuːmədli] *adv*. 脾气很好地；心情愉快地 in a good mood
⑪ Your(His/Her) Grace：大人，阁下，夫人 Your(His/Her) Lordship/Ladyship
⑫ charge [tʃɑːdʒ] *v*. 命令 order, demand, command
⑬ allegiance [əˈliːdʒəns] *n*. 效忠 loyalty, faithfulness
⑭ fall in with：赞成；和……一致 support, agree with
⑮ mute [mjuːt] *n*. 哑巴 a person who is not able to speak
⑯ depart [dɪˈpɑːt] *v*. 离去 leave, take leave
⑰ steadfast [ˈstedfɑːst] *adj*. 坚定的 firm, steady, constant
⑱ masquerade [ˌmæskəˈreɪd] *n*. 假面舞会 masked ball
⑲ union [ˈjuːniən] *n*. 结婚 match, marriage
⑳ wooing [ˈwuːɪŋ] *n*. 求婚 courting, courtship, suit

outwardly① a friend. This enemy was Don Pedro's stepbrother Don John, who was jealous of Claudio because Don Pedro preferred him to Don John.

It was to Don John that Borachio came with the interesting conversation which he had overheard②.[vii]

"I shall have some fun at that masquerade myself," said Don John when Borachio ceased speaking.

On the night of the masquerade, Don Pedro, masked and pretending he was Claudio, asked Hero if he might walk with her.

They moved away together, and Don John went up to Claudio and said, "Signor Benedick, I believe?" "The same," fibbed③ Claudio.

"I should be much obliged④ then," said Don John, "if you would use your influence with my brother to cure him of his love for Hero. She is beneath him in rank⑤."

"How do you know he loves her?" inquired⑥ Claudio.

"I heard him swear⑦ his affection⑧," was the reply, and Borachio chimed in⑨ with, "So did I too."

Claudio was then left to himself, and his thought was that his Prince had betrayed⑩ him. "Farewell, Hero," he muttered⑪. "I was a fool to trust to an agent⑫."

Meanwhile Beatrice and Benedick (who was masked) were having a brisk⑬ exchange of opinions.

"Did Benedick ever make you laugh?" she asked.

"Who is Benedick?" he inquired.

"A Prince's jester⑭," replied Beatrice, and she spoke so sharply that he declared afterwards, "I would not marry her, if her estate were the Garden of Eden⑮."[viii]

But the principal⑯ speaker at the masquerade was neither Beatrice nor Benedick. It was Don Pedro, who carried out his plan to the letter⑰, and brought the light back to Claudio's face in a

---

① outwardly ['aʊtwədli] *adv*. 表面上 apparently, seemingly
② overhear [ˌəʊvə'hɪə(r)] *v*. 偷听到 listen in, eavesdrop
③ fib [fɪb] *v*. 撒谎 lie, falsify, tell a lie
④ obliged [ə'blaɪdʒd] *adj*. 感激的 thankful, grateful, appreciative
⑤ rank [ræŋk] *n*. 地位 status, standing, position
⑥ inquire [ɪn'kwaɪə(r)] *v*. 询问 ask, question
⑦ swear [sweə(r)] *v*. 发誓 vow, promise, pledge
⑧ affection [ə'fekʃn] *n*. 爱情 love, fondness, attachment
⑨ chime in: 插话 interrupt
⑩ betray [bɪ'treɪ] *v*. 背叛 rebel
⑪ mutter ['mʌtə(r)] *v*. 嘀咕,嘟囔 grumble, mumble
⑫ agent ['eɪdʒənt] *n*. 代理人 representative, deputy
⑬ brisk [brɪsk] *adj*. 快的;忙碌的 quick, busy
⑭ jester ['dʒestə(r)] *n*. 弄臣 fool, clown, prankster, buffoon
⑮ the Garden of Eden ['iːdn]: 伊甸园
⑯ principal ['prɪnsəpl] *adj*. 主要的 main, chief, prime, primary
⑰ to the letter: 严格地 strictly, precisely, accurately

twinkling[1], by appearing before him with Leonato and Hero, and saying, "Claudio, when would you like to go to church?"

"Tomorrow," was the prompt[2] answer. "Time goes on crutches[3] till I marry Hero."

"Give her a week, my dear son," said Leonato, and Claudio's heart thumped[4] with joy.

"And now," said the amiable[5] Don Pedro, "we must find a wife for Signor Benedick. It is a task for Hercules[6]."

"I will help you," said Leonato, "if I have to sit up ten nights."

Then Hero spoke. "I will do what I can, My Lord, to find a good husband for Beatrice."

Thus, with happy laughter, ended the masquerade which had given Claudio a lesson for nothing.[ix]

Borachio cheered up Don John by laying a plan before him with which he was confident[7] he could persuade[8] both Claudio and Don Pedro that Hero was a fickle[9] girl who had two strings to her bow[10]. Don John agreed to this plan of hate.

Don Pedro, on the other hand, had devised[11] a cunning[12] plan of love. "If," he said to Leonato, "we pretend, when Beatrice is near enough to overhear us, that Benedick is pining for[13] her love, she will pity him, see his good qualities, and love him. And if, when Benedick thinks we don't know he is listening, we say how sad it is that the beautiful Beatrice should be in love with a heartless scoffer[14] like Benedick, he will certainly be on his knees before her in a week or less."

So one day, when Benedick was reading in a summer house[15], Claudio sat down outside it with Leonato, and said, "Your daughter told me something about a letter she wrote."

"Letter!" exclaimed Leonato. "She will get up twenty times in the night and write goodness

---

① in a twinkling：转瞬之间，一刹那
② prompt [prɒmpt] *adj*. 迅速的 immediate, rapid, instant
③ crutch [krʌtʃ] *n*. 拐杖 cane, stick, staff
④ thump [θʌmp] *v*. 怦怦跳 beat, throb, pound, pulsate
⑤ amiable ['eɪmiəbl] *adj*. 和蔼可亲的 pleasant, agreeable, friendly
⑥ Hercules ['hɜːkjʊliːz]：赫拉克勒斯(古希腊神话中的大力神)
⑦ confident ['kɒnfɪdənt] *adj*. 确信的 sure, certain, convinced
⑧ persuade [pə'sweɪd] *v*. 使相信 convince, cause to believe
⑨ fickle ['fɪkl] *adj*. 易变的 changeable, faithless, inconstant
⑩ have two strings to one's bow：有两手准备
⑪ devise [dɪ'vaɪz] *v*. 策划 plan, plot, design, think up
⑫ cunning ['kʌnɪŋ] *adj*. 巧妙的 clever, brilliant, ingenious
⑬ pine for：渴望 long for, crave, yearn, hanker after
⑭ scoffer ['skɒfə(r)] *n*. 嘲笑者 mocker, jeerer, flouter
⑮ summer house：凉亭 arbor, pavilion

knows[1] what. But once Hero peeped[2], and saw the words 'Benedick and Beatrice' on the sheet, and then Beatrice tore[3] it up."

"Hero told me," said Claudio, "that she cried, 'O sweet Benedick!'"

Benedick was touched to the core[4] by this improbable[5] story, which he was vain enough to believe. "She is fair and good," he said to himself. "I must not seem proud. I feel that I love her. People will laugh, of course, but their paper bullets[6] will do me no harm."

At this moment Beatrice came to the summer house, and said, "Against my will, I have come to tell you that dinner is ready."

"Fair Beatrice, I thank you," said Benedick.

"I took no more pains to come than you take pains to thank me," was the rejoinder[7], intended to freeze him.ˣ

But it did not freeze him. It warmed him. The meaning he squeezed[8] out of her rude speech was that she was delighted to come to him.

Hero, who had undertaken[9] the task of melting[10] the heart of Beatrice, took no trouble to seek an occasion[11]. She simply said to her maid Margaret one day, "Run into the parlor[12] and whisper to Beatrice that Ursula and I are talking about her in the orchard."

Having said this, she felt as sure that Beatrice would overhear what was meant for her ears as if she had made an appointment with her cousin.

In the orchard was a bower, screened from the sun by honeysuckles[13], and Beatrice entered it a few minutes after Margaret had gone on her errand[14].

"But are you sure," asked Ursula, who was one of Hero's attendants, "that Benedick loves Beatrice so devotedly[15]?"

"So say the Prince and my betrothed[16]," replied Hero, "and they wished me to tell her, but I

---

① goodness knows：上帝才知道，老天才知道
② peep [piːp] *v*. 窥视 peek, peer, spy on
③ tear [teə(r)] *v*. 撕碎 rip, split, shred
④ to the core：彻底；直至核心 deeply, utterly
⑤ improbable [ɪmˈprɒbəbl] *adj*. 不大可能的 unlikely
⑥ bullet [ˈbʊlɪt] *n*. 子弹 ball, shot
⑦ rejoinder [rɪˈdʒɔɪndə(r)] *n*. 回答 reply, answer, response
⑧ squeeze [skwiːz] *v*. 挤压 force, press, compress, squash
⑨ undertake [ˌʌndəˈteɪk] *v*. 承担 take on
⑩ melt [melt] *v*. 使软化，变得温柔 soften, relax, mollify
⑪ occasion [əˈkeɪʒn] *n*. 时机 chance, opportunity
⑫ parlor [ˈpɑːlə(r)] *n*. 客厅 sitting/living room
⑬ honeysuckle [ˈhʌnisʌkl] *n*. 忍冬，金银花
⑭ errand [ˈerənd] *n*. 差事 job, task, mission
⑮ devotedly [dɪˈvəʊtɪdli] *adv*. 忠实地 truly, faithfully
⑯ betrothed [bɪˈtrəʊðd] *n*. 未婚夫 fiancé, husband-to-be

said, 'No! Let Benedick get over it.'"

"Why did you say that?"

"Because Beatrice is unbearably① proud. Her eyes sparkle② with disdain and scorn③. She is too conceited④ to love. I should not like to see her making game of⑤ poor Benedick's love. I would rather see Benedick waste away⑥ like a covered fire."

"I don't agree with you," said Ursula. "I think your cousin is too clear-sighted⑦ not to see the merits⑧ of Benedick."

"He is the one man in Italy, except Claudio," said Hero.

The talkers then left the orchard, and Beatrice, excited and tender, stepped out of the summer house, saying to herself, "Poor dear Benedick, be true to me, and your love shall tame⑨ this wild heart of mine."

We now return to the plan of hate.

The night before the day fixed for Claudio's wedding, Don John entered a room in which Don Pedro and Claudio were conversing⑩, and asked Claudio if he intended to be married tomorrow.

"You know he does!" said Don Pedro.

"He may know differently," said Don John, "when he has seen what I will show him if he will follow me."

They followed him into the garden, and they saw a lady leaning out of Hero's window talking love to Borachio.

Claudio thought the lady was Hero, and said, "I will shame⑪ her for it tomorrow!" Don Pedro thought she was Hero, too, but she was not Hero; she was Margaret.

Don John chuckled⑫ noiselessly when Claudio and Don Pedro quitted⑬ the garden; he gave Borachio a purse containing a thousand ducats⑭.

The money made Borachio feel very gay, and when he was walking in the street with his friend Conrade, he boasted⑮ of his wealth and the giver, and told what he had done.

A watchman overheard them, and thought that a man who had been paid a thousand ducats for villainy⑯ was worth taking in charge⑰. He therefore arrested Borachio and Conrade, who spent the rest of the night in prison.

---

① unbearably [ʌn'beərəbli] *adv*. 无法容忍地 intolerably
② sparkle ['spɑːkl] *v*. 发亮 shine, glitter, glow, gleam
③ scorn [skɔːn] *n*. 蔑视 disdain, contempt, mockery
④ conceited [kən'siːtɪd] *adj*. 自负的 overconfident, vain
⑤ make game of: 嘲弄 taunt, mock, make fun of
⑥ waste away: 日渐衰弱,日益消瘦 decline
⑦ clear-sighted [ˌklɪə 'saɪtɪd] *adj*. 头脑清楚的 wise, insightful
⑧ merit ['merɪt] *n*. 优点 strength, advantage
⑨ tame [teɪm] *v*. 驯服 train, domesticate
⑩ converse [kən'vɜːs] *v*. 交谈 talk, communicate
⑪ shame [ʃeɪm] *v*. 使感到羞耻 disgrace, humiliate
⑫ chuckle ['tʃʌkl] *v*. 轻笑,暗笑 laugh, giggle, snigger
⑬ quit [kwɪt] *v*. 离开 leave, depart, exit
⑭ ducat ['dʌkət] *n*. 达克特(旧时多个欧洲国家通用的金币)
⑮ boast [bəʊst] *v*. 自夸 brag, flaunt, show off
⑯ villainy ['vɪləni] *n*. 坏事 crime, vice, sin, wickedness
⑰ take in charge: 逮捕 arrest, apprehend

Before noon of the next day half the aristocrats① in Messina were at church. Hero thought it was her wedding day, and she was there in her wedding dress, no cloud on her pretty face or in her frank and shining eyes.

The priest was Friar Francis. Turning to Claudio, he said, "You come hither②, My Lord, to marry this lady?" "No!" contradicted③ Claudio.

Leonato thought he was quibbling④ over grammar. "You should have said, Friar," he said, "'You come to be married to her.'"

Friar Francis turned to Hero. "Lady," he said, "you come hither to be married to this Count⑤?"

"I do," replied Hero.

"If either of you know any impediment⑥ to this marriage, I charge you to utter⑦ it," said the Friar.

"Do you know of any, Hero?" asked Claudio.

"None," she said.

"Know you of any, Count?" demanded the Friar. "I dare reply for him, 'None,'" said Leonato.

Claudio exclaimed bitterly, "O! What will not men dare say![xi] Father," he continued, "will you give me your daughter?"

"As freely," replied Leonato, "as God gave her to me."

"And what can I give you?" asked Claudio. "Which is worthy of this gift?"

"Nothing," said Don Pedro, "unless you give the gift back to the giver."

"Sweet Prince, you teach me," said Claudio. "There, Leonato, take her back."

These brutal words were followed by others which flew from Claudio, Don Pedro and Don John.

The church seemed no longer sacred⑧. Hero took her own part as long as she could, then she swooned⑨.[xii] All her persecutors⑩ left the church, except her father, who was befooled⑪ by the accusations⑫ against her, and cried, "Hence⑬ from her! Let her die!"

But Friar Francis saw Hero blameless with his clear eyes that probed⑭ the soul. "She is innocent⑮," he said. "A thousand signs have told me so."

---

① aristocrat [ˈærɪstəkræt] *n*. 贵族 noble, lord, peer
② hither [ˈhɪðə(r)] *adv*. 〈古〉到此处 here
③ contradict [ˌkɒntrəˈdɪkt] *v*. 否认 refute, rebut, deny
④ quibble [ˈkwɪbl] *v*. (为小事)争论;斤斤计较 argue, complain
⑤ count [kaʊnt] *n*. 伯爵 a nobleman of high rank
⑥ impediment [ɪmˈpedɪmənt] *n*. 障碍 obstacle, barrier, block
⑦ utter [ˈʌtə(r)] *v*. 说,讲 speak, state, articulate, put into words
⑧ sacred [ˈseɪkrɪd] *adj*. 神圣的 holy, hallowed, divine
⑨ swoon [swuːn] *v*. 昏厥 faint, collapse, pass/black out
⑩ persecutor [ˈpɜːsɪkjuːtə(r)] *n*. 迫害者 tormentor, oppressor
⑪ befool [bɪˈfuːl] *v*. 愚弄 fool, trick, cheat, deceive, mislead
⑫ accusation [ˌækjuˈzeɪʃn] *n*. 指控 charge, complaint
⑬ hence [hens] *int*. 去,滚开 begone, go away
⑭ probe [prəʊb] *v*. 探测 explore, examine, look into
⑮ innocent [ˈɪnəsnt] *adj*. 无辜的 guiltless, irreproachable

Hero revived[①] under his kind gaze. Her father, flurried[②] and angry, knew not what to think, and the Friar said, "They have left her as one dead with shame. Let us pretend that she is dead until the truth is declared, and slander[③] turns to remorse."

"The Friar advises well," said Benedick. Then Hero was led away into a retreat[④], and Beatrice and Benedick remained alone in the church.

Benedick knew she had been weeping[⑤] bitterly and long. "Surely I do believe your fair cousin is wronged[⑥]," he said. She still wept.

"Is it not strange," asked Benedick, gently, "that I love nothing in the world as well as you?"

"It were as possible for me to say I loved nothing as well as you," said Beatrice, "but I do not say it. I am sorry for my cousin."

"Tell me what to do for her," said Benedick. "Kill Claudio."

"Ha! Not for the wide world," said Benedick. "Your refusal kills me," said Beatrice. "Farewell."

"Enough! I will challenge him," cried Benedick.

During this scene Borachio and Conrade were in prison. There they were examined[⑦] by a constable[⑧] called Dogberry.

The watchman gave evidence to the effect that[⑨] Borachio had said that he had received a thousand ducats for conspiring[⑩] against Hero.

Leonato was not present at this examination[⑪], but he was nevertheless[⑫] now thoroughly[⑬] convinced[⑭] of Hero's innocence[⑮]. He played the part of bereaved[⑯] father very well, and when Don Pedro and Claudio called on him in a friendly way, he said to the Italian, "You have slandered[⑰] my child to death, and I challenge you to combat[⑱]."

"I cannot fight an old man," said Claudio.

"You could kill a girl," sneered[⑲] Leonato, and Claudio crimsoned[⑳].

Hot words grew from hot words, and both Don Pedro and Claudio were feeling scorched[㉑]

---

① revive [rɪˈvaɪv] *v*. 苏醒 awaken, wake up, come to life
② flurried [ˈflʌrid] *adj*. 慌乱的 upset, disturbed
③ slander [ˈslɑːndə(r)] *n*. 诽谤 defamation, calumny
④ retreat [rɪˈtriːt] *n*. 隐退处 refuge, hideaway
⑤ weep [wiːp] *v*. 哭泣 cry, sob, moan, shed tears
⑥ wrong [rɒŋ] *v*. 不公正对待 hurt, harm
⑦ examine [ɪgˈzæmɪn] *v*. 审问 question, quiz, interrogate
⑧ constable [ˈkʌnstəbl] *n*. 警察 policeman, police officer
⑨ to the effect that: 意思是,大意是说
⑩ conspire [kənˈspaɪə(r)] *v*. 图谋 plot, scheme, contrive
⑪ examination [ɪgˌzæmɪˈneɪʃn] *n*. 审问 questioning, inquiry
⑫ nevertheless [ˌnevəðəˈles] *adv*. 尽管如此 nonetheless
⑬ thoroughly [ˈθʌrəli] *adv*. 彻底地 fully, completely, entirely
⑭ convinced [kənˈvɪnst] *adj*. 确信的 assured, confident
⑮ innocence [ˈɪnəsns] *n*. 清白 guiltlessness
⑯ bereaved [bɪˈriːvd] *adj*. 丧失亲人的 bereft, grief-stricken
⑰ slander [ˈslɑːndə(r)] *v*. 诽谤 defame, backbite, calumniate
⑱ combat [ˈkɒmbæt] *n*. 决斗 fight, battle, duel
⑲ sneer [snɪə(r)] *v*. 嘲笑 scoff, mock, jeer
⑳ crimson [ˈkrɪmzn] *v*. (脸)变红 redden, blush, flush, go red
㉑ scorched [skɔːtʃt] *adj*. 烧焦的 burnt

when Leonato left the room and Benedick entered.

"The old man," said Claudio, "was like to have snapped[1] my nose off."[xiii]

"You are a villain!" said Benedick, shortly[2]. "Fight me when and with what weapon you please, or I call you a coward."

Claudio was astounded[3], but said, "I'll meet you. Nobody shall say I can't carve[4] a calf's head."

Benedick smiled, and as it was time for Don Pedro to receive officials, the Prince sat down in a chair of state and prepared his mind for justice[5].

The door soon opened to admit Dogberry and his prisoners.

"What offence[6]," said Don Pedro, "are these men charged with?"

Borachio thought the moment a happy one for making a clean breast of[7] it. He laid the whole blame on[8] Don John, who had disappeared. "The Lady Hero being dead," he said, "I desire nothing but the reward of a murderer."[xiv]

Claudio heard with anguish[9] and deep repentance[10].

Upon the reentrance of Leonato he said to him, "This slave makes clear your daughter's innocence. Choose your revenge[11]."

"Leonato," said Don Pedro, humbly, "I am ready for any penance[12] you may impose[13]."

"I ask you both, then," said Leonato, "to proclaim[14] my daughter's innocence, and to honor her tomb by singing her praise before it. As for you, Claudio, I have this to say: my brother has a daughter so like Hero that she might be a copy of her. Marry her, and my vengeful[15] feelings die."

"Noble sir," said Claudio, "I am yours." Claudio then went to his room and composed[16] a solemn song. Going to the church with Don Pedro and his attendants, he sang it before the monument of Leonato's family. When he had ended he said, "Good night, Hero. Yearly will I do this."

He then gravely[17], as became[18] a gentleman whose heart was Hero's, made ready to marry a girl whom he did not love. He was told to meet her in Leonato's house, and was faithful to his

---

① snap [snæp] *v*. 突然咬,猛咬 bite, nip, gnaw
② shortly [ˈʃɔːtli] *adv*. (说话)不耐烦,不友善地 sharply
③ astounded [əˈstaʊndɪd] *adj*. 震惊的 shocked, astonished
④ carve [kɑːv] *v*. 切下,割下 cut, slice, hack
⑤ justice [ˈdʒʌstɪs] *n*. 法律制裁 sentence, conviction
⑥ offence [əˈfens] *n*. 罪行 crime, sin, wrongdoing, misdeed
⑦ make a clean breast of: 完全承认,和盘托出
⑧ lay blame on: 归咎于 impute, attribute
⑨ anguish [ˈæŋgwɪʃ] *n*. 极度痛苦 suffering, agony, torment
⑩ repentance [rɪˈpentəns] *n*. 后悔 regret, guilt, remorse
⑪ revenge [rɪˈvendʒ] *n*. 报复 retaliation, vengeance
⑫ penance [ˈpenəns] *n*. 赎罪 self-punishment, penalty
⑬ impose [ɪmˈpəʊz] *v*. 强加 force, enforce, press
⑭ proclaim [prəˈkleɪm] *v*. 宣布 announce, declare
⑮ vengeful [ˈvendʒfl] *adj*. 复仇的 revengeful, vindictive
⑯ compose [kəmˈpəʊz] *v*. 创作 write, create
⑰ gravely [ˈgreɪvli] *adv*. 沉重地 seriously, solemnly, grimly
⑱ become [bɪˈkʌm] *v*. 适合 suit, fit, match, conform to

appointment①.

He was shown into a room where Antonio (Leonato's brother) and several masked ladies entered after him. Friar Francis, Leonato, and Benedick were present.

Antonio led one of the ladies towards Claudio.

"Sweet," said the young man, "let me see your face."

"Swear first to marry her," said Leonato.

"Give me your hand," said Claudio to the lady, "before this Holy Friar I swear to marry you if you will be my wife."

"Alive I was your wife," said the lady, as she drew off her mask.

"Another Hero!" exclaimed Claudio.

"Hero died," explained Leonato, "only while slander lived."[xv]

The Friar was then going to marry the reconciled② pair, but Benedick interrupted him with, "Softly③, Friar, which of these ladies is Beatrice?"

Hereat④ Beatrice unmasked, and Benedick said, "You love me, don't you?"

"Only moderately⑤," was the reply. "Do you love me?"

"Moderately," answered Benedick.

"I was told you were well-nigh⑥ dead for me," remarked⑦ Beatrice.

"Of you I was told the same," said Benedick.

"Here's your own hand in evidence of your love," said Claudio, producing a feeble sonnet which Benedick had written to his sweetheart. "And here," said Hero, "is a tribute⑧ to Benedick, which I picked out of the pocket of Beatrice."

"A miracle!" exclaimed Benedick. "Our hands are against our hearts![xvi] Come, I will marry you, Beatrice."

"You shall be my husband to save your life," was the rejoinder.

Benedick kissed her on the mouth, and the Friar married them after he had married Claudio and Hero.

"How is Benedick the married man?" asked Don Pedro.

"Too happy to be made unhappy," replied Benedick. "Crack what jokes⑨ you will. As for you, Claudio, I had hoped to run you through the body, but as you are now my kinsman, live whole and love my cousin.[xvii]"

"My cudgel⑩ was in love with you, Benedick, until today," said Claudio; but, "Come, come, let's dance," said Benedick.

---

① appointment [əˈpɔɪntmənt] *n*. 约定 arrangement

② reconcile [ˈrekənsaɪl] *v*. (此处为过去分词用作形容词)使和解 reunite, harmonize

③ softly [ˈsɒftli] *int*. 〈古〉等一等 stay, wait

④ hereat [ˌhɪərˈæt] *adv*. 因此 because of this, as a result of this

⑤ moderately [ˈmɒdərətli] *adv*. 一般地 reasonably, passably

⑥ well-nigh [ˌwel ˈnaɪ] *adv*. 几乎 almost, nearly, virtually

⑦ remark [rɪˈmɑːk] *v*. 谈论 say, comment

⑧ tribute [ˈtrɪbjuːt] *n*. 称赞 praise, eulogy

⑨ crack a joke: 开玩笑 tell a joke

⑩ cudgel [ˈkʌdʒl] *n*. 短棒 club, stick

And dance they did. Not even the news of the capture of Don John was able to stop the flying feet of the happy lovers, for revenge is not sweet against an evil man who has failed to do harm.[xviii]

ⅰ In Sicily there is a town called Messina, which is the scene of a curious storm in a teacup that raged several hundred years ago. 西西里有个小城叫墨西拿,几百年前,那里发生了一件不寻常的小事,结果闹得满城风雨。(which…, that…:定语从句;a storm in a teacup:"茶杯里的风暴,小题大做")

ⅱ Don Pedro, Prince of Arragon, in Spain, had gained so complete a victory over his foes that the very land whence they came is forgotten. 阿拉贡亲王唐·彼德罗在西班牙的一场战争中大获全胜,人们甚至连他们来自何方都不记得了。(so…that…:"如此……以至于……",that引导结果状语从句)

ⅲ Claudio, on the other hand, had no sooner arrived at Messina than he fell in love with Hero, the daughter of Leonato, Governor of Messina. 克劳狄奥与之相反,他刚来到墨西拿就爱上了希罗——墨西拿总督里奥那托的女儿。(no sooner…than…=hardly…when…:"一……就……")

ⅳ "Too short and brown for praise," was Benedick's reply. "But alter her color or height, and you spoil her." 培尼狄克答道:"她太矮,也太黑,不值得恭维;可是改变她的身高和肤色,又会破坏她的形象。"(莎剧原文:…she's too low for a high praise, too brown for a fair praise and too little for a great praise: only this commendation I can afford her, that were she other than she is, she were unhandsome; and being no other but as she is, I do not like her. ……她是太矮了点儿,不能给她太高的恭维;太黑了点儿,不能给她太美的恭维;又太小了点儿,不能给她太大的恭维。我所能给她的唯一的称赞,就是她倘不是像现在这样子,一定很不漂亮;可是她既然不能再好看一点,所以我一点不喜欢她。)

ⅴ She is like the last day of December compared with the first of May if you set her beside her cousin. 如果把她和她的堂姐比较,她就是十二月的岁暮,堂姐是五月的春朝。[like:明喻(simile)修辞]

ⅵ She amused herself by saying witty and severe things about Benedick, who called her dear Lady Disdain. She was wont to say that she was born under a dancing star, and could not therefore be dull. 她经常拿培尼狄克开玩笑取乐,说一些机智又挖苦的话,培尼狄克称她为亲爱的"傲慢小姐"。她常常说自己生在舞动的星空下,所以不会无聊。[Lady Disdain:以普通名词代替专有名词的换称(antonomasia)修辞]

ⅶ It was to Don John that Borachio came with the interesting conversation which he had overheard. 波拉契奥把听来的那场有意思的谈话告诉了唐·约翰。(It was…that…which…:包含定语从句的强调句)

ⅷ "I would not marry her, if her estate were the Garden of Eden." "我不会和她结婚,即使伊甸园的家产都是她的。"[if(=even if)…were…:"即使……是……",与现在事实相反的非真实条件句]

ⅸ Thus, with happy laughter, ended the masquerade which had given Claudio a lesson for nothing. 就这样,假面舞会在欢

声笑语中结束了,克劳狄奥无辜地遭受了愚弄。(主谓完全倒装)

x "I took no more pains to come than you take pains to thank me," was the rejoinder, intended to freeze him. "我来一趟也不是什么辛苦的事,就像你说多谢也不是什么辛苦的事。"贝特丽丝反驳道,想让他难堪。(more...than...: 比较状语从句)

xi O! What will not men dare say! 啊! 人们还有什么不敢说的!

xii Hero took her own part as long as she could, then she swooned. 希罗竭力保持仪态,却突然晕倒了。

xiii "The old man," said Claudio, "was like to have snapped my nose off." "那个老头子,"克劳狄奥说,"差点把我的鼻子咬下来。"(like=likely,be likely to do...:"有可能……,很可能……")

xiv "The Lady Hero being dead," he said, "I desire nothing but the reward of a murderer." "希罗小姐已经死了,"他说,"我不奢望别的,但求处我应得之罪。"(the Lady Hero being dead:独立主格结构作原因状语)

xv "Hero died," explained Leonato, "only while slander lived." 里奥那托解释道:"希罗没能活下来,流言却还在满天飞。"

xvi Our hands are against our hearts! 我们的手不听使唤,会写下违心的话!

xvii As for you, Claudio, I had hoped to run you through the body, but as you are now my kinsman, live whole and love my cousin. 克劳狄奥,你嘛,我原本想狠狠揍你一顿,但既然你现在成了我的亲戚,我就放过你,好好爱我的小姨子。

xviii Not even the news of the capture of Don John was able to stop the flying feet of the happy lovers, for revenge is not sweet against an evil man who has failed to do harm. 唐·约翰被捕的消息也不能阻挡幸福恋人们的飞舞脚步,因为报复一个诡计没有得逞的邪恶之人,并不是什么好事。

朱丽叶《罗密欧与朱丽叶》

O Romeo, Romeo! Wherefore art thou Romeo?	罗密欧啊,罗密欧!为什么你偏偏是罗密欧呢?
Deny thy father and refuse thy name;	否认你的父亲,抛弃你的姓名吧;
Or, if thou wilt not, be but sworn my love,	也许你不愿意这样做,那么只要你宣誓做我的爱人,
And I'll no longer be a Capulet.	我也不愿再姓凯普莱特了。
'Tis but thy name that is my enemy;	只有你的名字才是我的仇敌;
Thou art thyself though, not a Montague.	你即使不姓蒙太古,仍然是这样的一个你。
What's Montague? It is nor hand, nor foot,	姓不姓蒙太古又有什么关系呢?它又不是手,又不是脚,
Nor arm, nor face, nor any other part	又不是手臂,又不是脸,又不是身体上任何
Belonging to a man. O, be some other name!	其他的部分。啊!换一个姓名吧!

罗密欧与朱丽叶
Romeo and Juliet

主要人物

Capulet [ˈkæpjʊlet] 凯普莱特（维洛那城大家族）
Montague [ˈmɒntəgjuː] 蒙太古（维洛那城大家族）
Romeo [ˈrəʊmɪəʊ] 罗密欧（蒙太古之子）
Benvolio [benˈvəʊlɪəʊ] 班伏里奥（蒙太古之侄）
Mercutio [mɜːˈkjuːʃɪəʊ] 茂丘西奥（亲王的亲戚）
Tybalt [ˈtɪbəlt] 提伯尔特（凯普莱特夫人之内侄）
Juliet [ˈdʒuːlɪət] 朱丽叶（凯普莱特之女）
Paris [ˈpærɪs] 帕里斯（少年贵族，亲王的亲戚）
Friar [ˈfraɪə(r)] Lawrence [ˈlɒrəns] 劳伦斯神父（法兰西斯派教士）

Once upon a time there lived in Verona① two great families named Montague and Capulet. They were both rich, and I suppose they were as sensible②, in most things, as other rich people. But in one thing they were extremely③ silly. There was an old, old quarrel between the two families, and instead of making it up④ like reasonable⑤ folks, they made a sort of pet of their quarrel⑥, and would not let it die out⑦.[i] So that a Montague wouldn't speak to a Capulet if he or she met one in the street—nor a Capulet to a Montague—or if they did speak, it was to say rude and unpleasant things, which often ended in a fight. And their relations and servants were just as foolish, so that street fights and duels and uncomfortablenesses⑧ of that kind were always growing out of the Montague-and-Capulet quarrel.

Now Lord Capulet, the head of that family, gave a party—a grand supper and a dance—and he was so hospitable⑨ that he said anyone might come to it except (of course) the Montagues. But there was a young Montague named Romeo, who very much wanted to be there, because Rosaline, the lady he loved, had been asked. This lady had never been at all kind to him, and he had no reason to love her; but the fact was that he wanted to love somebody, and as he hadn't seen the right lady, he was obliged to love the wrong one.[ii] So to the Capulet's grand party he came, with his friends Mercutio and Benvolio.

---

① Verona [vəˈrəʊnə]：维罗纳（意大利北部城市，朱生豪译本中译为“维洛那”）
② sensible [ˈsensəbl] *adj*. 明智的 wise, intelligent, well-advised
③ extremely [ɪkˈstriːmli] *adv*. 极度 unusually, exceptionally
④ make up：和解 shake hands, make peace, come to terms
⑤ reasonable [ˈriːznəbl] *adj*. 通情达理的 sensible, logical, rational
⑥ make a pet of sth.：以……为乐
⑦ die out：消失 disappear, vanish, fade away, cease to exist
⑧ uncomfortableness [ʌnˈkʌmfətəblnəs] *n*. 不安 uneasiness
⑨ hospitable [hɒˈspɪtəbl] *adj*. 好客的 kind, friendly, sociable

Old Capulet welcomed him and his two friends very kindly—and young Romeo moved about among the crowd of courtly① folks dressed in their velvets② and satins③, the men with jeweled sword hilts④ and collars, and the ladies with brilliant gems⑤ on breast and arms, and stones of price set in their bright girdles⑥. Romeo was in his best too, and though he wore a black mask over his eyes and nose, everyone could see by his mouth and his hair, and the way he held his head, that he was twelve times handsomer than anyone else in the room.

Presently amid the dancers he saw a lady so beautiful and so lovable that from that moment he never again gave one thought to that Rosaline whom he had thought he loved.[iii] And he looked at this other fair lady, as she moved in the dance in her white satin and pearls, and all the world seemed vain⑦ and worthless to him compared with her. And he was saying this, or something like it, when Tybalt, Lady Capulet's nephew, hearing his voice, knew him to be Romeo. Tybalt, being very angry, went at once to his uncle, and told him how a Montague had come uninvited to the feast; but old Capulet was too fine a gentleman to be discourteous⑧ to any man under his own roof, and he bade Tybalt be quiet. But this young man only waited for a chance to quarrel with Romeo.

In the meantime Romeo made his way to⑨ the fair lady, and told her in sweet words that he loved her, and kissed her. Just then her mother sent for her⑩, and then Romeo found out that the lady on whom he had set his heart's hopes was Juliet, the daughter of Lord Capulet, his sworn foe⑪. So he went away, sorrowing⑫ indeed, but loving her none the less⑬.

Then Juliet said to her nurse:

"Who is that gentleman that would not dance?"

"His name is Romeo, and a Montague, the only son of your great enemy," answered the nurse.

Then Juliet went to her room, and looked out of her window, over the beautiful green-gray garden, where the moon was shining. And Romeo was hidden in that garden among the trees—because he could not bear to go right away without trying to see her again. So she—not knowing him to be there—spoke her secret thought aloud, and told the quiet garden how she loved Romeo.

And Romeo heard and was glad beyond measure⑭. Hidden below, he looked up and saw her

---

① courtly [ˈkɔːtli] *adj*. 有教养的 refined, dignified, elegant
② velvet [ˈvelvɪt] *n*. 天鹅绒
③ satin [ˈsætɪn] *n*. 缎子
④ hilt [hɪlt] *n*. 刀(或剑等的)柄 handle, handgrip
⑤ gem [dʒem] *n*. 宝石 stone, jewel, precious stone
⑥ girdle [ˈgɜːdl] *n*. 腰带 belt, sash, waistband, corset
⑦ vain [veɪn] *adj*. 徒劳的 useless, pointless, worthless
⑧ discourteous [dɪsˈkɜːtiəs] *adj*. 失礼的 rude, impolite
⑨ make one's way to: 想方设法前往;走近 go to, head for
⑩ send for sb.: 派人去请某人 summon, demand, call for
⑪ sworn foe: 不共戴天的仇敌 sworn enemy
⑫ sorrow [ˈsɒrəʊ] *v*. 感到悲伤 grieve, lament
⑬ none the less: 尽管如此 nevertheless, nonetheless
⑭ beyond measure: 无可估量,极度 immensely, profoundly

fair face in the moonlight, framed① in the blossoming creepers② that grew round her window, and as he looked and listened, he felt as though he had been carried away in a dream, and set down by some magician in that beautiful and enchanted garden.[iv]

"Ah—why are you called Romeo?" said Juliet. "Since I love you, what does it matter what you are called?"

"Call me but love, and I'll be new baptized③—henceforth I never will be Romeo," he cried, stepping into the full white moonlight from the shade of the cypresses④ and oleanders that had hidden him.

She was frightened⑤ at first, but when she saw that it was Romeo himself, and no stranger, she was too glad, and, he standing in the garden below and she leaning⑥ from the window, they spoke long together, each one trying to find the sweetest words in the world, to make that pleasant talk that lovers use. And the tale of all they said, as well as the sweet music their voices made together, is all set down⑦ in a golden book, where you children may read it for yourselves some day.[v]

And the time passed so quickly, as it does for folks who love each other and are together, that when the time came to part, it seemed as though they had met but that moment—and indeed they hardly knew how to part.

"I will send to you tomorrow," said Juliet.

And so at last, with lingering⑧ and longing⑨, they said goodbye.

Juliet went into her room, and a dark curtain hid her bright window. Romeo went away through the still⑩ and dewy⑪ garden like a man in a dream.

The next morning, very early, Romeo went to Friar Laurence, a priest, and, telling him all

---

① frame [freɪm] *v*. 围绕 surround, encircle, encompass
② creeper [ˈkriːpə(r)] *n*. 蔓生植物,攀缘植物
③ baptize [bæpˈtaɪz] *v*. 洗礼 christen
④ cypress [ˈsaɪprəs] *n*. 柏树
⑤ frightened [ˈfraɪtnd] *adj*. 害怕的 alarmed, scared, terrified
⑥ lean [liːn] *v*. 倚靠 rest, prop, recline
⑦ set down: 记下,写下来 record, write down, put in writing
⑧ linger [ˈlɪŋɡə(r)] *v*. 徘徊 stay, remain, delay, hang around
⑨ long [lɒŋ] *v*. 渴望 desire, hunger for, crave, yearn, dream of
⑩ still [stɪl] *adj*. 静谧的 silent, quiet, noiseless, hushed
⑪ dewy [ˈdjuːi] *adj*. 露水打湿的 wet, damp, moist, sodden

the story, begged him to marry him to Juliet without delay①. And this, after some talk, the priest consented② to do.

So when Juliet sent her old nurse to Romeo that day to know what he purposed③ to do, the old woman took back a a message that all was well, and all things ready for the marriage of Juliet and Romeo on the next morning.

The young lovers were afraid to ask their parents' consent④ to their marriage, as young people should do, because of this foolish old quarrel between the Capulets and the Montagues.

And Friar Laurence was willing to help the young lovers secretly, because he thought that when they were once married their parents might soon be told, and that the match⑤ might put a happy end to the old quarrel.

So the next morning early, Romeo and Juliet were married at Friar Laurence's cell, and parted with tears and kisses. And Romeo promised to come into the garden that evening, and the nurse got ready a rope-ladder to let down from the window, so that Romeo could climb up and talk to his dear wife quietly and alone.

But that very day a dreadful thing happened.

Tybalt, the young man who had been so vexed⑥ at Romeo's going to the Capulet's feast, met him and his two friends, Mercutio and Benvolio, in the street, called Romeo a villain, and asked him to fight. Romeo had no wish to fight with Juliet's cousin, but Mercutio drew his sword, and he and Tybalt fought. And Mercutio was killed. When Romeo saw that this friend was dead, he forgot everything except anger at the man who had killed him, and he and Tybalt fought till Tybalt fell dead.

So, on the very day of his wedding⑦, Romeo killed his dear Juliet's cousin, and was sentenced⑧ to be banished. Poor Juliet and her young husband met that night indeed; he climbed the rope-ladder among the flowers, and found her window, but their meeting was a sad one, and they parted with bitter⑨ tears and hearts heavy, because they could not know when they should meet again.

Now Juliet's father, who, of course, had no idea that she was married, wished her to wed⑩ a gentleman named Paris, and was so angry when she refused, that she hurried away to ask Friar Laurence what she should do. He advised her to pretend to consent, and then he said:

"I will give you a draught⑪ that will make you seem to be dead for two days, and then when

---

① without delay: 立即 immediately, instantly
② consent [kən'sent] *v*. 同意 agree, approve, permit, assent
③ purpose ['pɜːpəs] *v*. 打算 plan, mean, intend
④ consent [kən'sent] *n*. 同意 agreement, approval, sanction
⑤ match [mætʃ] *n*. 婚姻 marriage, union
⑥ vexed [vekst] *adj*. 恼怒的 annoyed, irritated
⑦ wedding ['wedɪŋ] *n*. 婚礼 nuptials, marriage (ceremony)
⑧ sentence ['sentəns] *v*. 判决 condemn, convict
⑨ bitter ['bɪtə(r)] *adj*. 痛苦的 miserable, painful
⑩ wed [wed] *v*. 结婚,嫁,娶 marry, get married, tie the knot
⑪ draught [drɑːft] *n*. 药水 potion, medicine

they take you to church it will be to bury① you, and not to marry you. They will put you in the vault② thinking you are dead, and before you wake up Romeo and I will be there to take care of you. Will you do this, or are you afraid?"

"I will do it; talk not to me of fear!" said Juliet. And she went home and told her father she would marry Paris. If she had spoken out and told her father the truth...well, then this would have been a different story.[vi]

Lord Capulet was very much pleased to get his own way③, and set about④ inviting his friends and getting the wedding feast ready. Everyone stayed up all night, for there was a great deal to do, and very little time to do it in. Lord Capulet was anxious⑤ to get Juliet married because he saw she was very unhappy. Of course she was really fretting⑥ about her husband Romeo, but her father thought she was grieving⑦ for the death of her cousin Tybalt, and he thought marriage would give her something else to think about.

Early in the morning the nurse came to call Juliet, and to dress her for her wedding; but she would not wake, and at last the nurse cried out suddenly—

"Alas⑧! Alas! Help! Help! My lady's dead! Oh, well-a-day⑨ that ever I was born!"

Lady Capulet came running in, and then Lord Capulet, and Lord Paris, the bridegroom. There lay Juliet cold and white and lifeless, and all their weeping could not wake her. So it was a burying that day instead of a marrying. Meantime⑩ Friar Laurence had sent a messenger to Mantua⑪ with a letter to Romeo telling him of all these things; and all would have been well, only the messenger was delayed, and could not go.[vii]

But ill news travels fast. Romeo's servant who knew the secret of the marriage, but not of Juliet's pretended⑫ death, heard of her funeral⑬, and hurried to Mantua to tell Romeo how his young wife was dead and lying in the grave.

"Is it so?" cried Romeo, heartbroken. "Then I will lie by Juliet's side tonight."

And he bought himself a poison, and went straight back to Verona. He hastened to the tomb where Juliet was lying. It was not a grave, but a vault. He broke open the door, and was just going down the stone steps that led to the vault where all the dead Capulets lay, when he heard a voice behind him calling on him to stop.[viii]

It was the Count Paris, who was to have married Juliet that very day.

"How dare you come here and disturb the dead bodies of the Capulets, you vile⑭ Montague?"

---

① bury [ˈberi] *v*. 埋葬 entomb, inter, inearth
② vault [vɔːlt] *n*. 地下墓室 crypt, tomb
③ get one's own way: 为所欲为
④ set about: 着手,开始做 begin, start, get down to
⑤ anxious [ˈæŋkʃəs] *adj*. 急切的 eager, keen, impatient
⑥ fret [fret] *v*. 烦恼 worry, anguish, agonize, distress oneself
⑦ grieve [griːv] *v*. 悲伤 mourn, lament, sorrow
⑧ alas [əˈlæs] *int*. 唉(表悲伤、遗憾、恐惧、关切等)
⑨ well-a-day [ˈwel ə ˌdeɪ] *int*. 呜呼
⑩ meantime [ˈmiːntaɪm] *adv*. 与此同时 meanwhile
⑪ Mantua [ˈmæntjʊə]: 曼图亚(意大利城市,朱生豪译本中译为"曼多亚")
⑫ pretended [prɪˈtendɪd] *adj*. 假装的 feigned, assumed
⑬ funeral [ˈfjuːnərəl] *n*. 葬礼 burial
⑭ vile [vaɪl] *adj*. 卑鄙的 wicked, evil, mean, disgraceful

cried Paris.

Poor Romeo, half mad with sorrow, yet tried to answer gently.

"You were told," said Paris, "that if you returned to Verona you must die."

"I must indeed," said Romeo. "I came here for nothing else. Good, gentle youth—leave me! Oh, go—before I do you any harm! I love you better than myself—go—leave me here—"

Then Paris said, "I defy① you, and I arrest you as a felon②." And Romeo, in his anger and despair③, drew his sword. They fought, and Paris was killed.

As Romeo's sword pierced④ him, Paris cried—

"Oh, I am slain⑤! If thou be merciful⑥, open the tomb, and lay me with Juliet!"

And Romeo said, "In faith I will."

And he carried the dead man into the tomb and laid him by the dear Juliet's side. Then he kneeled by Juliet and spoke to her, and held her in his arms, and kissed her cold lips, believing that she was dead, while all the while she was coming nearer and nearer to the time of her awakening. Then he drank the poison, and died beside his sweetheart and wife.

Now came Friar Laurence when it was too late, and saw all that had happened—and then poor Juliet woke out of her sleep to find her husband and her friend both dead beside her.

The noise of the fight had brought other folks to the place too, and Friar Laurence, hearing them, ran away, and Juliet was left alone. She saw the cup that had held the poison, and knew how all had happened, and since no poison was left for her, she drew her Romeo's dagger⑦ and thrust⑧ it through her heart—and so, falling with her head on her Romeo's breast, she died. And here ends the story of these faithful⑨ and most unhappy lovers.

And when the old folks knew from Friar Laurence of all that had befallen⑩, they sorrowed exceedingly⑪, and now, seeing all the mischief⑫ their wicked quarrel had wrought⑬, they repented them of it, and over the bodies of their dead children they clasped⑭ hands at last, in friendship and forgiveness.

---

① defy [dɪˈfaɪ] *v*. 反抗 resist, oppose, challenge, stand up to
② felon [ˈfelən] *n*. 重罪犯 criminal, convict, offender
③ despair [dɪˈspeə(r)] *n*. 绝望 hopelessness, desperation
④ pierce [pɪəs] *v*. 刺穿 stab, penetrate, puncture, stick into
⑤ slay [sleɪ] *v*. (slew, slain)杀死 kill, slaughter, do away with
⑥ merciful [ˈmɜːsɪfl] *adj*. 仁慈的 sympathetic, compassionate
⑦ dagger [ˈdæɡə(r)] *n*. 匕首,短剑 knife, poniard
⑧ thrust [θrʌst] *v*. 猛推;刺 push, force, stab, penetrate
⑨ faithful [ˈfeɪθfl] *adj*. 忠贞的 trusty, loyal, devoted
⑩ befall [bɪˈfɔːl] *v*. 发生 happen, occur
⑪ exceedingly [ɪkˈsiːdɪŋli] *adv*. 极度地 extremely, exceptionally
⑫ mischief [ˈmɪstʃɪf] *n*. 伤害 harm, damage, injury, detriment
⑬ work [wɜːk] *v*. (wrought 是 work 过去式的旧式)造成 cause, lead to, result in
⑭ clasp [klɑːsp] *v*. 抓紧 grasp, hold, press, grip, seize, clutch

ⅰ There was an old, old quarrel between the two families, and instead of making it up like reasonable folks, they made a sort of pet of their quarrel, and would not let it die out. 在很久很久以前，两家人吵了一架，他们不像明事理的人那样互相和好，而是对吵架的事耿耿于怀，怎么也不肯作罢。

ⅱ This lady had never been at all kind to him, and he had no reason to love her; but the fact was that he wanted to love somebody, and as he hadn't seen the right lady, he was obliged to love the wrong one. 这个女人对罗密欧一点也不好，他根本没有理由爱上她；但事实是，他满心想要爱上某个人，既然没有遇上合适的女人，就只能爱上这个错的。

ⅲ Presently amid the dancers he saw a lady so beautiful and so lovable that from that moment he never again gave one thought to that Rosaline whom he had thought he loved. 不一会儿，罗密欧在那些跳舞的人中间看见一个女人，那么美丽，那么可爱，他顿时就把自己以为爱着的那个罗瑟琳忘到了脑后，不再想起。

ⅳ Hidden below, he looked up and saw her fair face in the moonlight, framed in the blossoming creepers that grew round her window, and as he looked and listened, he felt as though he had been carried away in a dream, and set down by some magician in that beautiful and enchanted garden. 他躲在下面仰头望去，她的美丽脸庞正沐浴在月光下，她的窗户四周爬满茂盛的藤蔓。他边看边听，仿佛置身梦境，被某个魔法师带进这座美丽的魔幻花园。

ⅴ And the tale of all they said, as well as the sweet music their voices made together, is all set down in a golden book, where you children may read it for yourselves some day. 他们叙述的所有经历和声音汇聚成的美妙音乐全都记载在一本金册里，说不定有朝一日你们这些孩子会亲自读到它。

ⅵ If she had spoken out and told her father the truth...well, then this would have been a different story. 假如她把真相告诉父亲……好吧，那会是个不同的故事。（if...had done..., ...would have done...：与过去事实相反的虚拟语气）

ⅶ Meantime Friar Laurence had sent a messenger to Mantua with a letter to Romeo telling him of all these things; and all would have been well, only the messenger was delayed, and could not go. 与此同时，劳伦斯神父派出一名信使去曼多亚捎信给罗密欧，告知他所有事情。原本一切都会平安无事，信使却被耽搁了，没能动身。

ⅷ He broke open the door, and was just going down the stone steps that led to the vault where all the dead Capulets lay, when he heard a voice behind him calling on him to stop. 他撞开门，准备沿着石阶往下走，石阶通向凯普莱特家族的坟墓，突然他听到背后传来一个声音呵斥他停下。

玛丽娜《泰尔亲王配力克里斯》

I am a maid,	陛下，我是一个少女，
My Lord, that ne'er before invited eyes,	从来不曾勾引别人向我注目，
But have been gaz'd on like a comet. She speaks,	可是像一颗彗星一般，到处受尽世人的凝视。她现在在向您说话，
My Lord, that, may be, hath endur'd a grief	陛下，她所身受的种种不幸，
Might equal yours, if both were justly weigh'd.	要是放在准确的天平里衡量起来，
Though wayward fortune did malign my state,	也许正和您的不幸同样的沉重。

My derivation was from ancestors
Who stood equivalent with mighty kings,
But time hath rooted out my parentage,
And to the world and awkward casualties
Bound me in servitude.

虽然横逆的命运降低了我的身份，
我的祖先却是和庄严的君主们分庭抗礼的；
可是时间已经淹没了我的家世，
使我在这多难的人世失去自由，
忍受一切意外的折磨。

泰尔亲王配力克里斯
Pericles, Prince of Tyre

主要人物

Pericles [ˈperɪkliːz] 配力克里斯(泰尔亲王)
Antiochus [ænˈtaɪəkəs] 安提奥克斯(安提奥克国王)
Helicanus [ˌhelɪˈkeɪnəs] 赫力堪纳斯(泰尔大臣)
Thaisa [θeɪˈɪsə] 泰莎(潘塔波里斯公主)
Cerimon [ˈserɪmɒn] 萨利蒙(以弗所贵族)
Marina [məˈriːnə] 玛丽娜(配力克里斯及泰莎之女)
Dionyza [ˌdaɪəˈnaɪzə] 狄奥妮莎(塔萨斯总督之妻)
Lysimachus [laɪˈsɪməkəs] 拉西马卡斯(米提林总督)

Pericles, the Prince of Tyre①, was unfortunate enough to make an enemy of Antiochus, the powerful and wicked King of Antioch②; and so great was the danger in which he stood that, on the advice of his trusty counselor, Lord Helicanus, he determined to travel about the world for a time.[i] He came to this decision despite the fact that, by the death of his father, he was now King of Tyre. So he set sail for Tarsus③, appointing④ Helicanus Regent⑤ during his absence. That he did wisely in thus leaving his kingdom was soon made clear.

Hardly had he sailed on his voyage, when Lord Thaliard arrived from Antioch with instructions from his royal master to kill Pericles.[ii] The faithful Helicanus soon discovered the deadly purpose of this wicked lord, and at once sent messengers to Tarsus to warn the King of the danger which threatened⑥ him.

The people of Tarsus were in such poverty and distress⑦ that Pericles, feeling that he could find no safe refuge⑧ there, put to sea⑨ again. But a dreadful storm overtook⑩ the ship in which he was, and the good vessel⑪ was wrecked, while of all on board only Pericles was saved. Bruised⑫

---

① Tyre [ˈtaɪə(r)]：提尔(古代腓尼基著名港口，现属黎巴嫩，朱生豪译本中译为“泰尔”)
② Antioch [ˈæntɪɒk]：安条克(古罗马重要城市，现为土耳其南部城市，朱生豪译本中译为“安提奥克”)
③ Tarsus [ˈtɑːsəs]：塔尔苏斯(古罗马重要城市，现为土耳其南部城市，朱生豪译本中译为“塔萨斯”)
④ appoint [əˈpɔɪnt] *v*. 任命 assign, commission, nominate
⑤ regent [ˈriːdʒənt] *n*. 摄政王 ruler, director, governor
⑥ threaten [ˈθretn] *v*. 威胁 warn, intimidate, bully, menace
⑦ distress [dɪˈstres] *n*. 痛苦 sorrow, pain, suffering
⑧ refuge [ˈrefjuːdʒ] *n*. 避难 protection, shelter, asylum
⑨ put to sea：出航，离港出海 sail, set sail, leave port
⑩ overtake [ˌəʊvəˈteɪk] *v*. 突袭 hit, befall, take by surprise
⑪ vessel [ˈvesl] *n*. 船，舰 ship, boat, craft, barque
⑫ bruised [bruːzd] *adj*. 受了瘀伤的 injured, wounded

and wet and faint①, he was flung② upon the cruel rocks on the coast of Pentapolis③, the country of the good King Simonides. Worn out as he was, he looked for nothing but death, and that speedily.[iii] But some fishermen, coming down to the beach, found him there, and gave him clothes and bade him be of good cheer④.

"Thou shalt come home with me," said one of them, "and we will have flesh for holidays, fish for fasting⑤ days, and moreo'er, puddings and flapjacks⑥, and thou shalt be welcome."[iv]

They told him that on the morrow many princes and knights were going to the King's Court, there to joust⑦ and tourney⑧ for the love of his daughter, the beautiful Princess Thaisa.

"Were my fortunes equal to my desires," said Pericles, "I could wish to make one there."[v]

As he spoke, some of the fishermen came by, drawing their net, and it dragged⑨ heavily, resisting all their efforts, but at last they hauled⑩ it in, to find that it contained a suit of rusty⑪ armor⑫; and looking at it, he blessed Fortune⑬ for her kindness, for he saw that it was his own, which had been given to him by his dead father. He begged the fishermen to let him have it that he might go to Court and take part in the tournament⑭, promising that if ever his ill fortunes bettered, he would reward⑮ them well.[vi] The fishermen readily consented, and being thus fully equipped⑯, Pericles set off in his rusty armor to the King's Court.

In the tournament none bore himself⑰ so well as Pericles, and he won the wreath⑱ of victory, which the fair Princess herself placed on his brows. Then at her father's command she asked him who he was, and whence⑲ he came; and he answered that he was a knight of Tyre, by name

---

① faint [feɪnt] *adj*. 虚弱的；头晕目眩的 weak, dizzy, giddy
② fling [flɪŋ] *v*. 掷，抛 throw, toss, hurl, cast, let fly
③ Pentapolis [pen'tæpəlɪs]：潘塔波里斯(希腊文，意译为"五座城")
④ be of good cheer：振作起来 cheer/brighten up
⑤ fasting ['fɑːstɪŋ] *n*. 禁食，斋戒 fast, abstinence
⑥ flapjack ['flæpdʒæk] *n*. 煎饼 pancake, hot cake
⑦ joust [dʒaʊst] *v*. 骑马比武 compete, contest
⑧ tourney ['tʊəni] *v*. 参加骑马比武大会 contend, trade blows
⑨ drag [dræg] *v*. 拖，拽 pull, draw, haul, trail, tow, tug
⑩ haul [hɔːl] *v*. (用力)拖，拉 drag, draw, pull, hale, heave
⑪ rusty ['rʌsti] *adj*. 生锈的 rusted, corroded, rust-covered
⑫ armor ['ɑːmə(r)] *n*. 盔甲 protection, covering, shield
⑬ Fortune ['fɔːtʃuːn] *n*. 命运女神 Fate, Goddess of Destiny
⑭ tournament ['tʊənəmənt] *n*. 比赛(此处指骑马比武大会) competition, contest
⑮ reward [rɪ'wɔːd] *v*. 回报 repay, compensate, recompense
⑯ equip [ɪ'kwɪp] *v*. 装备 arm, supply, furnish, fit out
⑰ bear oneself：表现 behave, conduct
⑱ wreath [riːθ] *n*. 花环，花冠 garland, ring, crown
⑲ whence [wens] *adv*.〈古〉从何处 wherefrom, from where

Pericles, but he did not tell her that he was the King of that country, for he knew that if once his whereabouts① became known to Antiochus, his life would not be worth a pin's purchase②.

Nevertheless Thaisa loved him dearly, and the King was so pleased with his courage and graceful bearing③ that he gladly permitted his daughter to have her own way, when she told him she would marry the stranger knight or die.

Thus Pericles became the husband of the fair lady for whose sake he had striven④ with the knights who came in all their bravery to joust and tourney for her love.[vii]

Meanwhile the wicked King Antiochus had died, and the people in Tyre, hearing no news of their King, urged⑤ Lord Helicanus to ascend⑥ the vacant⑦ throne. But they could only get him to promise that he would become their King, if at the end of a year Pericles did not come back. Moreover, he sent forth messengers far and wide⑧ in search of the missing Pericles.

Some of these made their way to Pentapolis, and finding their King there, told him how discontented⑨ his people were at his long absence, and that, Antiochus being dead, there was nothing now to hinder⑩ him from returning to his kingdom. Then Pericles told his wife and father-in-law who he really was, and they and all the subjects of Simonides greatly rejoiced to know that the gallant⑪ husband of Thaisa was a king in his own right. So Pericles set sail with his dear wife for his native land. But once more the sea was cruel to him, for again a dreadful storm broke out, and while it was at its height, a servant came to tell him that a little daughter was born to him. This news would have made his heart glad indeed, but that the servant went on to add that his wife—his dear, dear Thaisa—was dead.[viii]

While he was praying the gods to be good to his little baby girl, the sailors came to him, declaring that the dead Queen must be thrown overboard, for they believed that the storm would never cease so long as a dead body remained in the vessel. So Thaisa was laid in a big chest with spices and jewels, and a scroll⑫ on which the sorrowful King wrote these lines:

"Here I give to understand
If e'er this coffin⑬ drive aland,
I, King Pericles, have lost
This Queen, worth all our mundane⑭ cost.
Who finds her, give her burying.
She was the daughter of a king.

---

① whereabouts [ˈweərəbaʊts] *n*. 所在之处 position, location
② not worth a pin's purchase: 一文不值
③ bearing [ˈbeərɪŋ] *n*. 举止 manner, conduct, behavior
④ strive [straɪv] *v*. (strove, striven)争斗 compete, contend
⑤ urge [ɜːdʒ] *v*. 敦促 press, prompt, plead, appeal to
⑥ ascend [əˈsend] *v*. 登上 climb, rise, scale, mount, move up
⑦ vacant [ˈveɪkənt] *adj*. 空着的 free, empty, unoccupied
⑧ far and wide: 到处 everywhere, worldwide, in all places
⑨ discontented [ˌdɪskənˈtentɪd] *adj*. 不满的 dissatisfied
⑩ hinder [ˈhɪndə(r)] *v*. 阻止 stop, block, prevent, hold back
⑪ gallant [ˈgælənt] *adj*. 勇敢的 brave, heroic, courageous, valiant
⑫ scroll [skrəʊl] *n*. 纸卷 roll, paper
⑬ coffin [ˈkɒfɪn] *n*. 棺材 casket
⑭ mundane [mʌnˈdeɪn] *adj*. 尘世的 earthly, worldly, terrestrial

Besides this treasure for a fee,
The gods requite① his charity②."[ix]

Then the chest was cast into the sea, and the waves taking it, by and by washed it ashore at Ephesus③, where it was found by the servants of a lord named Cerimon. He at once ordered it to be opened, and when he saw how lovely Thaisa looked, he doubted if she were dead, and took immediate steps to restore her. Then a great wonder happened, for she, who had been thrown into the sea as dead, came back to life. But feeling sure that she would never see her husband again, Thaisa retired④ from the world, and became a priestess⑤ of the Goddess Diana⑥.

While these things were happening, Pericles went on to Tarsus with his little daughter, whom he called Marina, because she had been born at sea.[x] Leaving her in the hands of his old friend the Governor of Tarsus, the King sailed for his own dominions⑦.

Now Dionyza, the wife of the Governor of Tarsus, was a jealous and wicked woman, and finding that the young Princess grew up a more accomplished⑧ and charming girl than her own daughter, she determined to take Marina's life. So when Marina was fourteen, Dionyza ordered one of her servants to take her away and kill her. This villain would have done so, but that he was interrupted by some pirates⑨ who came in and carried Marina off to sea with them, and took her to Mytilene⑩, where they sold her as a slave.[xi] Yet such was her goodness, her grace, and her beauty, that she soon became honored there, and Lysimachus, the young Governor, fell deep in love with her, and would have married her, but that he thought she must be of too humble parentage⑪ to become the wife of one in his high position.[xii]

The wicked Dionyza believed, from her servant's report, that Marina was really dead, and so she put up a monument to her memory, and showed it to King Pericles, when after long years of

---

① requite [rɪˈkwaɪt] *v*. 回报 repay, reward
② charity [ˈtʃærəti] *n*. 仁爱 kindness, humanity
③ Ephesus [ˈefɪsəs]：以弗所(古希腊小亚细亚西岸贸易城市)
④ retire [rɪˈtaɪə(r)] *v*. 退隐 retreat, remove, withdraw
⑤ priestess [ˈpriːstɪs] *n*. 女祭司 clergywoman
⑥ Diana [daɪˈænə]：狄安娜(月亮和狩猎女神,相当于古希腊神话中的阿尔忒弥斯)
⑦ dominion [dəˈmɪniən] *n*. 领土 kingdom, territory
⑧ accomplished [əˈkʌmplɪʃt] *adj*. 才华高的 able, talented, gifted
⑨ pirate [ˈpaɪrət] *n*. 海盗 buccaneer
⑩ Mytilene [ˌmɪtɪˈliːni]：米蒂利尼(位于希腊爱琴海中的一个岛屿,朱生豪译本中译为"米提林")
⑪ parentage [ˈpeərəntɪdʒ] *n*. 出身 family, birth, origin, descent

absence he came to see his much-loved child. When he heard that she was dead, his grief was terrible to see. He set sail once more, and putting on sackcloth①, vowed never to wash his face or cut his hair again. There was a pavilion② erected③ on deck, and there he lay alone, and for three months he spoke word to none.

At last it chanced that his ship came into the port of Mytilene, and Lysimachus, the Governor, went on board to enquire④ whence the vessel came. When he heard the story of Pericles' sorrow and silence, he bethought⑤ him of Marina, and believing that she could rouse the King from his stupor⑥, sent for her and bade her try her utmost⑦ to persuade the King to speak, promising whatever reward she would, if she succeeded. Marina gladly obeyed, and sending the rest away, she sat and sang to her poor grief-laden⑧ father, yet, sweet as was her voice, he made no sign. So presently she spoke to him, saying that her grief might equal⑨ his, for, though she was a slave, she came from ancestors⑩ that stood equal to⑪ mighty⑫ kings.

Something in her voice and story touched the King's heart, and he looked up at her, and as he looked, he saw with wonder how like she was to his lost wife, so with a great hope springing up⑬ in his heart, he bade her tell her story.

Then, with many interruptions⑭ from the King, she told him who she was and how she had escaped from the cruel Dionyza. So Pericles knew that this was indeed his daughter, and he kissed her again and again, crying that his great seas of joy drowned⑮ him with their sweetness. "Give me, my robes," he said. "O Heaven, bless my girl!"

Then there came to him, though none else could hear it, the sound of heavenly music, and falling asleep, he beheld the goddess Diana, in a vision.

---

① sackcloth [ˈsækklɒθ] *n*. 粗麻布
② pavilion [pəˈvɪliən] *n*. 大帐篷 tent, canvas, wigwam
③ erect [ɪˈrekt] *v*. 搭建 build, raise, construct, establish, set up
④ enquire [ɪnˈkwaɪə] *v*. (=inquire) 询问 ask, question, query
⑤ bethink [bɪˈθɪŋk] *v*. 使想起 recall, recollect
⑥ stupor [ˈstjuːpə(r)] *n*. 不省人事 daze, numbness, unconsciousness
⑦ try one's utmost: 竭尽全力 strain every nerve
⑧ grief-laden [ˈgriːf leɪdn] *adj*. 极度悲伤的 grief-stricken
⑨ equal [ˈiːkwəl] *v*. 比得上 match, equate, amount to
⑩ ancestor [ˈænsestə(r)] *n*. 祖先 forefather, predecessor, forebear
⑪ equal to: 赶得上 even/level with
⑫ mighty [ˈmaɪti] *adj*. 强有力的 strong, forceful, powerful
⑬ spring up: 出现 appear, come into existence/being
⑭ interruption [ˌɪntəˈrʌpʃn] *n*. 打岔 break, disturbance
⑮ drown [draʊn] *v*. 沉浸于 overwhelm, overcome

"Go," she said to him, "to my temple at Ephesus, and when my maiden priests are met together, reveal① how thou at sea didst lose thy wife."

Pericles obeyed the goddess and told his tale before her altar. Hardly had he made an end, when the chief priestess, crying out, "You are—you are—O royal Pericles!" fell fainting to the ground, and presently recovering, she spoke again to him, "O My Lord, are you not Pericles?"[xiii] "The voice of dead Thaisa!" exclaimed the King in wonder. "That Thaisa am I," she said, and looking at her he saw that she spoke the very truth.

Thus Pericles and Thaisa, after long and bitter suffering, found happiness once more, and in the joy of their meeting they forgot the pain of the past. To Marina great happiness was given, and not only in being restored to her dear parents; for she married Lysimachus, and became a princess in the land where she had been sold as a slave.[xiv]

ⅰ Pericles, the Prince of Tyre, was unfortunate enough to make an enemy of Antiochus, the powerful and wicked King of Antioch; and so great was the danger in which he stood that, on the advice of his trusty counselor, Lord Helicanus, he determined to travel about the world for a time. 配力克里斯是泰尔的亲王,他很不幸地与安提奥克斯结下了仇;而安提奥克斯是安提奥克的国王,他心肠歹毒,力量十分强大。配力克里斯的处境非常危险。在一位可靠的大臣赫力堪纳斯的建议下,配力克里斯决定暂时出去周游世界,避避风头。(so...that...:"如此……以至于……",so 前置时的完全倒装;in which...:定语从句)

ⅱ Hardly had he sailed on his voyage, when Lord Thaliard arrived from Antioch with instructions from his royal master to kill Pericles. 配力克里斯刚开始航行,来自安提奥克的泰利阿德勋爵就受主人之命来追杀他。(hardly...when...:"一……就……",否定词 hardly 前置时的部分倒装)

ⅲ Worn out as he was, he looked for nothing but death, and that speedily. 配力克里斯精疲力竭,只希望赶快一死了之。

ⅳ "Thou shalt come home with me," said one of them, "and we will have flesh for holidays, fish for fasting days, and moreo'er, puddings and flapjacks, and thou shalt be welcome." "你跟我回去吧,"其中一个渔夫说,"我们假日吃肉,斋日吃鱼,还有布丁和煎饼,你不要客气。"(thou=you;shalt=shall;moreo'er=moreover)

① reveal [rɪˈviːl] *v.* 透露 disclose, make known

ⅴ "Were my fortunes equal to my desires," said Pericles, "I could wish to make one there." 配力克里斯说:"要是我的命运可以帮助我达到我的愿望,我倒也想参加一试。"(were my fortunes...=if my fortunes were...:与现在事实相反的虚拟语气中条件句省略 if 时的部分倒装)

ⅵ He begged the fishermen to let him have it that he might go to Court and take part in the tournament, promising that if ever his ill fortunes bettered, he would reward them well. 他恳求渔夫们把铠甲给他,让他去王宫参加比武大赛;他还保证,如果他时来运转的话,一定会重重地奖赏他们所有人。

ⅶ Thus Pericles became the husband of the fair lady for whose sake he had striven with the knights who came in all their bravery to joust and tourney for her love. 就这样,配力克里斯成了这位美丽姑娘的丈夫,他为了她打败了那些勇敢地前来参加比武、向公主求爱的骑士们。

ⅷ This news would have made his heart glad indeed, but that the servant went on to add that his wife—his dear, dear Thaisa—was dead. 这个消息本来应该让他满心欢喜的,可是仆人接着禀报,他的夫人——他亲爱的、亲爱的泰莎——不幸死去了。

ⅸ

"Here I give to understand	"余为国王配力克里斯,死者为余王后,
If e'er this coffin drive aland,	罄世间所有之一切,均不足抵偿此无价之损失。
I, King Pericles, have lost	万一此棺被风吹卷上岸,为仁人君子发现启视,
This Queen, worth all our mundane cost.	务请依礼安葬,因彼系出天潢,
Who finds her, give her burying.	为一国王之爱女也。
She was the daughter of a king.	凡棺中所有宝物,一概作为酬劳,
Besides this treasure for a fee,	而君子泽及朽骨之德,亦必仰邀天眷,
The gods requite his charity."	奚止存亡同感而已。"

ⅹ While these things were happening, Pericles went on to Tarsus with his little daughter, whom he called Marina, because she had been born at sea. 这些事情发生的时候,配力克里斯带着他襁褓中的女儿继续航行,来到了塔萨斯。他给女儿取名玛丽娜,因为她是在大海上出生的。(Marina 在意大利语里是"大海"的意思)

ⅺ This villain would have done so, but that he was interrupted by some pirates who came in and carried Marina off to sea with them, and took her to Mytilene, where they sold her as a slave. 这个坏蛋差点儿就这么做了,但就在那节骨眼儿上,几个海盗闯了过来,把玛丽娜抢到了海上。他们航行到米提林,把她作为奴隶卖掉了。(would have done...:"本会……",与过去事实相反的虚拟语气)

ⅻ Yet such was her goodness, her grace, and her beauty, that she soon became honored there, and Lysimachus, the young Governor, fell deep in love with her, and would have married her, but that he thought she must be of too humble parentage to become the wife of one in his high position. 玛丽娜凭着自己的善良、美貌和典雅的风度,很快就赢得了人们的尊敬。年轻的总督拉西马卡斯深深地爱上了她,很想娶她为妻,可是又担心她的出身太低微了,配不上他这样地位显赫的人。(would have done...:"本会……",与过去事实相反的虚拟语气)

xiii Hardly had he made an end, when the chief priestess, crying out, "You are—you are—O royal Pericles!" fell fainting to the ground, and presently recovering, she spoke again to him, "O My Lord, are you not Pericles?" 他还没有讲完,女祭司长就大声喊道:"您是——您是——啊,尊贵的配力克里斯!"她晕倒在地,很快又苏醒过来,又对他说道:"啊,我的主,您不是配力克里斯吗?"(hardly...when...:"一……就……",否定词 hardly 前置时的部分倒装)

xiv To Marina great happiness was given, and not only in being restored to her dear parents; for she married Lysimachus, and became a princess in the land where she had been sold as a slave. 玛丽娜获得了极大的幸福。她不仅回到了亲爱的父母身边,而且嫁给了拉西马卡斯,在这片曾经被卖身为奴的土地上,成为尊贵的王后。

奥菲利娅《哈姆莱特》

O, what a noble mind is here o'erthrown!
The courtier's, soldier's, scholar's, eye, tongue, sword,
Th' expectancy and rose of the fair state,
The glass of fashion and the mould of form,
Th' observ'd of all observers, quite, quite down!

啊,一颗多么高贵的心是这样陨落了!
朝臣的眼睛、学者的辩舌、军人的利剑、
国家所瞩望的一朵娇花;
时流的明镜、人伦的雅范、举世注目的中心,
这样无可挽回地陨落了!

And I, of ladies most deject and wretched,	我是一切妇女中间最伤心而不幸的,我曾经
That sucked the honey of his music vows;	从他音乐一般的盟誓中吮吸芬芳的甘蜜,
Now see that noble and most sovereign reason	现在却眼看着他的高贵无上的理智,
Like sweet bells jangled, out of tune and harsh;	像一串美妙的银铃失去了谐和的音调,
That unmatched form and feature of blown youth,	无比的青春美貌,
Blasted with ecstasy. O, woe is me,	在疯狂中凋谢!啊!我好苦,
T' have seen what I have seen, see what I see!	谁料过去的繁华,变作今朝的泥土!

哈姆莱特
Hamlet

主要人物

Hamlet [ˈhæmlɪt] 哈姆莱特(前王之子,今王之侄)

Gertrude [ˈgɜːtruːd] 乔特鲁德(丹麦王后,哈姆莱特之母)

Claudius [ˈklɔːdɪəs] 克劳狄斯(丹麦国王)

Horatio [həˈreɪʃɪəʊ] 霍拉旭(哈姆莱特之友)

Polonius [pəˈləʊnɪəs] 波洛涅斯(御前大臣)

Ophelia [ɒˈfiːljə] 奥菲利娅(波洛涅斯之女)

Laertes [leɪˈɜːtiːz] 雷欧提斯(波洛涅斯之子)

Ghost of Hamlet's Father 哈姆莱特父亲的鬼魂

Hamlet was the only son of the King of Denmark. He loved his father and mother dearly—and was happy in the love of a sweet lady named Ophelia. Her father, Polonius, was the King's Chamberlain[1].

While Hamlet was away studying at Wittenberg[2], his father died. Young Hamlet hastened home in great grief to hear that a serpent[3] had stung[4] the King, and that he was dead. The young Prince had loved his father so tenderly[5] that you may judge what he felt when he found that the Queen, before yet the King had been laid in the ground a month, had determined to marry again—and to marry the dead King's brother.

Hamlet refused to put off mourning[6] for the wedding.

"It is not only the black I wear on my body," he said, "that proves my loss. I wear mourning in my heart for my dead father. His son at least remembers him, and grieves still."

Then said Claudius the King's brother, "This grief is unreasonable. Of course you must sorrow at the loss of your father, but—"

"Ah," said Hamlet, bitterly, "I cannot in one little month forget those I love."

With that the Queen and Claudius left him, to make merry[7] over their wedding, forgetting the poor good King who had been so kind to them both.

And Hamlet, left alone, began to wonder and to question as to[8] what he ought to do. For he

---

① chamberlain [ˈtʃeɪmbəlɪn] *n*. (国王或女王的)内侍

② Wittenberg [ˈwɪtnbɜːg]: 维滕堡(德国城市,朱生豪译本中译为"威登堡")

③ serpent [ˈsɜːpənt] *n*. 蛇 a snake, especially a large one

④ sting [stɪŋ] *v*. 蜇,刺;使刺痛 hurt, wound, nip, prick, bite

⑤ tenderly [ˈtendəli] *adv*. 温柔地;亲切地 gently, lovingly, kindly

⑥ mourning [ˈmɔːnɪŋ] *n*. 丧服 weeds

⑦ make merry: 行乐 have fun, enjoy oneself

⑧ as to: 至于 as for, in/with regard to, in the matter of

could not believe the story about the snake-bite. It seemed to him all too plain that the wicked Claudius had killed the King, so as to get the crown and marry the Queen. Yet he had no proof①, and could not accuse② Claudius.

And while he was thus thinking came Horatio, a fellow student of his, from Wittenberg.

"What brought you here?" asked Hamlet, when he had greeted his friend kindly.

"I came, My Lord, to see your father's funeral."

"I think it was to see my mother's wedding," said Hamlet, bitterly. "My father! We shall not look upon his like③ again."

"My Lord," answered Horatio, "I think I saw him yesternight④."

Then, while Hamlet listened in surprise, Horatio told how he, with two gentlemen of the guard, had seen the King's ghost on the battlements⑤. Hamlet went that night, and true enough, at midnight, the ghost of the King, in the armor he had been wont to wear, appeared on the battlements in the chill⑥ moonlight. Hamlet was a brave youth. Instead of running away from the ghost he spoke to it—and when it beckoned⑦ him he followed it to a quiet place, and there the ghost told him that what he had suspected⑧ was true. The wicked Claudius had indeed killed his good brother the King, by dropping poison into his ear as he slept in his orchard in the afternoon.

"And you," said the ghost, "must avenge⑨ this cruel murder—on my wicked brother. But do nothing against the Queen—for I have loved her, and she is your mother. Remember me."

Then seeing the morning approach⑩, the ghost vanished.

"Now," said Hamlet, "there is nothing left but revenge. Remember thee—I will remember nothing else—books, pleasure, youth—let all go—and your commands alone live on my brain."

So when his friends came back he made them swear⑪ to keep the secret of the ghost, and then went in from the battlements, now gray with mingled⑫ dawn and moonlight, to think how he might best avenge his murdered father.

The shock of seeing and hearing his father's ghost made him feel almost mad, and for fear that his uncle might notice that he was not himself, he determined to hide his mad longing for revenge under a pretended madness in other matters.[ii]

And when he met Ophelia, who loved him—and to whom he had given gifts, and letters, and many loving words—he behaved so wildly to her, that she could not but think⑬ him mad. For she loved him so that she could not believe he would be as cruel as this, unless he were quite mad. So

---

① proof [pruːf] *n*. 证据 evidence
② accuse [əˈkjuːz] *v*. 控诉 charge, indict, arraign
③ like [laɪk] *n*. 类似的人 equal, parallel
④ yesternight [ˌjestəˈnaɪt] *adv*. 昨晚,昨夜
⑤ battlements [ˈbætlmənts] *n*. 城垛 wall, rampart
⑥ chill [tʃɪl] *adj*. 寒冷的 cold, chilly, freezing, frigid
⑦ beckon [ˈbekən] *v*. 示意 sign, signal, gesture, gesticulate
⑧ suspect [səˈspekt] *v*. 猜想 surmise, guess, suppose, believe
⑨ avenge [əˈvendʒ] *v*. 报仇 revenge, retaliate, hit back
⑩ approach [əˈprəʊtʃ] *v*. 临近 near, come close, draw near
⑪ swear [sweə(r)] *v*. 发誓 vow, avow, promise, pledge, commit
⑫ mingle [ˈmɪŋgl] *v*. (使)混合 mix, combine, blend
⑬ can not but do: 不得不 have no choice but to do

she told her father, and showed him a pretty letter from Hamlet. And in the letter was much folly, and this pretty verse①—

"Doubt thou the stars are fire;
Doubt that the sun doth move;
Doubt truth to be a liar;
But never doubt I love."[iii]

And from that time everyone believed that the cause of Hamlet's supposed madness was love.

Poor Hamlet was very unhappy. He longed to obey his father's ghost—and yet he was too gentle and kindly to wish to kill another man, even his father's murderer. And sometimes he wondered whether, after all, the ghost spoke truly.

Just at this time some actors came to the Court, and Hamlet ordered them to perform a certain play before the King and Queen. Now, this play was the story of a man who had been murdered in his garden by a near relation, who afterwards married the dead man's wife.

You may imagine the feelings of the wicked King, as he sat on his throne, with the Queen beside him and all his Court around, and saw, acted on the stage, the very wickedness that he had himself done.[iv] And when, in the play, the wicked relation poured poison into the ear of the sleeping man, the wicked Claudius suddenly rose, and staggered from the room—the Queen and others following.

Then said Hamlet to his friends—

"Now I am sure the ghost spoke true. For if Claudius had not done this murder, he could not have been so distressed② to see it in a play.[v]"

Now the Queen sent for Hamlet, by the King's desire, to scold him for his conduct during the play, and for other matters; and Claudius, wishing to know exactly what happened, told old Polonius to hide himself behind the hangings③ in the Queen's room. And as they talked, the Queen got frightened at Hamlet's rough, strange words, and cried for help, and Polonius behind the curtain cried out too. Hamlet, thinking it was the King who was hidden there, thrust with his sword at the hangings, and killed, not the King, but poor old Polonius.

So now Hamlet had offended④ his uncle and his mother, and by bad hap⑤ killed his true love's father.

"Oh! What a rash⑥ and bloody⑦ deed is this," cried the Queen.

And Hamlet answered bitterly, "Almost as bad as to kill a king, and marry his brother." Then Hamlet told the Queen plainly all his thoughts and how he knew of the murder, and begged her, at least, to have no more friendship or kindness of the base⑧ Claudius, who had killed the good King.[vi] And as they spoke the King's ghost again appeared before Hamlet, but the Queen could not

---

① verse [vɜːs] *n*. 诗,韵文 poem, rhyme
② distressed [dɪˈstrest] *adj*. 苦恼的 upset, troubled
③ hanging [ˈhæŋɪŋ] *n*. 墙幔 curtain, drape, arras
④ offend [əˈfend] *v*. 冒犯 insult, displease
⑤ hap [hæp] *n*. 机会;偶然 chance, accident
⑥ rash [ræʃ] *adj*. 鲁莽的 hasty, ill-advised, hot-headed
⑦ bloody [ˈblʌdi] *adj*. 血腥的;残暴的 cruel, savage, brutal
⑧ base [beɪs] *adj*. 卑鄙的 immoral, mean, ignoble

see it. So when the ghost had gone, they parted.

When the Queen told Claudius what had passed, and how Polonius was dead, he said, "This shows plainly that Hamlet is mad, and since he has killed the Chancellor①, it is for his own safety that we must carry out our plan, and send him away to England."[vii]

So Hamlet was sent, under charge of two courtiers who served the King, and these bore② letters to the English Court, requiring that Hamlet should be put to death. But Hamlet had the good sense to get at these letters, and put in others instead, with the names of the two courtiers who were so ready to betray him.[viii] Then, as the vessel went to England, Hamlet escaped on board a pirate ship, and the two wicked courtiers left him to his fate, and went on to meet theirs.

Hamlet hurried home, but in the meantime a dreadful③ thing had happened. Poor pretty Ophelia, having lost her lover and her father, lost her wits④ too, and went in sad madness about the Court, with straws, and weeds, and flowers in her hair, singing strange scraps⑤ of songs, and talking poor, foolish, pretty talk with no heart of meaning to it.[ix] And one day, coming to a stream where willows grew, she tried to hang a flowery garland⑥ on a willow, and fell into the water with all her flowers, and so died.

And Hamlet had loved her, though his plan of seeming⑦ madness had made him hide it; and when he came back, he found the King and Queen, and the Court, weeping at the funeral of his dear love and lady.

Ophelia's brother, Laertes, had also just come to Court to ask justice for the death of his father, old Polonius; and now, wild with grief, he leaped into his sister's grave, to clasp her in his arms once more.

"I loved her more than forty thousand brothers," cried Hamlet, and leapt into the grave after him, and they fought till they were parted.

Afterwards Hamlet begged Laertes to forgive him.

"I could not bear⑧," he said, "that any, even a brother, should seem to love her more than I."

But the wicked Claudius would not let them be friends. He told Laertes how Hamlet had killed old Polonius, and between them they made a plot to slay Hamlet by treachery⑨.

---

① chancellor [ˈtʃɑːnsələ(r)] *n*. 御前大臣 chief/prime minister
② bear [beə(r)] *v*. 携带 carry, take, convey
③ dreadful [ˈdredfl] *adj*. 可怕的 terrible, horrible, fearful
④ lose one's wits: 失魂落魄 lose one's head/mind/senses
⑤ scrap [skræp] *n*. 片段 piece, fragment, bit
⑥ garland [ˈgɑːlənd] *n*. 花环 wreath
⑦ seeming [ˈsiːmɪŋ] *adj*. 表面上的 apparent
⑧ bear [beə(r)] *v*. 忍受 stand, tolerate, endure
⑨ treachery [ˈtretʃəri] *n*. 背叛 betrayal

Laertes challenged him to a fencing① match, and all the Court were present. Hamlet had the blunt② foil③ always used in fencing, but Laertes had prepared for himself a sword, sharp, and tipped④ with poison. And the wicked King had made ready a bowl of poisoned wine, which he meant to give poor Hamlet when he should grow warm with the sword play, and should call for drink.

So Laertes and Hamlet fought, and Laertes, after some fencing, gave Hamlet a sharp sword thrust⑤. Hamlet, angry at this treachery—for they had been fencing, not as men fight, but as they play—closed with Laertes in a struggle; both dropped their swords, and when they picked them up again, Hamlet, without noticing it, had exchanged his own blunt sword for Laertes' sharp and poisoned one.[x] And with one thrust of it he pierced Laertes, who fell dead by his own treachery.

At this moment the Queen cried out, "The drink, the drink! Oh, my dear Hamlet! I am poisoned!"

She had drunk of the poisoned bowl the King had prepared for Hamlet, and the King saw the Queen, whom, wicked as he was, he really loved, fall dead by his means⑥.[xi]

Then Ophelia being dead, and Polonius, and the Queen, and Laertes, and the two courtiers who had been sent to England, Hamlet at last found courage to do the ghost's bidding and avenge his father's murder—which, if he had braced up his heart⑦ to do long before, all these lives would had been spared⑧, and none had suffered but the wicked King, who well deserved to die.[xii]

Hamlet, his heart at last being great enough to do the deed he ought, turned the poisoned sword on the false King.[xiii]

"Then—venom⑨—do thy work!" he cried, and the King died.

So Hamlet in the end kept the promise he had made his father. And all being now accomplished, he himself died.[xiv] And those who stood by saw him die, with prayers and tears, for his friends and his people loved him with their whole hearts. Thus ends the tragic tale of Hamlet, Prince of Denmark.

---

① fencing ['fensɪŋ] *n*. 击剑 the sport of fighting with long thin swords
② blunt [blʌnt] *adj*. 钝的,不锋利的 dull, edgeless
③ foil [fɔɪl] *n*. 花剑 a long thin light sword used in fencing
④ tip [tɪp] *v*. 覆盖……的末端 cap, top, crown
⑤ thrust [θrʌst] *n*. 刺,戳 stab, lunge
⑥ means [miːnz] *n*. 手段 way, method, tactic
⑦ brace up one's heart: 鼓起勇气 pluck up (the) courage
⑧ spare [speə(r)] *v*. 幸免 survive
⑨ venom ['venəm] *n*. 毒药 poison, toxin, bane

ⅰ The young Prince had loved his father so tenderly that you may judge what he felt when he found that the Queen, before yet the King had been laid in the ground a month, had determined to marry again—and to marry the dead King's brother. 年轻的王子是那么深爱他的父亲,因此你可以想象,当他发现国王刚安葬一个月,王后就决定再婚,而且是跟已故国王的弟弟结婚时,他内心是一种什么感受。

ⅱ The shock of seeing and hearing his father's ghost made him feel almost mad, and for fear that his uncle might notice that he was not himself, he determined to hide his mad longing for revenge under a pretended madness in other matters. 和父王的鬼魂会面并听到父王说的话,让他激动得要发疯。因为担心他的叔叔可能会注意到他的改变,所以他决定假装自己因其他事情发了疯,以隐藏他急于复仇的欲望。

ⅲ "Doubt thou the stars are fire; "你可以疑心星星是火把;
Doubt that the sun doth move; 你可以疑心太阳会移转;
Doubt truth to be a liar; 你可以疑心真理是谎话;
But never doubt I love." 可是我的爱永没有改变。"

ⅳ You may imagine the feelings of the wicked King, as he sat on his throne, with the Queen beside him and all his Court around, and saw, acted on the stage, the very wickedness that he had himself done. 那个恶毒的国王坐在宝座上,王后陪在他身边,朝臣们簇拥在周围,当他看到舞台上演的正是他的罪恶行径时,你可以想象他内心的感受。

ⅴ For if Claudius had not done this murder, he could not have been so distressed to see it in a play. 因为要是克劳狄斯没有下这种毒手,那他看到这出戏时就不会这么苦恼了。(if...had done..., ...could have done...:与过去事实相反的虚拟语气)

ⅵ Then Hamlet told the Queen plainly all his thoughts and how he knew of the murder, and begged her, at least, to have no more friendship or kindness of the base Claudius, who had killed the good King. 然后,哈姆莱特把他的想法全都明明白白地告诉了王后,并说了他是怎么得知这桩谋杀案的。他恳求母亲,至少不要再对卑鄙的克劳狄斯怀有温情和善意,因为是他谋杀了贤明的国王。

ⅶ "This shows plainly that Hamlet is mad, and since he has killed the Chancellor, it is for his own safety that we must carry out our plan, and send him away to England." "这显然说明哈姆莱特已经疯了,考虑到他杀死了御前大臣,为了他自身的安全,现在必须执行我们的计划,把他立刻送到英国去。"(it is...that...:强调句型,强调目的状语)

viii But Hamlet had the good sense to get at these letters, and put in others instead, with the names of the two courtiers who were so ready to betray him. 但是哈姆莱特非常机智,他偷偷拿到信,把它们换掉了——把里面的名字换成了那两个打算背叛他的朝臣。

ix Poor pretty Ophelia, having lost her lover and her father, lost her wits too, and went in sad madness about the Court, with straws, and weeds, and flowers in her hair, singing strange scraps of songs, and talking poor, foolish, pretty talk with no heart of meaning to it. 美丽而不幸的奥菲利娅,失去了自己的恋人和父亲,也失去了自己的理智,她神色忧愁、疯疯癫癫地在王宫里走来走去,头发上插着稻秸、野草和鲜花,嘴里哼着支离破碎的奇怪的歌,还有口无心地说着一些莫名其妙的傻话。

x Hamlet, angry at this treachery—for they had been fencing, not as men fight, but as they play—closed with Laertes in a struggle; both dropped their swords, and when they picked them up again, Hamlet, without noticing it, had exchanged his own blunt sword for Laertes' sharp and poisoned one. 哈姆莱特对他的背叛大为恼火——因为他们的比剑不是决斗,只是表演——便和雷欧提斯打起来。他们都打掉了剑,就在他们拾剑时,哈姆莱特无意中把自己的钝剑换成了雷欧提斯的尖头毒剑。

xi She had drunk of the poisoned bowl the King had prepared for Hamlet, and the King saw the Queen, whom, wicked as he was, he really loved, fall dead by his means. 她喝下了国王为哈姆莱特预备的那碗毒酒,国王眼看着王后——尽管他很邪恶,但他真心爱她——倒地死去,她被他的诡计害死了。(wicked as he was:表语前置的部分倒装)

xii Then Ophelia being dead, and Polonius, and the Queen, and Laertes, and the two courtiers who had been sent to England, Hamlet at last found courage to do the ghost's bidding and avenge his father's murder—which, if he had braced up his heart to do long before, all these lives had been spared, and none had suffered but the wicked King, who well deserved to die. 奥菲利娅死了,波洛涅斯、王后、雷欧提斯,还有那两个被派往英国的朝臣也死了,哈姆莱特终于有了勇气,去完成鬼魂的命令,为冤死的父王报仇——如果他很早之前就有胆量做这件事,这些人的性命就都能保住,受到惩罚的就只有那个罪该万死的狠毒的国王。(Ophelia being...:独立主格结构;if... had done..., ...would have done...:与过去事实相反的虚拟语气)

xiii Hamlet, his heart at last being great enough to do the deed he ought, turned the poisoned sword on the false King. 哈姆莱特终于振作起来做了他应该做的事,把毒剑刺向篡位的国王。(his heart...being...:独立主格结构)

xiv And all being now accomplished, he himself died. 大功告成后,他自己也死了。(all being...:独立主格结构)

伊摩琴《辛白林》

O, learn'd indeed were that astronomer
That knew the stars as I his characters;
He'ld lay the future open. You good gods,
Let what is here contain'd relish of love,

啊！要是有哪一个占星的术士熟悉天上的星辰，
正像我熟悉他的字迹一样，那才真算得学术湛深，
他的慧眼可以观察到未来的一切。仁慈的神明啊，
但愿这儿写着的，只是爱，

Of My Lord's health, of his content, yet not	是我主的健康，是他的满足，可是并不是他对于我
That we two are asunder; let that grieve him:	们两人远别的满足；让这一件事使他悲哀吧，
Some griefs are med'cinable; that is one of them,	有些悲哀是有药饵的作用的，这一种悲哀也是，
For it doth physic love: of his content,	因为它可以滋养爱情；但愿他一切满足，
All but in that!	只除了这一件事！

辛白林
Cymbeline

主要人物

Cymbeline [ˈsɪmbəliːn] 辛白林（英国国王）

Imogen [ˈɪməʊdʒən] 伊摩琴（辛白林及其前后所生之女）

Leonatus [liːəˈneɪtəs] 里奥那托斯（绅士，伊摩琴之夫）

Iachimo [ɪˈækɪməʊ] 阿埃基摩（意大利人）

Pisanio [pɪˈzɑːnɪəʊ] 毕萨尼奥（里奥那托斯之仆）

Belarius [bəˈleərɪəs] 培拉律斯（被放逐的贵族）

Guiderius [gwɪˈdɪərɪəs] 吉德律斯（辛白林之子）

Arviragus [ɑːˈvɪrəgəs] 阿维拉古斯（辛白林之子）

Lucius [ˈluːsjəs] 路歇斯（罗马主将）

Cymbeline was the King of Britain. He had three children. The two sons were stolen away from him when they were quite little children, and he was left with only one daughter, Imogen. The King married a second time, and brought up Leonatus, the son of a dear friend, as Imogen's playfellow; and when Leonatus was old enough, Imogen secretly married him. This made the King and Queen very angry, and the King, to punish Leonatus, banished him from Britain.

Poor Imogen was nearly heartbroken at parting from Leonatus, and he was not less unhappy. For they were not only lovers and husband and wife, but they had been friends and comrades ever since they were quite little children. With many tears and kisses, they said, "Goodbye." They promised never to forget each other, and that they would never care for anyone else as long as they lived.

"This diamond was my mother's, love," said Imogen. "Take it, my heart, and keep it as long as you love me."

"Sweetest, fairest," answered Leonatus, "wear this bracelet① for my sake."

"Ah!" cried Imogen, weeping, "When shall we meet again?"

And while they were still in each other's arms, the King came in, and Leonatus had to leave

---

① bracelet [ˈbreɪslət] *n*. 手镯 bangle, wristlet

without more farewell.

When he was come to Rome, where he had gone to stay with an old friend of his father's, he spent his days still in thinking of his dear Imogen, and his nights in dreaming of her.[i] One day at a feast some Italian and French noblemen were talking of their sweethearts, and swearing that they were the most faithful and honorable① and beautiful ladies in the world. And a Frenchman reminded Leonatus how he had said many times that his wife Imogen was more fair, wise, and constant than any of the ladies in France.

"I say so still," said Leonatus.

"She is not so good but that she would deceive②," said Iachimo, one of the Italian nobles.[ii]

"She never would deceive," said Leonatus.

"I wager③," said Iachimo, "that, if I go to Britain, I can persuade your wife to do whatever I wish, even if it should be against your wishes."

"That you will never do," said Leonatus. "I wager this ring upon my finger," which was the very ring Imogen had given him at parting, "that my wife will keep all her vows to me, and that you will never persuade her to do otherwise④."[iii]

So Iachimo wagered half his estate against the ring on Leonatus's finger, and started forthwith⑤ for Britain, with a letter of introduction to Leonatus's wife. When he reached there he was received with all kindness; but he was still determined to win his wager⑥.

He told Imogen that her husband thought no more of her, and went on to tell many cruel lies about him. Imogen listened at first, but presently perceived what a wicked person Iachimo was, and ordered him to leave her. Then he said—

"Pardon me, fair lady. All that I have said is untrue. I only told you this to see whether you would believe me, or whether you were as much to be trusted as your husband thinks. Will you forgive me?"

"I forgive you freely⑦," said Imogen.

"Then," went on Iachimo, "perhaps you will prove it by taking charge of⑧ a trunk, containing a number of jewels which your husband and I and some other gentlemen have bought as a present for the Emperor of Rome."

"I will indeed," said Imogen, "do anything for my husband and a friend of my husband's. Have the jewels sent into my room, and I will take care of them."

"It is only for one night," said Iachimo, "for I leave Britain again tomorrow."

So the trunk was carried into Imogen's room, and that night she went to bed and to sleep. When she was fast asleep⑨, the lid of the trunk opened and a man got out. It was Iachimo. The

---

① honorable [ˈɒnərəbl] *adj*. 可敬的 respectable
② deceive [dɪˈsiːv] *v*. 欺骗 fool, trick, cheat, take in
③ wager [ˈweɪdʒə(r)] *v*. 打赌 bet, stake, gamble
④ otherwise [ˈʌðəwaɪz] *adv*. 不同地 differently, in another way
⑤ forthwith [ˌfɔːθˈwɪθ] *adv*. 立刻 immediately, at once, instantly
⑥ wager [ˈweɪdʒə(r)] *n*. 赌注 bet, stake, gamble, ante
⑦ freely [ˈfriːli] *adv*. 自愿地 readily, willingly, voluntarily
⑧ take charge of: 照管 see to, look after, take care of
⑨ fast asleep: 熟睡,酣睡 sound asleep

story about the jewels was as untrue as the rest of the things he had said. He had only wished to get into her room to win his wicked wager. He looked about him and noticed the furniture, and then crept to the side of the bed where Imogen was asleep and took from her arm the gold bracelet which had been the parting gift of her husband. Then he crept back to the trunk, and next morning sailed for Rome.

When he met Leonatus, he said—

"I have been to Britain and I have won the wager, for your wife no longer thinks about you. She stayed talking with me all one night in her room, which is hung with tapestry① and has a carved chimney piece②, and silver andirons③ in the shape of two winking④ Cupids⑤."

"I do not believe she has forgotten me; I do not believe she stayed talking with you in her room. You have heard her room described by the servants."

"Ah!" said Iachimo, "but she gave me this bracelet. She took it from her arm. I see her yet. Her pretty action did outsell⑥ her gift, and yet enriched⑦ it too.[iv] She gave it me, and said she prized⑧ it once."

"Take the ring," cried Leonatus, "you have won; and you might have won my life as well, for I care nothing for it now I know my lady has forgotten me."[v]

And mad with anger, he wrote letters to Britain to his old servant, Pisanio, ordering him to take Imogen to Milford Haven⑨, and to murder her, because she had forgotten him and given away his gift. At the same time he wrote to Imogen herself, telling her to go with Pisanio, his old servant, to Milford Haven, and that he, her husband, would be there to meet her.

Now when Pisanio got this letter he was too good to carry out its orders, and too wise to let them alone altogether.[vi] So he gave Imogen the letter from her husband, and started with her for Milford Haven. Before he left, the wicked Queen gave him a drink which, she said, would be useful in sickness. She hoped he would give it to Imogen, and that Imogen would die, and the wicked Queen's son could be King. For the Queen thought this drink was a poison, but really and truly it was only a sleeping draft⑩.

When Pisanio and Imogen came near to Milford Haven, he told her what was really in the letter he had had from her husband.

"I must go on to Rome, and see him myself," said Imogen.

And then Pisanio helped her to dress in boy's clothes, and sent her on her way, and went back to the Court. Before he went he gave her the drink he had had from the Queen.

Imogen went on, getting more and more tired, and at last came to a cave. Someone seemed to

---

① tapestry [ˈtæpəstri] *n*. 壁毯 arras, wall hanging
② chimney piece: 壁炉台 mantelpiece
③ andiron [ˈændaɪən] *n*. 柴架 firedog
④ wink [wɪŋk] *v*. 眨眼 blink, bat, flutter
⑤ Cupid [ˈkjuːpɪd] *n*. (古罗马神话中的爱神)丘比特(的画像或雕塑)
⑥ outsell [ˌaʊtˈsel] *v*. 胜过 beat, surpass, overtake, outdo
⑦ enrich [ɪnˈrɪtʃ] *v*. 使丰富;使富有 improve, enhance, make rich
⑧ prize [praɪz] *v*. 珍视 value, treasure, cherish, hold dear
⑨ Milford Haven: 米尔福德港(英国)
⑩ sleeping draft: 安眠剂(draft=draught)

live there, but no one was in just then. So she went in, and as she was almost dying of hunger, she took some food she saw there, and had just done so, when an old man and two boys came into the cave. She was very much frightened when she saw them, for she thought that they would be angry with her for taking their food, though she had meant to leave money for it on the table. But to her surprise they welcomed her kindly. She looked very pretty in her boy's clothes and her face was good, as well as pretty.

"You shall be our brother," said both the boys; and so she stayed with them, and helped to cook the food, and make things comfortable. But one day when the old man, whose name was Belarius, was out hunting with the two boys, Imogen felt ill, and thought she would try the medicine Pisanio had given her. So she took it, and at once became like a dead creature, so that when Belarius and the boys came back from hunting, they thought she was dead, and with many tears and funeral songs, they carried her away and laid her in the wood, covered with flowers.

They sang sweet songs to her, and strewed① flowers on her, pale primroses②, and the azure③ harebell④, and eglantine, and furred⑤ moss⑥, and went away sorrowful. No sooner had they gone than Imogen awoke, and not knowing how she came there, nor where she was, went wandering through the wood.[vii]

Now while Imogen had been living in the cave, the Romans had decided to attack Britain, and their army had come over, and with them Leonatus, who had grown sorry for his wickedness against Imogen, so had come back, not to fight with the Romans against Britain, but with the Britons against Rome.[viii] So as Imogen wandered alone, she met with Lucius, the Roman General, and took service with him as his page.

When the battle was fought between the Romans and Britons, Belarius and his two boys fought for their own country, and Leonatus, disguised as a British peasant, fought beside them. The Romans had taken Cymbeline prisoner⑦, and old Belarius, with his sons and Leonatus, bravely rescued the King. Then the Britons won the battle, and among the prisoners brought before the King were Lucius, with Imogen, Iachimo, and Leonatus, who had put on the uniform of a Roman soldier. He was tired of his life since he had cruelly ordered his wife to be killed, and he hoped that, as a Roman soldier, he would be put to death.

---

① strew [struː] *v*. 撒满 scatter, spread, sprinkle
② primrose [ˈprɪmrəʊz] *n*. 报春花
③ azure [ˈæʒə(r)] *adj*. 天蓝色的 bright blue, sky blue, sky-colored
④ harebell [ˈheəbel] *n*. 风铃草
⑤ furred [fɜːd] *adj*. 长着软毛的 covered with fur
⑥ moss [mɒs] *n*. 苔藓,地衣 lichen
⑦ take prisoner: 俘获 capture, seize, arrest, take into custody

When they were brought before the King, Lucius spoke out—

"A Roman with a Roman's heart can suffer," he said. "If I must die, so be it. This one thing only will I entreat①. My boy, a Briton② born, let him be ransomed③. Never master had a page so kind, so duteous④, diligent⑤, true. He has done no Briton harm, though he has served a Roman. Save him, Sir."

Then Cymbeline looked on the page, who was his own daughter, Imogen, in disguise, and though he did not recognize her, he felt such a kindness that he not only spared the boy's life, but he said—

"He shall have any boon⑥ he likes to ask of me, even though he ask a prisoner, the noblest taken."

Then Imogen said, "The boon I ask is that this gentleman shall say from whom he got the ring he has on his finger." And she pointed to Iachimo.

"Speak," said Cymbeline, "how did you get that diamond?"

Then Iachimo told the whole truth of his villainy. At this, Leonatus was unable to contain⑦ himself, and casting aside⑧ all thought of disguise, he came forward, cursing⑨ himself for his folly in having believed Iachimo's lying story, and calling again and again on his wife whom he believed dead.

"Oh, Imogen, my love, my life!" he cried. "Oh, Imogen!"

Then Imogen, forgetting she was disguised, cried out, "Peace, My Lord—here, here!"

Leonatus turned to strike the forward⑩ page who thus interfered⑪ in his great trouble, and then he saw that it was his wife, Imogen, and they fell into each other's arms.

The King was so glad to see his dear daughter again, and so grateful to the man who had rescued him (whom he now found to be Leonatus), that he gave his blessing on their marriage, and then he turned to Belarius, and the two boys. Now Belarius spoke—

"I am your old servant, Belarius. You accused me of treason when I had only been loyal to

① entreat [ɪn'triːt] *v*. 恳求 beg, petition, implore, plead with
② Briton ['brɪtn] *n*. 英国人 Britisher
③ ransom ['rænsəm] *v*. 赎出 redeem
④ duteous ['djuːtɪəs] *adj*. 顺从的 dutiful, obedient
⑤ diligent ['dɪlɪdʒənt] *adj*. 勤勉的 hard-working, industrious
⑥ boon [buːn] *n*. 恩惠 blessing
⑦ contain [kən'teɪn] *v*. 克制 control, restrain, hold back
⑧ cast aside: 抛弃 abandon, discard, throw away
⑨ curse [kɜːs] *v*. 咒骂 swear, abuse
⑩ forward ['fɔːwəd] *adj*. 冒失的 presumptuous
⑪ interfere [ˌɪntə'fɪə(r)] *v*. 干预 meddle, intervene

you, and to be doubted, made me disloyal①. So I stole your two sons, and see—they are here!" And he brought forward the two boys, who had sworn to be brothers to Imogen when they thought she was a boy like themselves.

The wicked Queen was dead of some of her own poisons, and the King, with his three children about him, lived to a happy old age.

So the wicked were punished, and the good and true lived happy ever after. So may the wicked suffer, and honest folk prosper till the world's end.

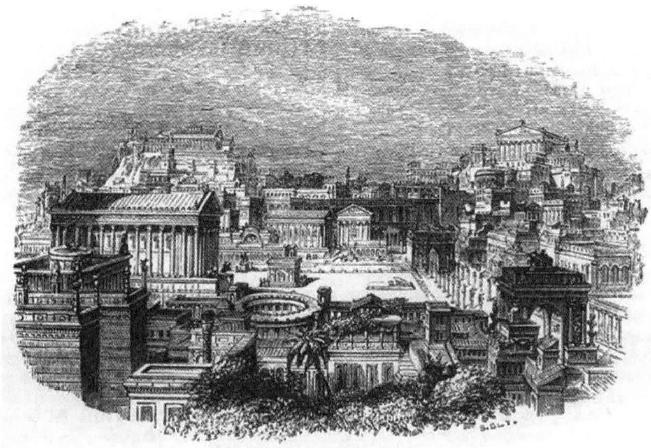

ⅰ When he was come to Rome, where he had gone to stay with an old friend of his father's, he spent his days still in thinking of his dear Imogen, and his nights in dreaming of her. 里奥那托斯来到罗马,投靠他父亲的一个老朋友,他整日思念他亲爱的伊摩琴,夜夜梦见她。(he was come=he had come:过时用法,受法语复合过去时的影响)

ⅱ "She is not so good but that she would deceive," said Iachimo, one of the Italian nobles. "她没有那么好,她有可能会背叛你。"其中一名意大利贵族阿埃基摩说道。(but:强调事实)

ⅲ "I wager this ring upon my finger," which was the very ring Imogen had given him at parting, "that my wife will keep all her vows to me, and that you will never persuade her to do otherwise." "我用我手指上的这个戒指跟你打赌,"这正是两人分别时伊摩琴送给他的戒指,"我的妻子一定会坚守对我的承诺,永远不可能接受你的诱惑。"(that..., and that...:双重并列宾语从句)

ⅳ Her pretty action did outsell her gift, and yet enriched it too. 她那优美的姿态,比这份礼物更有价值,也使礼物变得更为贵重。

ⅴ "Take the ring," cried Leonatus, "you have won; and you might have won my life as well, for I care nothing for it now I know my lady has forgotten me." "把戒指拿去吧,"里奥那托斯喊道,"你赢了。你同时也赢去了我的生命。现在我知道我的妻子已经把我遗忘,我的生命不足为惜。"(now=now that)

ⅵ Now when Pisanio got this letter he was too good to carry out its orders, and too wise to let them alone altogether. 毕萨尼奥收到了信,他心地十分善良,不忍心照信中吩咐的去做;同时他又很机智,没有置之不理。

ⅶ No sooner had they gone than Imogen awoke, and not knowing how she came there, nor where she was, went

① disloyal [dɪsˈlɔɪəl] *adj*. 不忠的 false, unfaithful, faithless

wandering through the wood. 他们刚走，伊摩琴就醒了，她不知道自己怎么会来到这里，也不知道这是什么地方，她只是漫无目的地在树林里游荡。

viii Now while Imogen had been living in the cave, the Romans had decided to attack Britain, and their army had come over, and with them Leonatus, who had grown sorry for his wickedness against Imogen, so had come back, not to fight with the Romans against Britain, but with the Britons against Rome. 当伊摩琴住在山洞里的时候，罗马人决定对英国发起进攻。他们的军队浩浩荡荡地过来，里奥那托斯也在其中。他非常后悔自己那样狠毒地对待伊摩琴，所以又回来了——不是为了跟罗马人一起进攻英国，而是为了跟英国人一起抗击罗马人。

麦克白夫人《麦克白》

Come, you spirits
That tend on mortal thoughts, unsex me here,
And fill me from the crown to the toe, top-full
Of direst cruelty, make thick my blood,
Stop up the access and passage to remorse,
That no compunctious visitings of nature

来,注视着人类恶念的魔鬼们!
解除我的女性的柔弱,用最凶恶的残忍
自顶至踵贯注在我的全身;
凝结我的血液,
不要让怜悯钻进我的心头,
不要让天性中的恻隐

Shake my fell purpose nor keep peace between
The effect and it. Come to my woman's breasts,
And take my milk for gall...
That my keen knife see not the wound it makes,
Nor heaven peep through the blanket of the dark
To cry "Hold, hold!"

摇动我的狠毒的决意！
进入我的妇人的胸中，把我的乳水
当作胆汁吧！……
让我的锐利的刀瞧不见它自己切开的伤口，
让青天不能从黑暗的重衾里探出头来，
高喊"住手，住手！"

麦克白
Macbeth

主要人物

Duncan [ˈdʌŋkən] 邓肯(苏格兰国王)
Macbeth [məkˈbeθ] 麦克白(苏格兰军中大将)
Banquo [ˈbæŋkwəʊ] 班柯(苏格兰军中大将)
Malcolm [ˈmælkəm] 马尔康(邓肯之子)
Donalbain [ˈdɒnlbeɪn] 道纳本(邓肯之子)
Fleance [ˈfliːəns] 弗里恩斯(班柯之子)
Macduff [məkˈdʌf] 麦克德夫(苏格兰贵族)
Lennox [ˈlenəks] 列诺克斯(苏格兰贵族)
Lady Macbeth　麦克白夫人
The Three Witches　三女巫

When a person is asked to tell the story of Macbeth, he can tell two stories. One is of a man called Macbeth who came to the throne of Scotland by a crime in the year of our Lord① 1039, and reigned justly and well, on the whole②, for fifteen years or more. This story is part of Scottish history. The other story issues from③ a place called Imagination; it is gloomy④ and wonderful, and you shall hear it.

A year or two before Edward the Confessor⑤ began to rule England, a battle was won in Scotland against a Norwegian⑥ King by two generals named Macbeth and Banquo. After the battle, the generals walked together towards Forres, in Elginshire⑦, where Duncan, King of Scotland, was awaiting them.

While they were crossing a lonely heath, they saw three bearded⑧ women, sisters, hand in hand, withered in appearance and wild⑨ in their attire.

"Speak, who are you?" demanded Macbeth.

"Hail⑩, Macbeth, chieftain⑪ of Glamis⑫," said the first woman.

---

① year of our Lord：公元某年 year of grace
② on the whole：总的来说 altogether, all in all, by and large
③ issue from：从……中出来 come out of
④ gloomy [ˈgluːmi] *adj*. 忧郁的 depressing, sorrowful, dismal
⑤ Edward [ˈedwəd] the Confessor [kənˈfesə(r)]：忏悔者爱德华(约 1001—1066)
⑥ Norwegian [nɔːˈwiːdʒən] *adj*. 挪威的
⑦ Elginshire [ˈelgɪnʃə(r)]：埃尔金郡(位于英国苏格兰东北部)
⑧ bearded [ˈbɪədɪd] *adj*. 有胡子的 whiskered
⑨ wild [waɪld] *adj*. 凌乱的 untidy, disordered, dishevelled
⑩ hail [heɪl] *int*. (招呼用语)万安,万福,万岁
⑪ chieftain [ˈtʃiːftən] *n*. 首领 chief, leader, headman
⑫ Glamis [glɑːmz]：格拉姆斯(英国地名)

"Hail, Macbeth, chieftain of Cawdor[1]," said the second woman.

"Hail, Macbeth, King that is to be," said the third woman.

Then Banquo asked, "What of me?" And the third woman replied, "Thou shalt be the father of kings."

"Tell me more," said Macbeth. "By my father's death I am chieftain of Glamis, but the chieftain of Cawdor lives, and the King lives, and his children live. Speak, I charge you!"

The women replied only by vanishing, as though suddenly mixed with the air.

Banquo and Macbeth knew then that they had been addressed[2] by witches, and were discussing their prophecies[3] when two nobles[4] approached. One of them thanked Macbeth, in the King's name, for his military[5] services, and the other said, "He bade me call you chieftain of Cawdor."

Macbeth then learned that the man who had yesterday borne that title was to die for treason, and he could not help thinking, "The third witch called me, 'King that is to be.'"

"Banquo," he said, "you see that the witches spoke truth concerning[6] me. Do you not believe, therefore, that your child and grandchild will be kings?"

Banquo frowned[7]. Duncan had two sons, Malcolm and Donalbain, and he deemed[8] it disloyal to hope that his son Fleance should rule Scotland. He told Macbeth that the witches might have intended to tempt[9] them both into villainy by their prophecies concerning the throne. Macbeth, however, thought the prophecy that he should be King too pleasant to keep to himself, and he mentioned it to his wife in a letter.[i]

Lady Macbeth was the granddaughter of a King of Scotland who had died in defending his crown against the King who preceded[10] Duncan, and by whose order her only brother was slain.[ii] To her, Duncan was a reminder of bitter wrongs. Her husband had royal blood in his veins[11], and when she read his letter, she was determined that he should be King.

When a messenger arrived to inform her that Duncan would pass a night in Macbeth's castle, she nerved herself for[12] a very base action.

She told Macbeth almost as soon as she saw him

① Cawdor ['kɔːdə(r)]：考德(英国地名)
② address [ə'dres] *v*. 向……说话 communicate with
③ prophecy ['prɒfəsi] *n*. 预言 prediction, forecast, foretelling
④ noble ['nəʊbl] *n*. 贵族成员 nobleman/noblewoman, peer, aristocrat
⑤ military ['mɪlətri] *adj*. 军事的 warlike, martial
⑥ concerning [kən'sɜːnɪŋ] *prep*. 关于 regarding, touching
⑦ frown [fraʊn] *v*. 皱眉 knit one's brow(s)
⑧ deem [diːm] *v*. 认为 think, believe, suppose, consider
⑨ tempt [tempt] *v*. 引诱 invite, attract, allure, entice, seduce
⑩ precede [prɪ'siːd] *v*. 先于 predate, forego, come before/ahead of
⑪ vein [veɪn] *n*. 静脉
⑫ nerve oneself for：鼓起勇气 give yourself the courage or strength

that Duncan must spend a sunless morrow. She meant that Duncan must die, and that the dead are blind. "We will speak further," said Macbeth uneasily, and at night, with his memory full of Duncan's kind words, he would fain① have spared his guest.

"Would you live a coward?" demanded Lady Macbeth, who seems to have thought that morality and cowardice② were the same.

"I dare do all that may become a man," replied Macbeth. "Who dare do more is none." iii

"Why did you write that letter to me?" she inquired fiercely③, and with bitter words she egged him on④ to murder, and with cunning words she showed him how to do it.

After supper Duncan went to bed, and two grooms⑤ were placed on guard at his bedroom door. Lady Macbeth caused them to drink wine till they were stupefied⑥. She then took their daggers and would have killed the King herself if his sleeping face had not looked like her father's. iv

Macbeth came later, and found the daggers lying by the grooms; and soon with red hands he appeared before his wife, saying, "Methought I heard a voice cry, 'Sleep no more! Macbeth destroys the sleeping.'"

"Wash your hands," she said. "Why did you not leave the daggers by the grooms? Take them back, and smear⑦ the grooms with blood."

"I dare not," said Macbeth.

His wife dared, and she returned to him with hands red as his own, but a heart less white, she proudly told him, for she scorned his fear. v

The murderers heard a knocking, and Macbeth wished it was a knocking which could wake the dead. It was the knocking of Macduff, the chieftain of Fife⑧, who had been told by Duncan to visit him early. Macbeth went to him, and showed him the door of the King's room.

Macduff entered, and came out again crying, "O horror! Horror! Horror!"

Macbeth appeared as horror-stricken⑨ as Macduff, and pretending that he could not bear to see life in Duncan's murderers, he slew the two grooms with their own daggers before they could proclaim their innocence. vi

These murders did not shriek⑩ out, and Macbeth was crowned⑪ at Scone. One of Duncan's sons went to Ireland, the other to England. Macbeth was King. But he was discontented. The prophecy concerning Banquo oppressed⑫ his mind. If Fleance were to rule, a son of Macbeth

---

① fain [feɪn] *adv*. 欣然地 gladly, willingly
② cowardice [ˈkaʊədɪs] *n*. 懦弱 cowardliness, weakness
③ fiercely [ˈfɪəsli] *adv*. 凶狠地 furiously, ferociously, savagely
④ egg sb. on: 怂恿某人 push, urge, incite, encourage, spur
⑤ groom [gruːm] *n*. 马夫;王室侍从官 servant, stableman
⑥ stupefied [ˈstjuːpɪfaɪd] *adj*. 神志不清的 dazed, numb
⑦ smear [smɪə(r)] *v*. 涂抹 daub
⑧ Fife [faɪf]: 法夫(苏格兰东部一地区)
⑨ horror-stricken [ˈhɔrə strɪkən] *adj*. 惊恐万分的 horror-struck
⑩ shriek [ʃriːk] *v*. 尖叫 scream, cry, yell, howl, wail, squeal
⑪ crown [kraʊn] *v*. 加冕 coronate
⑫ oppress [əˈpres] *v*. 使烦恼 weigh down, burden

would not rule. Macbeth determined, therefore, to murder both Banquo and his son. He hired two ruffians①, who slew Banquo one night when he was on his way with Fleance to a banquet which Macbeth was giving to his nobles. Fleance escaped.

Meanwhile Macbeth and his Queen received their guests very graciously②, and he expressed a wish for them which has been uttered thousands of times since his day—"Now good digestion③ wait on appetite④, and health on both."[vii]

"We pray Your Majesty to sit with us," said Lennox, a Scotch noble; but ere⑤ Macbeth could reply, the ghost of Banquo entered the banqueting hall and sat in Macbeth's place.

Not noticing the ghost, Macbeth observed⑥ that, if Banquo were present, he could say that he had collected under his roof the choicest⑦ chivalry⑧ of Scotland.[viii] Macduff, however, had curtly⑨ declined his invitation.

The King was again pressed⑩ to take a seat, and Lennox, to whom Banquo's ghost was invisible, showed him the chair where it sat.

But Macbeth, with his eyes of genius, saw the ghost. He saw it like a form of mist and blood, and he demanded passionately⑪, "Which of you have done this?"

Still none saw the ghost but he, and to the ghost Macbeth said, "Thou canst not say I did it."

The ghost glided⑫ out, and Macbeth was impudent⑬ enough to raise a glass of wine "to the general joy of the whole table, and to our dear friend Banquo, whom we miss."

The toast⑭ was drunk as the ghost of Banquo entered for the second time.

"Begone⑮!" cried Macbeth. "You are senseless⑯, mindless! Hide in the earth, thou horrible shadow."

---

① ruffian ['rʌfiən] *n*. 恶棍 thug, villain, rogue, rascal, scoundrel
② graciously ['greɪʃəsli] *adv*. 和蔼地 genially, agreeably, affably, amiably
③ digestion [daɪ'dʒestʃən] *n*. 消化 digesting
④ appetite ['æpɪtaɪt] *n*. 食欲 hunger, stomach
⑤ ere [eə(r)] *prep*. 〈古〉(=before) 在……之前
⑥ observe [əb'zɜːv] *v*. 评论 remark, comment
⑦ choice [tʃɔɪs] *adj*. 上等的 select
⑧ chivalry ['ʃɪvəlri] *n*. 骑兵(总称) cavalry
⑨ curtly ['kɜːtli] *adv*. 唐突无礼地 brusquely, abruptly
⑩ press [pres] *v*. 催促;逼迫 urge, force, push
⑪ passionately ['pæʃənətli] *adv*. 生气地 angrily, furiously
⑫ glide [glaɪd] *v*. 滑行;悄悄地走 slip, sail, slide, ghost, skim
⑬ impudent ['ɪmpjədənt] *adj*. 不恭的 rude, impertinent
⑭ toast [təʊst] *n*. 祝酒 pledge
⑮ begone [bɪ'gɒn] *int*. 〈古〉走开 go away
⑯ senseless ['sensləs] *adj*. 愚蠢的 foolish

Again none saw the ghost but he.

"What is it Your Majesty sees?" asked one of the nobles.

The Queen dared not permit an answer to be given to this question. She hurriedly begged her guests to quit a sick man who was likely to grow worse if he was obliged to talk.

Macbeth, however, was well enough next day to converse with the witches whose prophecies had so depraved① him.

He found them in a cavern② on a thunderous day. They were revolving round③ a cauldron④ in which were boiling particles⑤ of many strange and horrible creatures, and they knew he was coming before he arrived.

"Answer me what I ask you," said the King.

"Would you rather hear it from us or our masters?" asked the first witch.

"Call them," replied Macbeth.

Thereupon⑥ the witches poured blood into the cauldron and grease⑦ into the flame that licked⑧ it, and a helmeted⑨ head appeared with the visor⑩ on, so that Macbeth could only see its eyes.

He was speaking to the head, when the first witch said gravely, "He knows thy thought," and a voice in the head said, "Macbeth, beware⑪ Macduff, the chieftain of Fife." The head then descended⑫ into the cauldron till it disappeared.

"One word more," pleaded Macbeth.

"He will not be commanded," said the first witch, and then a crowned⑬ child ascended from

---

① deprave [dɪˈpreɪv] *v*. 使堕落 corrupt
② cavern [ˈkævən] *n*. 大洞穴 cave
③ revolve round: 围绕……旋转 move around in a circle
④ cauldron [ˈkɔːldrən] *n*. 大锅 pot
⑤ particle [ˈpɑːtɪkl] *n*. 碎片 bit, piece, scrap, shred, crumb
⑥ thereupon [ˌðeərəˈpɒn] *adv*. 随即;于是 immediately, presently
⑦ grease [griːs] *n*. 油脂 fat, oil, dripping
⑧ lick [lɪk] *v*. (火舌)舔食 touch
⑨ helmeted [ˈhelmɪtɪd] *adj*. 戴着头盔的 wearing a helmet
⑩ visor [ˈvaɪzə(r)] *n*. (头盔上的)面罩
⑪ beware [bɪˈweə(r)] *v*. 小心 be careful/cautious, watch out
⑫ descend [dɪˈsend] *v*. 下降 fall, drop, sink, go down
⑬ crowned [kraʊnd] *adj*. 戴有王冠的 wearing a crown

the cauldron bearing a tree in his hand. The child said—

"Macbeth shall be unconquerable① till

The Wood of Birnam② climbs Dunsinane Hill③."

"That will never be," said Macbeth; and he asked to be told if Banquo's descendants④ would ever rule Scotland.

The cauldron sank into the earth; music was heard, and a procession⑤ of phantom⑥ kings filed⑦ past Macbeth; behind them was Banquo's ghost. In each king, Macbeth saw a likeness to Banquo, and he counted eight kings.

Then he was suddenly left alone.

His next proceeding⑧ was to send murderers to Macduff's castle. They did not find Macduff, and asked Lady Macduff where he was. She gave a stinging answer, and her questioner called Macduff a traitor⑨. "Thou liest!" shouted Macduff's little son, who was immediately stabbed⑩, and with his last breath entreated his mother to fly. The murderers did not leave the castle while one of its inmates⑪ remained alive.

Macduff was in England listening, with Malcolm, to a doctor's tale of cures wrought by Edward the Confessor when his friend Ross came to tell him that his wife and children were no more. At first Ross dared not speak the truth, and turn Macduff's bright sympathy with sufferers relieved by royal virtue into sorrow and hatred.[ix] But when Malcolm said that England was sending an army into Scotland against Macbeth, Ross blurted out⑫ his news, and Macduff cried, "All dead, did you say? All my pretty ones and their mother? Did you say all?"

His sorry hope was in revenge, but if he could have looked into Macbeth's castle on Dunsinane Hill, he would have seen at work a force more solemn than revenge.[x] Retribution⑬ was working, for Lady Macbeth was mad. She walked in her sleep amid ghastly⑭ dreams. She was wont to wash her hands for a quarter of an hour at a time; but after all her washing, would still see a red spot of blood upon her skin. It was pitiful to hear her cry that all the perfumes of Arabia⑮ could not sweeten her little hand.

"Canst thou not minister to⑯ a mind diseased⑰?" inquired Macbeth of the doctor, but the doctor replied that his patient must minister to her own mind. This reply gave Macbeth a scorn of

---

① unconquerable [ʌn'kɒŋkərəbl] *adj*. 不可战胜的 unbeatable, invincible

② Birnam ['bɜːnəm]: 伯纳姆(英国地名,朱生豪译本中译为"勃南")

③ Dunsinane [dʌn'sɪnən] Hill: 邓西嫩山

④ descendant [dɪ'sendənt] *n*. 后裔 offspring, issue

⑤ procession [prə'seʃn] *n*. 队伍 train, file

⑥ phantom ['fæntəm] *adj*. 虚幻的 imaginary, illusory

⑦ file [faɪl] *v*. 列队行进 march, troop, parade, walk in line

⑧ proceeding [prə'siːdɪŋ] *n*. 行动 action, move

⑨ traitor ['treɪtə(r)] *n*. 叛徒 betrayer, turncoat

⑩ stab [stæb] *v*. 刺 pierce, jab, puncture

⑪ inmate ['ɪnmeɪt] *n*. (监狱或精神病院里的)居住者;〈古〉(房屋的)同住者 dweller

⑫ blurt out: 脱口而出 exclaim, ejaculate

⑬ retribution [ˌretrɪ'bjuːʃn] *n*. 报应 judgement

⑭ ghastly ['gɑːstli] *adj*. 可怕的 terrible, horrible, awful, dreadful

⑮ Arabia [ə'reɪbɪə]: 阿拉伯半岛(位于亚洲西南部)

⑯ minister to: 照顾 tend, take care of

⑰ diseased [dɪ'ziːzd] *adj*. 患病的 sick, ailing

medicine. "Throw physic① to the dogs," he said. "I'll none of it."

One day he heard a sound of women crying. An officer approached him and said, "The Queen, Your Majesty, is dead." "Out, brief candle," muttered Macbeth, meaning that life was like a candle, at the mercy of a puff of air. He did not weep; he was too familiar with death.

Presently a messenger told him that he saw Birnam Wood on the march. Macbeth called him a liar and a slave, and threatened to hang him if he had made a mistake. "If you are right you can hang me," he said.

From the turret② windows of Dunsinane Castle, Birnam Wood did indeed appear to be marching. Every soldier of the English army held aloft③ a bough which he had cut from a tree in that wood, and like human trees they climbed Dunsinane Hill.

Macbeth had still his courage. He went to battle to conquer④ or die, and the first thing he did was to kill the English general's son in single combat. Macbeth then felt that no man could fight him and live, and when Macduff came to him blazing⑤ for revenge, Macbeth said to him, "Go back. I have spilt⑥ too much of your blood already."

"My voice is in my sword," replied Macduff, and hacked⑦ at him and bade him yield⑧.

"I will not yield!" said Macbeth, but his last hour had struck. He fell.

Macbeth's men were in retreat⑨ when Macduff came before Malcolm holding a King's head by the hair.

"Hail, King!" he said, and the new King looked at the old.

So Malcolm reigned after Macbeth; but in years that came afterwards the descendants of Banquo were kings.

① physic [ˈfɪzɪk] *n*. 药物 drug, medicine, medication, remedy
② turret [ˈtʌrət] *n*. 炮塔,角楼 tower
③ aloft [əˈlɒft] *adv*. 在空中 in the air
④ conquer [ˈkɒŋkə(r)] *v*. 战胜 beat, defeat, overpower, triumph
⑤ blaze [bleɪz] *v*. (怒火)燃烧 glower, glare
⑥ spill [spɪl] *v*. 使洒出 slop, splatter
⑦ hack [hæk] *v*. 砍,劈 cut, chop, hew, gash, slash
⑧ yield [jiːld] *v*. 屈服 surrender, give in, throw in the towel
⑨ retreat [rɪˈtriːt] *n*. 撤退 withdrawal, pullback

i Macbeth, however, thought the prophecy that he should be King too pleasant to keep to himself, and he mentioned it to his wife in a letter. 然而,要当国王的预言让麦克白兴奋不已,他在一封信里把这件事告诉了他妻子。(that…:同位语从句解释说明 prophecy 的内容)

ii Lady Macbeth was the granddaughter of a King of Scotland who had died in defending his crown against the King who preceded Duncan, and by whose order her only brother was slain. 麦克白夫人是苏格兰国王的孙女。她的爷爷在同邓肯之前的那位国王争夺王位时死去了,对方还下令杀死了她唯一的兄弟。(who…, who…, and by whose order…:三重定语从句的嵌套)

iii "I dare do all that may become a man," replied Macbeth. "Who dare do more is none." 麦克白回答道:"只要是男子汉做的事,我都敢做。没有人比我更胆大。"

iv She then took their daggers and would have killed the King herself if his sleeping face had not looked like her father's. 然后,她拿走了他们的匕首,要不是国王睡着的样子活像她的父亲,她早就亲手杀了他。(…would have done…if…had done…:与过去事实相反的虚拟语气)

v His wife dared, and she returned to him with hands red as his own, but a heart less white, she proudly told him, for she scorned his fear. 可是他的妻子不怕,于是她也和他一样双手沾满鲜血地回来了,但是她骄傲地告诉他,自己的心却没有他那般胆怯,她还嘲笑他的担心。

vi Macbeth appeared as horror-stricken as Macduff, and pretending that he could not bear to see life in Duncan's murderers, he slew the two grooms with their own daggers before they could proclaim their innocence. 麦克白和麦克德夫一样也是吓坏了的模样,他假装绝不能饶恕谋害邓肯的凶手,就用那两名侍卫的匕首杀死了他们——在他们还来不及证明自己的清白之前。

vii "Now good digestion wait on appetite, and health on both." "来,请放量醉饱吧,愿各位胃纳健旺,身强力壮!"(朱生豪译)/"愿诸位食欲大开,消化良好,敬祝二者齐备!"(梁实秋译)

viii Not noticing the ghost, Macbeth observed that, if Banquo were present, he could say that he had collected under his roof the choicest chivalry of Scotland. 还没有察觉到鬼魂的麦克白表示,要是班柯在场的话,那真可以说是苏格兰的贤士都齐聚一堂了。(not noticing…:现在分词的否定式作状语;if…were…, …could do…:与现在事实相反的虚拟语气)

ix At first Ross dared not speak the truth, and turn Macduff's bright sympathy with sufferers relieved by royal virtue into sorrow and hatred. 起初,洛斯不敢说出真相,因为麦克德夫充满同情心,他高贵的情操可以缓解受难者的痛苦,洛斯怕麦克德夫由这种人转变成充满哀伤和恨意的人。

x His sorry hope was in revenge, but if he could have looked into Macbeth's castle on Dunsinane Hill, he would have seen at work a force more solemn than revenge. 他可悲的愿望就是报仇雪恨,但如果能到邓西嫩山上麦克白的城堡里探个究竟,他就会看到有股比复仇更庄严的力量正在发挥作用。(if…could have done…, …would have done…:与过去事实相反的虚拟语气)

阿德里安娜《错误的喜剧》

Come, I will fasten on this sleeve of thine.
Thou art an elm, my husband, I a vine,
Whose weakness, married to thy stronger state,
Makes me with thy strength to communicate.
If aught possess thee from me, it is dross,
Usurping ivy, brier, or idle moss,
Who, all for want of pruning, with intrusion
Infect thy sap and live on thy confusion.

来，让我来把你的袖子抓住，
我是藤萝，丈夫，你是榆树。
我枝条柔弱，靠在你的干上，
让我来分享你的倔强的力量；
若有谁把你从我身边夺去，
那必是野蔓荆棘青苔，无聊的东西；
它们因为没有人加以修剪，
硬把你的汁浆吮吸得精干。

错误的喜剧
The Comedy of Errors

主要人物

Egeon [iːˈdʒɪən] 伊勤（叙拉古商人）

Emilia [ɪˈmɪlɪə] 爱米利娅（伊勤的妻子，以弗所尼庵中住持）

Antipholus [ænˈtɪfələs] of Ephesus [ˈefɪsəs] 小安提福勒斯（伊勤及爱米利娅的孪生子）

Antipholus of Syracuse [ˈsaɪrəkjuːz] 大安提福勒斯（伊勤及爱米利娅的孪生子）

Dromio [ˈdrəʊmɪəʊ] of Ephesus 小德洛米奥（侍奉安提福勒斯兄弟的孪生兄弟）

Dromio of Syracuse 大德洛米奥（侍奉安提福勒斯兄弟的孪生兄弟）

Adriana [ˌeɪdrɪˈeɪnə] 阿德里安娜（小安提福勒斯的妻子）

Luciana [ˌluːsɪˈɑːnə] 露西安娜（阿德里安娜的妹妹）

Solinus [səˈlaɪnəs] 索列纳斯（以弗所公爵）

Angelo [ˈændʒɪləʊ] 安哲鲁（金匠）

Egeon was a merchant of Syracuse①, which is a seaport in Sicily. His wife was Emilia, and they were very happy until Egeon's manager died, and he was obliged to go by himself to a place called Epidamnum② on the Adriatic③. As soon as she could, Emilia followed him, and after they had been together some time two baby boys were born to them. The babies were exactly alike; even when they were dressed differently they looked the same.

And now you must believe a very strange thing. At the same inn where these children were born, and on the same day, two baby boys were born to a much poorer couple than Emilia and Egeon; so poor, indeed, were the parents of these twins that they sold them to the parents of the other twins.[i]

Emilia was eager to show her children to her friends in Syracuse, and in treacherous④ weather she and Egeon and the four babies sailed homewards.

---

① Syracuse [ˈsaɪrəkjuːz]：叙拉古（古希腊城邦，今属意大利）

② Epidamnum [ˌepɪˈdæmnəm]：厄匹达姆纽姆（朱生豪译本中译为"埃必丹农"）

③ Adriatic [ˌeɪdrɪˈætɪk]：亚得里亚海

④ treacherous [ˈtretʃərəs] *adj*. 危险的 dangerous, risky, hazardous

They were still far from Syracuse when their ship sprang[1] a leak[2], and the crew left it in a body[3] by the only boat, caring little what became of[4] their passengers.

Emilia fastened[5] one of her children to a mast and tied one of the slave children to him; Egeon followed her example with the remaining children. Then the parents secured[6] themselves to the same masts, and hoped for safety.

The ship, however, suddenly struck a rock and was split[7] in two, and Emilia, and the two children whom she had tied, floated away from Egeon and the other children. Emilia and her charges[8] were picked up by some people of Epidamnum, but some fishermen of Corinth[9] took the babies from her by force, and she returned to Epidanmum alone, and very miserable[10]. Afterwards she settled in Ephesus, a famous town in Asia Minor[11].

Egeon and his charges were also saved; and, more fortunate than Emilia, he was able to return to Syracuse and keep them till they were eighteen. His own child he called Antipholus, and the slave child he called Dromio; and, strangely enough, these were the names given to the children who floated away from him.

At the age of eighteen the son who was with Egeon grew restless[12] with a desire to find his brother. Egeon let him depart with his servant, and the young men are henceforth known as Antipholus of Syracuse and Dromio of Syracuse.

Let alone, Egeon found his home too dreary[13] to dwell[14] in, and traveled for five years. He did not, during his absence, learn all the news of Syracuse, or he would never have gone to Ephesus.[ii]

As it was, his melancholy wandering ceased in that town, where he was arrested almost as soon as he arrived. He then found that the Duke of Syracuse had been acting in so tyrannical[15] a manner to Ephesians[16] unlucky enough to fall into his hands, that the Government of Ephesus had angrily passed a law which punished by death or a fine of a thousand pounds any Syracusan who should come to Ephesus.[iii] Egeon was brought before Solinus, Duke of Ephesus, who told him that he must die or pay a thousand pounds before the end of the day.

You will think there was fate in this when I tell you that the children who were kidnapped[17]

---

① spring [sprɪŋ] *v*. 突然出现 appear suddenly
② leak [liːk] *n*. 裂缝 hole, opening, crack
③ in a body: 全体,整体 all together
④ what became of: (遭遇)如何,(结果)怎么样 what happened to
⑤ fasten [ˈfɑːsn] *v*. 系牢 tie, bind, tie up, secure, do up
⑥ secure [sɪˈkjʊə(r)] *v*. 拴牢 fasten
⑦ split [splɪt] *v*. 使裂开 break, crack, snap
⑧ charge [tʃɑːdʒ] *n*. 需要照管的人 ward, dependant, minor
⑨ Corinth [ˈkɒrɪnθ]: 科林斯(古希腊城邦)
⑩ miserable [ˈmɪzrəbl] *adj*. 痛苦的 sad, sorrowful, melancholy
⑪ Asia Minor [ˌeɪʃə ˈmaɪnə(r)]: 小亚细亚(亚洲西部半岛)
⑫ restless [ˈrestləs] *adj*. 坐立不安的 worried, nervous, disturbed
⑬ dreary [ˈdrɪəri] *adj*. 令人沮丧的 dull, dismal, depressing
⑭ dwell [dwel] *v*. 居住 live, reside, abide
⑮ tyrannical [tɪˈrænɪkl] *adj*. 残暴的 cruel, brutal
⑯ Ephesian [ɪˈfiːʒən] *n*. 以弗所人
⑰ kidnap [ˈkɪdnæp] *v*. 绑架 abduct, seize

by the fishermen of Corinth were now citizens of Ephesus, whither they had been brought by Duke Menaphon, an uncle of Duke Solinus. They will henceforth be called Antipholus of Ephesus and Dromio of Ephesus.

Moreover, on the very day when Egeon was arrested, Antipholus of Syracuse landed in Ephesus and pretended that he came from Epidamnum in order to avoid a penalty①. He handed his money to his servant Dromio of Syracuse, and bade him take it to the Centaur Inn② and remain there till he came.

In less than ten minutes he was met on the Mart③ by Dromio of Ephesus, his brother's slave, and immediately mistook him for④ his own Dromio. "Why are you back so soon? Where did you leave the money?" asked Antipholus of Syracuse.

This Dromio knew of no money except six pence, which he had received on the previous Wednesday and given to the saddler⑤; but he did know that his mistress was annoyed because his master was not in to dinner, and he asked Antipholus of Syracuse to go to a house called The Phoenix without delay. His speech angered the hearer, who would have beaten him if he had not fled.[iv] Antipholus of Syracuse then went to The Centaur, found that his gold had been deposited⑥ there, and walked out of the inn.

He was wandering about Ephesus when two beautiful ladies signaled⑦ to him with their hands. They were sisters, and their names were Adriana and Luciana. Adriana was the wife of his brother Antipholus of Ephesus, and she had made up her mind, from the strange account⑧ given her by Dromio of Ephesus, that her husband preferred another woman to his wife. "Ay, you may look as if you did not know me," she said to the man who was really her brother-in-law, "but I can remember when no words were sweet unless I said them, no meat flavorsome⑨ unless I carved it."

"Is it I you address?"[v] said Antipholus of Syracuse stiffly⑩. "I do not know you."

"Fie, brother," said Luciana. "You know perfectly well that she sent Dromio to you to bid you come to dinner." And Adriana said, "Come, come. I have been made a fool of long enough.

---

① penalty ['penəlti] *n*. 惩罚 punishment
② Centaur ['sentɔː(r)] Inn: 圣陶尔酒店(centaur 意为"古希腊神话中半人半马的怪物")
③ mart [mɑːt] *n*. 集市 marketplace
④ mistake for: 把……错认为 confuse with, mix up with
⑤ saddler ['sædlə(r)] *n*. 马具商,制造马鞍的人
⑥ deposit [dɪ'pɒzɪt] *v*. 存放 put, keep
⑦ signal ['sɪgnəl] *v*. 示意 gesture, sign, beckon
⑧ account [ə'kaʊnt] *n*. 叙述 report, relation, description
⑨ flavorsome ['fleɪvəsəm] *adj*. 很有滋味的 tasty, delicious
⑩ stiffly ['stɪfli] *adv*. 生硬地 awkwardly, clumsily, gracelessly

My truant① husband shall dine with me and confess his silly pranks② and be forgiven."

They were determined ladies, and Antipholus of Syracuse grew weary of disputing③ with them, and followed them obediently④ to The Phoenix, where a very late "midday" dinner awaited them.

They were at dinner when Antipholus of Ephesus and his slave Dromio demanded admittance. "Maud, Bridget, Marian, Cecily, Gillian, Ginn!" shouted Dromio of Ephesus, who knew all his fellow servants' names by heart.

From within came the reply, "Fool, dray horse⑤, coxcomb⑥, idiot!" It was Dromio of Syracuse that unconsciously insulting his brother.

Master and man did their best to get in, short of⑦ using a crowbar⑧, and finally went away; but Antipholus of Ephesus felt so annoyed with his wife that he decided to give a gold chain which he had promised her, to another woman.

Inside The Phoenix, Luciana, who believed Antipholus of Syracuse to be her sister's husband, attempted, by a discourse⑨ in rhyme⑩, when alone with him, to make him kinder to Adriana. In reply he told her that he was not married, but that he loved her so much that, if Luciana were a mermaid, he would gladly lie on the sea if he might feel beneath him her floating golden hair.[vi]

Luciana was shocked and left him, and reported his lovemaking⑪ to Adriana, who said that her husband was old and ugly, and not fit to be seen or heard, though secretly she was very fond of him.

Antipholus of Syracuse soon received a visitor in the shape of Angelo the goldsmith⑫, of whom Antipholus of Ephesus had ordered the chain which he had promised his wife and intended to give to another woman.

The goldsmith handed the chain to Antipholus of Syracuse, and treated his "I bespoke⑬ it

---

① truant [ˈtruːənt] *adj*. 逃避责任的;闲荡的 irresponsible, idle
② prank [præŋk] *n*. 恶作剧 practical joke, trick
③ dispute [dɪˈspjuːt] *v*. 争论 argue, quarrel, squabble
④ obediently [əˈbiːdiəntli] *adv*. 顺从地 submissively, unresistingly
⑤ dray horse: 运货马车的马
⑥ coxcomb [ˈkɒkskəʊm] *n*. 花花公子 dandy, beau, prig, fop
⑦ short of: 除……以外 except, save, apart from, other than
⑧ crowbar [ˈkrəʊbɑː(r)] *n*. 铁撬棍 jemmy
⑨ discourse [ˈdɪskɔːs] *n*. 谈话 talk, conversation, discussion
⑩ in rhyme: 押韵
⑪ lovemaking [ˈlʌvmeɪkɪŋ] *n*. 调情,求爱
⑫ goldsmith [ˈgəʊldsmɪθ] *n*. 金匠
⑬ bespeak [bɪˈspiːk] *v*. (bespoke, bespoken)预定 predetermine

not" as mere fun, so that the puzzled merchant took the chain as good-humoredly as he had partaken① of Adriana's dinner.[vii] He offered payment, but Angelo foolishly said he would call again.

The consequence was that Angelo was without money when a creditor② of the sort that stands no nonsense③, threatened him with arrest unless he paid his debt immediately.[viii] This creditor had brought a police officer with him, and Angelo was relieved to see Antipholus of Ephesus coming out of the house where he had been dining because he had been locked out of The Phoenix. Bitter was Angelo's dismay④ when Antipholus denied receipt of the chain. Angelo could have sent his mother to prison if she had said that, and he gave Antipholus of Ephesus in charge.[ix]

At this moment up came Dromio of Syracuse and told the wrong Antipholus that he had shipped his goods, and that a favorable wind was blowing. To the ears of Antipholus of Ephesus this talk was simple nonsense. He would gladly have beaten the slave, but contented himself with crossly⑤ telling him to hurry to Adriana and bid her send to her arrested husband a purse of money which she would find in his desk.

Though Adriana was furious⑥ with her husband because she thought he had been making love to⑦ her sister, she did not prevent Luciana from getting the purse, and she bade Dromio of Syracuse bring home his master immediately.

Unfortunately, before Dromio could reach the police station he met his real master, who had never been arrested, and did not understand what he meant by offering him a purse. Antipholus of Syracuse was further surprised when a lady whom he did not know asked him for a chain that he had promised her. She was, of course, the lady with whom Antipholus of Ephesus had dined⑧ when his brother was occupying his place at table. "Avaunt⑨, thou witch!" was the answer which, to her astonishment, she received.

Meanwhile Antipholus of Ephesus waited vainly for the money which was to have released him. Never a good-tempered man, he was crazy with anger when Dromio of Ephesus, who, of course, had not been instructed to fetch a purse, appeared with nothing more useful than a rope.[x] He beat the slave in the street despite the remonstrance⑩ of the police officer; and his temper did not mend⑪ when Adriana, Luciana, and a doctor arrived under the impression that⑫ he was mad and must have his pulse⑬ felt. He raged⑭ so much that men came forward to bind him. But the kindness of Adriana spared him this shame. She promised to pay the sum demanded of him, and

① partake of: 吃,喝 eat, drink
② creditor [ˈkredɪtə(r)] *n*. 债主
③ stand no nonsense: 不好惹;不允许放肆
④ dismay [dɪsˈmeɪ] *n*. 惊愕 alarm, consternation
⑤ crossly [ˈkrɒsli] *adv*. 生气地 angrily
⑥ furious [ˈfjʊəriəs] *adj*. 狂怒的 angry, rageful, wrathful
⑦ make love to: 向……示爱 court, woo, show love to
⑧ dine [daɪn] *v*. 进餐 eat, feast
⑨ avaunt [əˈvɔːnt] *int*. 滚,走开 begone, go away
⑩ remonstrance [rɪˈmɒnstrəns] *n*. 抗议 objection, protest
⑪ mend [mend] *v*. 好转 improve, enhance, get better
⑫ under the impression that: (误)认为……
⑬ pulse [pʌls] *n*. 脉搏 heartbeat
⑭ rage [reɪdʒ] *v*. 发脾气 rail, fume, lose one's temper

asked the doctor to lead him to The Phoenix.

Angelo's merchant creditor being paid, the two were friendly again, and might soon have been seen chatting before an abbey① about the odd② behavior of Antipholus of Ephesus.[xi] "Softly," said the merchant at last, "that's he, I think."

It was not; it was Antipholus of Syracuse with his servant Dromio, and he wore Angelo's chain round his neck! The reconciled pair fairly pounced③ upon him to know what he meant by denying the receipt of the chain he had the impudence④ to wear. Antipholus of Syracuse lost his temper, and drew his sword, and at that moment Adriana and several others appeared. "Hold!" shouted the careful wife. "Hurt him not; he is mad. Take his sword away. Bind him—and Dromio too."

Dromio of Syracuse did not wish to be bound, and he said to his master, "Run, master! Into that abbey, quick, or we shall be robbed!"

They accordingly retreated into the abbey.

Adriana, Luciana, and a crowd remained outside, and the Abbess⑤ came out, and said, "People, why do you gather here?"

"To fetch my poor distracted⑥ husband," replied Adriana.

Angelo and the merchant remarked that they had not known that he was mad.

Adriana then told the Abbess rather too much about her wifely worries, for the Abbess received the idea that Adriana was a shrew⑦, and that if her husband was distracted he had better not return to her for the present.

Adriana determined, therefore, to complain to Duke Solinus, and, lo and behold⑧! A minute afterwards the great man appeared with officers and two others. The others were Egeon and the headsman⑨. The thousand marks⑩ had not been found, and Egeon's fate seemed sealed⑪.

Ere the Duke could pass the abbey Adriana knelt before him, and told a woeful⑫ tale of a mad husband rushing about stealing jewelry and drawing his sword, adding that the Abbess refused to allow her to lead him home.

The Duke bade the Abbess be summoned⑬, and no sooner had he given the order than a servant from The Phoenix ran to Adriana with the tale that his master had singed⑭ off the doctor's beard.

"Nonsense!" said Adriana. "He's in the abbey."

---

① abbey [ˈæbi] *n*. 修道院 monastery, convent, priory
② odd [ɒd] *adj*. 怪异的 strange, unusual, peculiar, abnormal
③ pounce [paʊns] *v*. 突袭 attack, strike, jump, swoop
④ impudence [ˈɪmpjədəns] *n*. 粗鲁 rudeness
⑤ abbess [ˈæbes] *n*. 女修道院院长
⑥ distracted [dɪˈstræktɪd] *adj*. 精神错乱的 mad
⑦ shrew [ʃruː] *n*. 悍妇 virago, tigress, termagant
⑧ lo and behold：你瞧(用于引起对令人惊讶或讨厌之事的注意)
⑨ headsman [ˈhedzmən] *n*. 刽子手 hangman, executioner
⑩ mark [mɑːk] *n*. 马克(古代欧洲的货币计量单位)
⑪ seal [siːl] *v*. 确定,使成定局 settle
⑫ woeful [ˈwəʊfl] *adj*. 悲伤的 sad, wretched, miserable
⑬ summon [ˈsʌmən] *v*. 召唤 call
⑭ singe [sɪndʒ] *v*. 烧焦 burn, sear, scorch, char

“As sure as I live I speak the truth,” said the servant.

Antipholus of Syracuse had not come out of the abbey, before his brother of Ephesus prostrated[1] himself in front of the Duke, exclaiming, “Justice, most gracious[2] Duke, against that woman.” He pointed to Adriana. “She has treated another man like her husband in my own house.”

Even while he was speaking Egeon said, “Unless I am delirious[3], I see my son Antipholus.”

No one noticed him, and Antipholus of Ephesus went on to say how the doctor, whom he called “a threadbare[4] juggler[5],” had been one of a gang[6] who tied him to his slave Dromio, and thrust them into a vault whence he had escaped by gnawing[7] through his bonds[8].[xii]

The Duke could not understand how the same man who spoke to him was seen to go into the abbey, and he was still wondering when Egeon asked Antipholus of Ephesus if he was not his son. He replied, “I never saw my father in my life.” But so deceived was Egeon by his likeness to the brother whom he had brought up, that he said, “Thou art ashamed to acknowledge me in misery.”[xiii]

Soon, however, the Abbess advanced[9] with Antipholus of Syracuse and Dromio of Syracuse.

Then cried Adriana, “I see two husbands or mine eyes deceive me.” And Antipholus, espying[10] his father, said, “Thou art Egeon or his ghost.”

It was a day of surprises, for the Abbess said, “I will free that man by paying his fine, and gain my husband whom I lost. Speak, Egeon, for I am thy wife Emilia.”

The Duke was touched. “He is free without a fine,” he said.

So Egeon and Emilia were reunited, and Adriana and her husband reconciled; but no one was happier than Antipholus of Syracuse, who, in the Duke's presence, went to Luciana and said, “I told you I loved you. Will you be my wife?”

Her answer was given by a look, and therefore is not written.

The two Dromios were glad to think they would receive no more beatings.

---

① prostrate [ˈprɒstreɪt] *v*. 使……俯伏 prone

② gracious [ˈgreɪʃəs] *adj*. 仁慈的 benignant

③ delirious [dɪˈlɪriəs] *adj*. 神志不清的 insane

④ threadbare [ˈθredbeə(r)] *adj*. 俗套的 conventional

⑤ juggler [ˈdʒʌglə(r)] *n*. 变戏法的人；骗子 magician, conjuror, fraud

⑥ gang [gæŋ] *n*. 团伙 group, pack, crew, company

⑦ gnaw [nɔː] *v*. 咬，啃，啮 bite, chew

⑧ bond [bɒnd] *n*. 绳索 cord, rope

⑨ advance [ədˈvɑːns] *v*. 向前移动 move forward

⑩ espy [eˈspaɪ] *v*. 突然看见 spy, catch sight of

ⅰ ...so poor, indeed, were the parents of these twins that they sold them to the parents of the other twins. 这对双胞胎的父母是如此穷苦,只能把他们的孩子卖给了另一对双胞胎的父母。(so...that...:"如此……以至于……",so 前置时的完全倒装)

ⅱ He did not, during his absence, learn all the news of Syracuse, or he would never have gone to Ephesus. 外出期间,他没有听到任何有关叙拉古的消息,要不然他永远不会去以弗所。(or ... would have done...:与过去事实相反的含蓄条件句)

ⅲ He then found that the Duke of Syracuse had been acting in so tyrannical a manner to Ephesians unlucky enough to fall into his hands, that the Government of Ephesus had angrily passed a law which punished by death or a fine of a thousand pounds any Syracusan who should come to Ephesus. 后来他才知道叙拉古公爵对待不幸落到自己手里的以弗所人非常残酷暴虐,以弗所政府恼羞成怒地通过了一项法律,规定叙拉古人胆敢进入以弗所,就要处以死刑或者缴纳一千镑的罚款。(that...so..., that...which...who...:宾语从句、结果状语从句和双重定语从句的嵌套)

ⅳ His speech angered the hearer, who would have beaten him if he had not fled. 他的话惹恼了听的人,要不是他逃走了,准挨一顿打。(...would have done...if...had done...:与过去事实相反的虚拟语气)

ⅴ "Is it I you address?" "你是在对我说话吗?"(it is I...:省略 that 的强调结构)

ⅵ In reply he told her that he was not married, but that he loved her so much that, if Luciana were a mermaid, he would gladly lie on the sea if he might feel beneath him her floating golden hair. 他回复她说,他没有结婚,但是他很喜欢她。如果露西安娜是一条美人鱼,并且他能够沉醉在她金色的发浪里,他愿意高兴地躺卧在海面上。(that..., but that..., so...that, if...were..., ...would do...:并列宾语从句、结果状语从句和条件状语从句的嵌套,与现在事实相反的虚拟语气)

ⅶ The goldsmith handed the chain to Antipholus of Syracuse, and treated his "I bespoke it not" as mere fun, so that the puzzled merchant took the chain as good-humoredly as he had partaken of Adriana's dinner. 金匠把项链交给大安提福勒斯,并把他说的"我没有订购它"当作玩笑话。于是这名一头雾水的商人就认为项链和在阿德里安娜家吃晚餐都是善意的恶作剧。

ⅷ The consequence was that Angelo was without money when a creditor of the sort that stands no nonsense, threatened him with arrest unless he paid his debt immediately. 结果,安哲鲁碰到他的债主时,已经身无分文,债主不愿和他纠缠,威胁他要是不立即还钱就逮捕他。

ⅸ Angelo could have sent his mother to prison if she had said that, and he gave Antipholus of Ephesus in charge. 即使是他的母亲这么说,安哲鲁也会把她送进监狱坐牢,因此他把小安提福勒斯交给了官差。(could have done...if...had done...:与过去事实相反的虚拟语气)

ⅹ Never a good-tempered man, he was crazy with anger when Dromio of Ephesus, who, of course, had not been instructed to fetch a purse, appeared with nothing more useful than a rope. 他从来就不是一个好脾气的人,当小德洛米奥只带着一根绳子出现时,他简直气得发疯。当然,小德洛米奥并没有受命去取钱袋子。

ⅺ Angelo's merchant creditor being paid, the two were friendly again, and might soon have been seen chatting before an abbey about the odd behavior of Antipholus of Ephesus. 安哲鲁的商人债主拿到了钱,他们两人重归于好。没过多久,有人看到他们在一座修道院前面聊起小安提福勒斯古怪的行为。(...being...:独立主格结构作原因状语)

ⅻ No one noticed him, and Antipholus of Ephesus went on to say how the doctor, whom he called "a threadbare juggler," had been one of a gang who tied him to his slave Dromio, and thrust them into a vault whence he had escaped by gnawing through his bonds. 没有人注意到他,小安提福勒斯继续说他和他的仆人德洛米奥如何被一个团伙捆在一起然后被扔进一个地下室,他又如何咬断绳子逃了出来。那个被他称为"江湖术士"的医生是团伙的一员。[whom..., who..., whence(=where)...:三重定语从句的嵌套]

xiii But so deceived was Egeon by his likeness to the brother whom he had brought up, that he said, "Thou art ashamed to acknowledge me in misery." 可是他和伊勤抚养大的儿子——他的亲兄弟——实在太像,连伊勤都被骗了,于是他说:"你看我潦倒,就不愿意认我。"(so...that...:"如此……以至于……",so 前置时的完全倒装)

鲍西娅《威尼斯商人》

The quality of mercy is not strain'd.	慈悲不是出于勉强，
It droppeth as the gentle rain from heaven	它是像甘霖一样从天上降下尘世；
Upon the place beneath. It is twice blest：	它不但给幸福于受施的人，
It blesseth him that gives and him that takes.	也同样给幸福于施与的人；
'Tis mightiest in the mightiest；it becomes	它有超乎一切的无上威力，
The throned monarch better than his crown；	比皇冠更足以显出一个帝王的高贵：

His sceptre shows the force of temporal power,	御杖不过象征着俗世的威权，
The attribute to awe and majesty,	使人民对于君上的尊严
Wherein doth sit the dread and fear of kings;	凛然生畏；
But mercy is above this sceptred sway...	慈悲的力量却高出于权力之上……

杰西卡《威尼斯商人》

Alack, what heinous sin is it in me
To be ashamed to be my father's child!
But though I am a daughter to his blood,
I am not to his manners. O Lorenzo,
If thou keep promise, I shall end this strife,
Become a Christian and thy loving wife.

唉，我真是罪恶深重，
竟会羞于做我父亲的孩子！
可是虽然我在血统上是他的女儿，
在行为上却不是他的女儿。罗兰佐啊！
你要是能够守信不渝，我将要结束我内心的冲突，
皈依基督教，做你的亲爱的妻子。

威尼斯商人
The Merchant of Venice

主要人物

Shylock [ˈʃaɪlɒk] 夏洛克(犹太富翁)
Antonio [ænˈtəʊnɪəʊ] 安东尼奥(威尼斯商人)
Bassanio [bəˈsɑːnɪəʊ] 巴萨尼奥(安东尼奥的朋友)
Portia [ˈpɔːʃɪə] 鲍西娅(富家嗣女)
Jessica [ˈdʒesɪkə] 杰西卡(夏洛克的女儿)
Prince of Morocco [məˈrɒkəʊ] 摩洛哥亲王
Prince of Arragon [ˈærəgən] 阿拉贡亲王

Antonio was a rich and prosperous① merchant of Venice②. His ships were on nearly every sea, and he traded with Portugal, with Mexico, with England, and with India. Although proud of his riches, he was very generous with them, and delighted to use them in relieving the wants of his friends, among whom his relation, Bassanio, held the first place.

Now Bassanio, like many another gay and gallant gentleman, was reckless③ and extravagant, and finding that he had not only come to the end of his fortune, but was also unable to pay his creditors, he went to Antonio for further help.[i]

"To you, Antonio," he said, "I owe the most in money and in love; and I have thought of a plan to pay everything I owe if you will but help me."

"Say what I can do, and it shall be done," answered his friend.

Then said Bassanio, "In Belmont④ is a lady richly left, and from all quarters⑤ of the globe renowned⑥ suitors come to woo her, not only because she is rich, but because she is beautiful and good as well. She looked on me with such favor when last we met, that I feel sure that I should win her away from all rivals⑦ for her love had I but the means to go to Belmont, where she lives.[ii]"

"All my fortunes," said Antonio, "are at sea, and so I have no ready money; but luckily my credit⑧ is good in Venice, and I will borrow for you what you need."

There was living in Venice at this time a rich moneylender⑨, named Shylock. Antonio

---

① prosperous [ˈprɒspərəs] *adj*. 成功的 successful, prospering
② Venice [ˈvenɪs]: 威尼斯(意大利港市)
③ reckless [ˈrekləs] *adj*. 鲁莽的 rash, foolhardy
④ Belmont [ˈbelmɒnt]: 贝尔蒙特(虚构的意大利城市)
⑤ quarter[ˈkwɔːtə(r)] *n*. 城镇的区(或一部分) part, district, region
⑥ renowned [rɪˈnaʊnd] *adj*. 有名的 famous, well-known, noted
⑦ rival [ˈraɪvl] *n*. 竞争对手 opponent, adversary, antagonist
⑧ credit [ˈkredɪt] *n*. 信誉 reputation, esteem
⑨ moneylender [ˈmʌnilendə(r)] *n*. 放高利贷者 usurer

despised and disliked this man very much, and treated him with the greatest harshness and scorn. He would thrust him, like a cur[1], over his threshold, and would even spit[2] on him. Shylock submitted[3] to all these indignities[4] with a patient shrug, but deep in his heart he cherished[5] a desire for revenge on the rich, smug[6] merchant. For Antonio both hurt his pride and injured his business. "But for him," thought Shylock, "I should be richer by half a million ducats.[iii] On the market place, and wherever he can, he denounces[7] the rate of interest[8] I charge, and—worse than that—he lends out money freely."

So when Bassanio came to him to ask for a loan of three thousand ducats to Antonio for three months, Shylock hid his hatred, and turning to Antonio, said—

"Harshly as you have treated me, I would be friends with you and have your love.[iv] So I will lend you the money and charge you no interest. But, just for fun, you shall sign a bond[9] in which it shall be agreed that if you do not repay me in three months' time, then I shall have the right to a pound of your flesh, to be cut from what part of your body I choose.[v]"

"No," cried Bassanio to his friend, "you shall run no such risk for me."

"Why, fear not," said Antonio, "my ships will be home a month before the time. I will sign the bond."

Thus Bassanio was furnished[10] with the means to go to Belmont, there to woo the lovely Portia. The very night he started, the moneylender's pretty daughter, Jessica, ran away from her father's house with her lover, and she took with her from her father's hoards[11] some bags of ducats and precious stones. Shylock's grief and anger were terrible to see. His love for her changed to hate. "I would she were dead at my feet and the jewels in her ear," he cried.[vi] His only comfort now was in hearing of the serious losses which had befallen Antonio, some of whose ships were wrecked. "Let him look to his bond," said Shylock, "let him look to his bond."

Meanwhile Bassanio had reached Belmont, and had visited the fair Portia. He found, as he

---

① cur [kɜː(r)] *n*. 杂种狗 mongrel, mutt

② spit [spɪt] *v*. 啐唾沫(常表示愤怒或鄙视) force saliva out of one's mouth

③ submit [səbˈmɪt] *v*. 屈服 surrender, yield, give in

④ indignity [ɪnˈdɪɡnəti] *n*. 侮辱 insult, humiliation, dishonor

⑤ cherish [ˈtʃerɪʃ] *v*. 抱有 hold, harbor

⑥ smug [smʌg] *adj*. 自鸣得意的 self-satisfied, complacent

⑦ denounce [dɪˈnaʊns] *v*. 谴责 condemn, attack, censure

⑧ rate of interest: 利率

⑨ bond [bɒnd] *n*. 契约 agreement, contract, compact

⑩ furnish [ˈfɜːnɪʃ] *v*. 提供 supply, provide

⑪ hoard [hɔːd] *n*. 贮藏物 store, stash, supply, reserve

had told Antonio, that the rumor① of her wealth and beauty had drawn to her suitors from far and near. But to all of them Portia had but one reply. She would only accept that suitor who would pledge② himself to abide③ by the terms④ of her father's will. These were conditions that frightened away many an ardent⑤ wooer⑥. For he who would win Portia's heart and hand, had to guess which of three caskets⑦ held her portrait⑧. If he guessed aright⑨, then Portia would be his bride; if wrong, then he was bound⑩ by oath⑪ never to reveal which casket he chose, never to marry, and to go away at once.

The caskets were of gold, silver, and lead. The gold one bore this inscription⑫:—"Who chooseth⑬ me shall gain what many men desire;" the silver one had this:—"Who chooseth me shall get as much as he deserves;" while on the lead one were these words:—"Who chooseth me must give and hazard⑭ all he hath." The Prince of Morocco⑮, as brave as he was black, was among the first to submit to this test. He chose the gold casket, for he said neither base lead nor silver could contain her picture. So he chose the gold casket, and found inside the likeness⑯ of what many men desire—death.

After him came the haughty⑰ Prince of Arragon, and saying, "Let me have what I deserve—surely I deserve the lady," he chose the silver one, and found inside a fool's head. "Did I deserve no more than a fool's head?" he cried.

Then at last came Bassanio, and Portia would have delayed him from making his choice from very fear of his choosing wrong.[vii] For she loved him dearly, even as he loved her. "But," said Bassanio, "let me choose at once, for, as I am, I live upon the rack⑱."

Then Portia bade her servants to bring music and play while her gallant lover made his choice.

---

① rumor [ˈruːmə(r)] *n*. 传闻 story, gossip, hearsay
② pledge [pledʒ] *v*. 保证 promise, vow, swear
③ abide [əˈbaɪd] *v*. 遵守 obey, observe, comply with
④ terms [tɜːmz] *n*. 条件 conditions, provisions
⑤ ardent [ˈɑːdnt] *adj*. 热情的 enthusiastic, zealous, passionate
⑥ wooer [ˈwuːə(r)] *n*. 求婚者 admirer, suitor, courter
⑦ casket [ˈkɑːskɪt] *n*. 匣子 box, case
⑧ portrait [ˈpɔːtreɪt] *n*. 肖像 portraiture
⑨ aright [əˈraɪt] *adv*. 正确地 rightly, correctly, without error
⑩ bind [baɪnd] *v*. 迫使 force, oblige
⑪ oath [əʊθ] *n*. 誓言 promise, pledge, vow, commitment
⑫ inscription [ɪnˈskrɪpʃn] *n*. 题词 epigraph
⑬ chooseth: chooses 的古体形式,即 choose 的第三人称单数形式
⑭ hazard [ˈhæzəd] *v*. 使处于危险 endanger, risk, imperil
⑮ Morocco [məˈrɒkəʊ]: 摩洛哥(非洲一国家名)
⑯ likeness [ˈlaɪknəs] *n*. 画像 portrait
⑰ haughty [ˈhɔːti] *adj*. 傲慢的 proud, arrogant
⑱ upon the rack: 倍感压力;焦虑万分;痛苦不堪

And Bassanio took the oath and walked up to the caskets—the musicians playing softly the while. "Mere outward show," he said, "is to be despised. The world is still deceived with ornament①, and so no gaudy② gold or shining silver for me. I choose the lead casket; joy be the consequence!" And opening it, he found fair Portia's portrait inside, and he turned to her and asked if it were true that she was his.

"Yes," said Portia, "I am yours, and this house is yours, and with them I give you this ring, from which you must never part."

And Bassanio, saying that he could hardly speak for joy, found words to swear that he would never part with the ring③ while he lived.

Then suddenly all his happiness was dashed④ with sorrow, for messengers came from Venice to tell him that Antonio was ruined⑤, and that Shylock demanded from the Duke the fulfilment⑥ of the bond, under which he was entitled⑦ to a pound of the merchant's flesh. Portia was as grieved as Bassanio to hear of the danger which threatened his friend.

"First," she said, "take me to church and make me your wife, and then go to Venice at once to help your friend. You shall take with you money enough to pay his debt twenty times over."

But when her newly-made husband had gone, Portia went after him, and arrived in Venice disguised as a lawyer, and with an introduction from a celebrated lawyer Bellario, whom the Duke of Venice had called in to decide the legal questions raised by Shylock's claim⑧ to a pound of Antonio's flesh. When the Court met, Bassanio offered Shylock twice the money borrowed, if he would withdraw⑨ his claim. But the moneylender's only answer was—

"If every ducat in six thousand ducats,
Were in six parts, and every part a ducat,
I would not draw them; I would have my bond."[viii]

It was then that Portia arrived in her disguise, and not even her own husband knew her. The Duke gave her welcome on account of⑩ the great Bellario's introduction, and left the settlement of the case to her. Then in noble words she bade Shylock have mercy. But he was deaf to her entreaties⑪. "I will have the pound of flesh," was his reply.

"What have you to say?" asked Portia of the merchant.

"But little," he answered. "I am armed⑫ and well prepared."

"The Court awards⑬ you a pound of Antonio's flesh," said Portia to the moneylender.

---

① ornament [ˈɔːnəmənt] *n*. 装饰 decoration, adornment
② gaudy [ˈgɔːdi] *adj*. 俗丽的 garish
③ part with sth.: 放弃,交出(尤指不舍得的东西)
④ dash [dæʃ] *v*. 使破灭 break, shatter, destroy
⑤ ruin [ˈruːɪn] *v*. 使破产 bankrupt
⑥ fulfilment [fʊlˈfɪlmənt] *n*. 履行 completion, realization
⑦ entitle [ɪnˈtaɪtl] *v*. 给予权利 enable, permit, sanction
⑧ claim [kleɪm] *n*. 索要 demand, request, requirement
⑨ withdraw [wɪðˈdrɔː] *v*. 撤回 recall, retract, revoke, take back
⑩ on account of: 由于 due to, owing to, by reason of
⑪ entreaty [ɪnˈtriːti] *n*. 恳求 plea, petition, appeal
⑫ armed [ɑːmd] *adj*. 备有所需的 ready, prepared
⑬ award [əˈwɔːd] *v*. 判给 give, grant, accord

"Most righteous① judge!" cried Shylock. "A sentence: come, prepare."

"Tarry② a little. This bond gives you no right to Antonio's blood, only to his flesh. If, then, you spill a drop of his blood, all your property③ will be forfeited④ to the State. Such is the Law."

And Shylock, in his fear, said, "Then I will take Bassanio's offer."

"No," said Portia sternly⑤, "you shall have nothing but your bond. Take your pound of flesh, but remember, that if you take more or less, even by the weight of a hair, you will lose your property and your life."

Shylock now grew very much frightened. "Give me my three thousand ducats that I lent him, and let him go."

Bassanio would have paid it to him, but said Portia, "No! He shall have nothing but his bond."

"You, a foreigner," she added, "have sought to take the life of a Venetian⑥ citizen, and thus by the Venetian law, your life and goods are forfeited. Down, therefore, and beg mercy of the Duke."

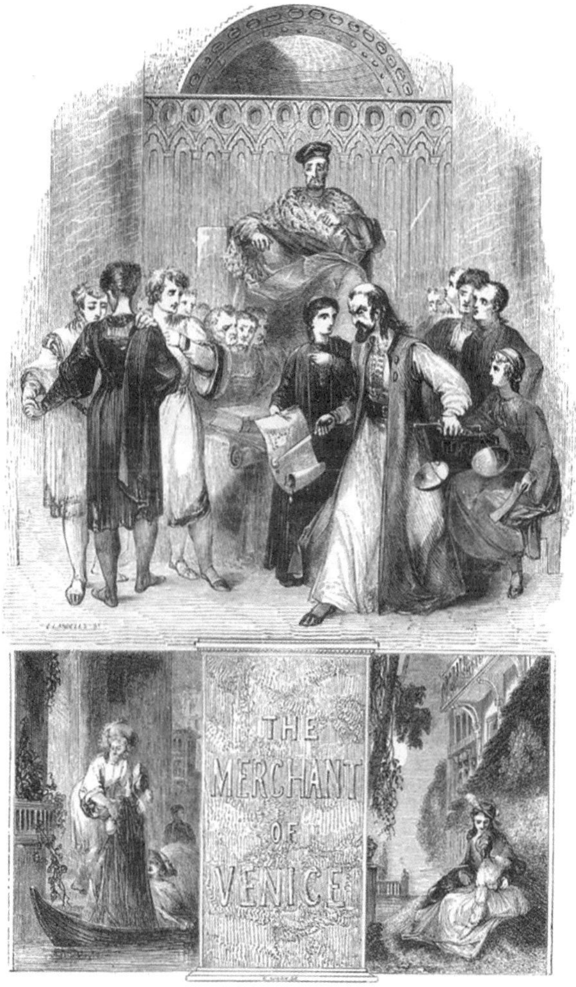

Thus were the tables turned, and no mercy would have been shown to Shylock had it not been for Antonio.[ix] As it was, the moneylender forfeited half his fortune to the State, and he had to settle the other half on his daughter's husband, and with this he had to be content.

Bassanio, in his gratitude to the clever lawyer, was induced⑦ to part with the ring his wife had given him, and with which he had promised never to part, and when on his return to Belmont he confessed as much to Portia, she seemed very angry, and vowed she would not be friends with him until she had her ring again.[x] But at last she told him that it was she who, in the disguise of

---

① righteous [ˈraɪtʃəs] *adj*. 公正的 just, fair, impartial, rightful
② tarry [ˈtæri] *v*. 耽搁 wait, stay, linger
③ property [ˈprɒpəti] *n*. 财产 possessions, holdings, belongings
④ forfeit [ˈfɔːfɪt] *v*. 被没收 lose, relinquish, surrender, give up
⑤ sternly [ˈstɜːnli] *adv*. 严厉地 seriously, severely, strictly
⑥ Venetian [vəˈniːʃn] *adj*. 威尼斯的;威尼斯人的
⑦ induce [ɪnˈdjuːs] *v*. 诱使 persuade, convince, entice

the lawyer, had saved his friend's life, and got the ring from him. So Bassanio was forgiven, and made happier than ever, to know how rich a prize he had drawn in the lottery[1] of the caskets.

ⅰ Now Bassanio, like many another gay and gallant gentleman, was reckless and extravagant, and finding that he had not only come to the end of his fortune, but was also unable to pay his creditors, he went to Antonio for further help. 这位巴萨尼奥,像许多其他风流倜傥的绅士一样,不拘小节、挥金如土。如今,巴萨尼奥发现自己不仅身无分文,还欠下了一屁股债,于是找到安东尼奥,再一次请求帮助。

ⅱ She looked on me with such favor when last we met, that I feel sure that I should win her away from all rivals for her love had I but the means to go to Belmont, where she lives. 我们上次见面时,她对我情有独钟,我感觉只要我有能力前往她所在的贝尔蒙特,就肯定能战胜所有的求婚者,赢得她的芳心。(such...that...:"如此……以至于……",结果状语从句;I should...had I=I should...if I had...:错综时间条件句省略 if 时的部分倒装)

ⅲ But for him, I should be richer by half a million ducats. 如果不是他,我的财产还会多上五十万。(but for him=if it had not been for him:与过去事实相反的含蓄条件句;I should...:主句为与现在事实相反的虚拟语气)

ⅳ Harshly as you have treated me, I would be friends with you and have your love. 您那么粗暴地对待我,我还是愿意跟您交朋友,获得与您的情谊。(as:"尽管……",引导让步状语从句时的部分倒装)

ⅴ But, just for fun, you shall sign a bond in which it shall be agreed that if you do not repay me in three months' time, then I shall have the right to a pound of your flesh, to be cut from what part of your body I choose. 但是,为了开个玩笑,您得签一份契约,上面要规定清楚:如果三个月内您还不出钱,我就有权随我的意愿,在您身上任何部位割下整整一磅肉来。

ⅵ "I would she were dead at my feet and the jewels in her ear," he cried. "我希望她死在我脚下,耳朵上挂着珠宝。"他大叫道。(would=wish;I wish...were...:与现在事实相反的虚拟语气)

---

① lottery [ˈlɒtəri] *n*. 碰运气的事 gamble

ⅶ Then at last came Bassanio，and Portia would have delayed him from making his choice from very fear of his choosing wrong. 最后进来的是巴萨尼奥。因为担心他选错，鲍西娅本想拖延不让他做出选择。(then...came...：完全倒装；would have done...："本会……"，与过去事实相反的虚拟语气)

ⅷ

"If every ducat in six thousand ducats，	"即使这六千块钱中间的每一块钱
Were in six parts，and every part a ducat，	都可以分作六份，每一份都可以变成一块钱，
I would not draw them；I would have my bond."	我也不要它们；我只要照约处罚。"

ⅸ Thus were the tables turned，and no mercy would have been shown to Shylock had it not been for Antonio. 局面就这样扭转了。如果不是安东尼奥的宽容大度，夏洛克是不会得到饶恕的。[would have been...had it not been...(＝...if it had not been...)：与过去事实相反的虚拟语气，非真实条件句省略 if 时的部分倒装；turn the tables："扭转局势"]

ⅹ Bassanio，in his gratitude to the clever lawyer，was induced to part with the ring his wife had given him，and with which he had promised never to part，and when on his return to Belmont he confessed as much to Portia，she seemed very angry，and vowed she would not be friends with him until she had her ring again. 巴萨尼奥为了感谢这位机智的律师，在对方的诱导下，交出了妻子给他的戒指——他答应过永远不和它分离。回到贝尔蒙特后，他向鲍西娅坦白了实情，鲍西娅看上去十分生气，发誓要跟他一刀两断，除非他把戒指重新找回来。

泰门《雅典的泰门》

O you gods, think I, what need we have any friends, if we should ne'er have need of 'em? They were the most needless creatures living, should we ne'er have use for 'em, and would most resemble sweet instruments hung up in cases that keep their sounds to themselves.

神啊！要是我们永远没有需用我们的朋友的时候，那么我们何必要朋友呢？要是我们永远不需要他们的帮助，那么他们便是世上最无用的东西，就像深藏不用的乐器一样，没有人听得见它们美妙的声音。

雅典的泰门
Timon of Athens

主要人物

Timon [ˈtaɪmən] 泰门（雅典贵族）
Lucullus [luːˈkʌləs] 路库勒斯（谄媚的贵族）
Sempronius [semˈprəʊnɪəs] 辛普洛涅斯（谄媚的贵族）
Ventidius [venˈtɪdɪəs] 文提狄斯（泰门的负心友人之一）
Apemantus [ˌæpɪˈmæntəs] 艾帕曼特斯（性情乖僻的哲学家）
Alcibiades [ˌælsɪˈbaɪədiːz] 艾西巴第斯（雅典将官）
Flavius [ˈfleɪvɪəs] 弗莱维斯（泰门的管家）
Flaminius [fləˈmɪnɪəs] 弗莱米涅斯（泰门的仆人）

Four hundred years before the birth of Christ①, a man lived in Athens whose generosity was not only great, but absurd②. He was very rich, but no worldly wealth was enough for a man who spent and gave like Timon. If anybody gave Timon a horse, he received from Timon twenty better horses. If anybody borrowed money of Timon and offered to repay it, Timon was offended. If a poet had written a poem and Timon had time to read it, he would be sure to buy it; and a painter had only to hold up his canvas③ in front of Timon to receive double its market price.

Flavius, his steward, looked with dismay at his reckless mode of life. When Timon's house was full of noisy lords drinking and spilling costly④ wine, Flavius would sit in a cellar⑤ and cry. He would say to himself, "There are ten thousand candles burning in this house, and each of those singers braying⑥ in the concert room costs a poor man's yearly income a night." And he would remember a terrible thing said by Apemantus, one of his master's friends, "O what a number of men eat Timon, and Timon sees them not!"

Of course, Timon was much praised.

A jeweler who sold him a diamond pretended that it was not quite perfect till Timon wore it. "You mend the jewel by wearing it," he said. Timon gave the diamond to a lord called Sempronius, and the lord exclaimed, "O, he's the very soul of bounty." "Timon is infinitely⑦ dear to me," said another lord, called Lucullus, to whom he gave a beautiful horse; and other

① Christ [kraɪst] *n*. 基督，耶稣基督 Jesus Christ
② absurd [əbˈsɜːd] *adj*. 荒谬的 silly, ridiculous
③ canvas [ˈkænvəs] *n*. 油画 painting
④ costly [ˈkɒstli] *adj*. 昂贵的 expensive, dear
⑤ cellar [ˈselə(r)] *n*. 地窖 vault, basement, underground room
⑥ bray [breɪ] *v*. 以刺耳的高声讲话(或笑) screech
⑦ infinitely [ˈɪnfɪnətli] *adv*. 非常，极其 very much, extremely

Athenians paid him compliments① as sweet.

But when Apemantus had listened to some of them, he said, "I'm going to knock out an honest Athenian's brains."

"You will die for that," said Timon.

"Then I shall die for doing nothing," said Apemantus. And now you know what a joke was like four hundred years before Christ.

This Apemantus was a frank despiser② of mankind, but a healthy one, because he was not unhappy. In this mixed world anyone with a number of acquaintances③ knows a person who talks bitterly of men, but does not shun④ them, and boasts that he is never deceived by their fine speeches, and is inwardly cheerful and proud.[i] Apemantus was a man like that.

Timon, you will be surprised to hear, became much worse than Apemantus, after the dawning of a day which we call Quarter Day⑤.

Quarter Day is the day when bills pour in. The grocer, the butcher, and the baker are all thinking of their debtors⑥ on that day, and the wise man has saved enough money to be ready for them. But Timon had not; and he did not only owe money for food. He owed it for jewels and horses and furniture; and, worst of all, he owed it to moneylenders, who expected him to pay twice as much as he had borrowed.

Quarter Day is a day when promises to pay are scorned⑦, and on that day Timon was asked for a large sum of money. "Sell some land," he said to his steward. "You have no land," was the reply. "Nonsense! I had a hundred, thousand acres," said Timon. "You could have spent the price of the world if you had possessed it," said Flavius.[ii]

"Borrow some then," said Timon; "try Ventidius." He thought of Ventidius because he had once got Ventidius out of prison by paying a creditor of this young man. Ventidius was now rich. Timon trusted in his gratitude. But not for all; so much did he owe![iii] Servants were despatched⑧ with requests for loans of money to several friends:

---

① compliment [ˈkɒmplɪmənt] n. 称赞 praise, admiration
② despiser [dɪˈspaɪzə(r)] n. 鄙视者
③ acquaintance [əˈkweɪntəns] n. 泛泛之交 a person that you know slightly, but not well
④ shun [ʃʌn] v. 避开 avoid, evade, keep/shy away from
⑤ Quarter Day：季度结算日(季度的第一天)
⑥ debtor [ˈdetə(r)] n. 债务人 borrower, loanee
⑦ scorn [skɔːn] v. 轻蔑地拒绝 refuse
⑧ despatch [dɪˈspætʃ] v. (=dispatch)派遣 send

One servant (Flaminius) went to Lucullus. When he was announced Lucullus said, "A gift, I warrant①. I dreamt of a silver jug and basin last night." Then, changing his tone, "How is that honorable, free-hearted, perfect gentleman, your master, eh?"

"Well in health, sir," replied Flaminius.

"And what have you got there under your cloak?" asked Lucullus, jovially②.

"Faith③, sir, nothing but an empty box, which, on my master's behalf④, I beg you to fill with money, sir."

"La! La! La!" said Lucullus, who could not pretend to mean, "Ha! Ha! Ha!"[iv] "Your master's one fault is that he is too fond of giving parties. I've warned him that it was expensive. Now, look here, Flaminius, you know this is no time to lend money without security⑤, so suppose you act like a good boy and tell him that I was not at home. Here's three solidares⑥ for yourself."

"Back, wretched money," cried Flaminius, "to him who worships⑦ you!"

Others of Timon's friends were tried and found stingy⑧. Amongst them was Sempronius.

"Hum," he said to Timon's servant, "has he asked Ventidius? Ventidius is beholden⑨ to him."

"He refused."

"Well, have you asked Lucullus?"

"He refused."

"A poor compliment to apply to me last of all," said Sempronius, in affected⑩ anger. "If he had sent to me at first, I would gladly have lent him money, but I'm not going to be such a fool as to lend him any now."[v]

"Your Lordship makes a good villain," said the servant.

When Timon found that his friends were so mean, he took advantage of⑪ a lull⑫ in his storm of creditors to invite Ventidius and Company⑬ to a banquet. Flavius was horrified, but Ventidius and Company, were not in the least ashamed, and they assembled⑭ accordingly in Timon's house,

---

① warrant [ˈwɒrənt] *v*. 保证 guarantee, promise, ensure
② jovially [ˈdʒəʊviəli] *adv*. 快活地 happily, friendly, cheerfully
③ faith [feɪθ] *int*. 〈古〉千真万确 indeed, in truth/faith, to be sure
④ on one's behalf: 代表某人 as a representative of
⑤ security [sɪˈkjʊərəti] *n*. 担保 pledge, assurance, guarantee
⑥ solidare [ˈsɒlɪdeə] *n*. (莎士比亚戏剧中的)小硬币 a small coin
⑦ worship [ˈwɜːʃɪp] *v*. 崇拜 love, adore, idolize, glorify, deify
⑧ stingy [ˈstɪndʒi] *adj*. 吝啬的 mean, miserly, parsimonious
⑨ beholden [bɪˈhəʊldən] *adj*. 蒙恩的 indebted
⑩ affected [əˈfektɪd] *adj*. 假装的 feigned, pretended, artificial
⑪ take advantage of: 利用 use, make use of
⑫ lull [lʌl] *n*. 间歇 respite, pause
⑬ company [ˈkʌmpəni] *n*. 宾客 guests, visitors, callers
⑭ assemble [əˈsembl] *v*. 聚集 gather, meet, come together

and said to one another that their princely host had been jesting① with them.

"I had to put off an important engagement② in order to come here," said Lucullus, "but who could refuse Timon?"

"It was a real grief to me to be without ready money when he asked for some," said Sempronius.

"The same here," chimed in a third lord.

Timon now appeared, and his guests vied③ with one another in apologies and compliments. Inwardly sneering, Timon was gracious to them all.

In the banqueting hall was a table resplendent④ with covered dishes. Mouths watered. These summer friends loved good food.

"Be seated, worthy friends," said Timon. He then prayed aloud to the gods of Greece. "Give each man enough," he said, "for if you, who are our gods, were to borrow of men they would cease to adore⑤ you. Let men love the joint⑥ more than the host. Let every score of guests contain twenty villains. Bless my friends as much as they have blessed me. Uncover the dishes, dogs, and lap⑦!"[vi]

The hungry lords were too much surprised by this speech to resent⑧ it. They thought Timon was unwell, and, although he had called them dogs, they uncovered the dishes.

There was nothing in them but warm water.

① jest [dʒest] *v*. 开玩笑 joke
② engagement [ɪn'geɪdʒmənt] *n*. 约会 appointment
③ vie [vaɪ] *v*. 争夺 compete, contend
④ resplendent [rɪ'splendənt] *adj*. 辉煌的 glorious, splendid
⑤ adore [ə'dɔː(r)] *v*. 崇敬 worship, revere, glorify, venerate
⑥ joint [dʒɔɪnt] *n*. 一块烤肉 a piece of roast meat
⑦ lap [læp] *v*. 舔食 lick
⑧ resent [rɪ'zent] *v*. 怨恨 dislike, grudge, be angry about

"May you never see a better feast," wished Timon. "I wash off the flatteries[1] with which you plastered[2] me and sprinkle[3] you with your villainy."[vii] With these words he threw the water into his guests' faces, and then he pelted[4] them with the dishes. Having thus ended the banquet, he went into an outhouse, seized a spade, and quitted Athens forever.

His next dwelling[5] was a cave near the sea.

Of all his friends, the only one who had not refused him aid was a handsome soldier named Alcibiades, and he had not been asked because, having quarreled with the Government of Athens, he had left that town. The thought that Alcibiades might have proved a true friend did not soften Timon's bitter feeling. He was too weak-minded to discern[6] the fact that good cannot be far from evil in this mixed world. He determined to see nothing better in all mankind than the ingratitude[7] of Ventidius and the meanness[8] of Lucullus.

He became a vegetarian[9], and talked pages to himself as he dug in the earth for food.

One day, when he was digging for roots near the shore, his spade struck gold. If he had been a wise man, he would have enriched himself quickly, and returned to Athens to live in comfort[10].[viii] But the sight of the gold vein[11] gave no joy but only scorn to Timon. "This yellow slave," he said, "will make and break religions. It will make black white and foul fair. It will buy murder and bless the accursed[12]."

He was still ranting[13] when Alcibiades, now an enemy of Athens, approached with his soldiers and two beautiful women who cared for nothing but pleasure.

Timon was so changed by his bad thoughts and rough[14] life that Alcibiades did not recognize him at first.

"Who are you?" he asked.

"A beast, as you are," was the reply.

Alcibiades knew his voice, and offered him help and money. But Timon would none of it, and began to insult[15] the women. They, however, when they found he had discovered a gold mine, cared not a jot[16] for his opinion of them, but said, "Give us some gold, good Timon. Have you more?"

---

① flattery [ˈflætəri] *n*. 奉承 adulation, court, fawning
② plaster [ˈplɑːstə(r)] *v*. 使过分承受 overwhelm
③ sprinkle [ˈsprɪŋkl] *v*. 洒 scatter
④ pelt [pelt] *v*. 投掷 throw, bombard
⑤ dwelling [ˈdwelɪŋ] *n*. 住所 house, residence
⑥ discern [dɪˈsɜːn] *v*. 觉察出 perceive, recognize
⑦ ingratitude [ɪnˈɡrætɪtjuːd] *n*. 忘恩负义 ungratefulness
⑧ meanness [ˈmiːnnəs] *n*. 卑鄙 baseness, vileness
⑨ vegetarian [ˌvedʒəˈteəriən] *n*. 素食主义者 a person who does not eat meat or fish
⑩ in comfort: 舒适地 comfortably, with ease
⑪ gold vein: 金矿脉 a vein of gold
⑫ accursed [əˈkɜːsɪd] *adj*. 被诅咒的;该死的 cursed
⑬ rant [rænt] *v*. 咆哮 shout, roar, yell, rave, bellow
⑭ rough [rʌf] *adj*. 艰难的 hard, harsh, tough
⑮ insult [ɪnˈsʌlt] *v*. 侮辱 offend, humiliate
⑯ not a jot: 一点也没有 not a bit, not at all

With further insults, Timon filled their aprons with gold ore[①].

"Farewell," said Alcibiades, who deemed[②] that Timon's wits were lost; and then his disciplined[③] soldiers left without profit the mine which could have paid their wages, and marched towards Athens.

Timon continued to dig and curse, and affected great delight when he dug up a root and discovered that it was not a grape.

Just then Apemantus appeared. "I am told that you imitate[④] me," said Apemantus.

"Only," said Timon, "because you haven't a dog which I can imitate."

"You are revenging yourself on your friends by punishing yourself," said Apemantus. "That is very silly, for they live just as comfortably as they ever did. I am sorry that a fool should imitate me."

"If I were like you," said Timon, "I should throw myself away."[ix]

"You have done so," sneered Apemantus. "Will the cold brook[⑤] make you a good morning drink, or an east wind warm your clothes as a valet[⑥] would?"

"Off with you!" said Timon. But Apemantus stayed a while longer and told him he had a passion for extremes, which was true. Apemantus even made a pun[⑦], but there was no good laughter to be got out of Timon.

Finally, they lost their temper[⑧] like two schoolboys, and Timon said he was sorry to lose the stone which he flung at Apemantus, who left him with an evil wish.

This was almost an "at-home" day for Timon, for when Apemantus had departed, he was visited by some robbers. They wanted gold.

"You want too much," said Timon. "Here are water, roots and berries."

"We are not birds and pigs," said a robber.

"No, you are cannibals[⑨]," said Timon. "Take the gold, then, and may it poison[⑩] you! Henceforth rob one another."

He spoke so frightfully[⑪] to them that, though they went away with full pockets, they almost

---

① ore [ɔː(r)] *n*. 矿石 rock from which metal can be obtained

② deem [diːm] *v*. 认为 think, believe, suppose, consider, regard

③ disciplined [ˈdɪsəplɪnd] *adj*. 训练有素的 trained

④ imitate [ˈɪmɪteɪt] *v*. 模仿 copy, mimic, counterfeit, simulate

⑤ brook [brʊk] *n*. 小溪 stream, rivulet, runnel

⑥ valet [ˈvæleɪ] *n*. 贴身男仆 manservant

⑦ pun [pʌn] *n*. 双关语 wordplay

⑧ lose one's temper: 发脾气 blow up

⑨ cannibal [ˈkænɪbl] *n*. 食人族 man-eater, anthropophagus

⑩ poison [ˈpɔɪzn] *v*. 毒害

⑪ frightfully [ˈfraɪtfəli] *adv*. 可怕地 terribly, horribly, dreadfully

repented of their trade. His last visitor on that day of visits was his good steward Flavius. “My dearest master!” he cried.

“Away! What are you?” said Timon.

“Have you forgotten me, sir?” asked Flavius, mournfully[1].

“I have forgotten all men,” was the reply, “and if you'll allow[2] that you are a man, I have forgotten you.”

“I was your honest servant,” said Flavius.

“Nonsense! I never had an honest man about me,” retorted Timon.

Flavius began to cry.

“What! Shedding[3] tears?” said Timon. “Come nearer, then. I will love you because you are a woman, and unlike men, who only weep when they laugh or beg.”

They talked awhile[4], then Timon said, “Yon[5] gold is mine. I will make you rich, Flavius, if you promise me to live by yourself and hate mankind. I will make you very rich if you promise me that you will see the flesh[6] slide off[7] the beggar's bones before you feed him, and let the debtor die in jail before you pay his debt.[×]”

Flavius simply said, “Let me stay to comfort you, my master.”

“If you dislike cursing, leave me,” replied Timon, and he turned his back on Flavius, who went sadly back to Athens, too much accustomed to[8] obedience[9] to force his services upon his ailing[10] master.

The steward had accepted nothing, but a report got about that a mighty nugget of gold[11] had been given him by his former master, and Timon therefore received more visitors. They were a painter and a poet, whom he had patronized[12] in his prosperity.

“Hail, worthy Timon!” said the poet. “We heard with astonishment how your friends deserted[13] you. No whip[14]'s large enough for their backs!”

“We have come,” put in the painter, “to offer our services.”

“You've heard that I have gold,” said Timon.

“There was a report,” said the painter, blushing, “but my friend and I did not come for that.”

“Good honest men!” jeered[15] Timon. “All the same, you shall have plenty of gold if you will

---

① mournfully [ˈmɔːnfəli] *adv*. 悲哀地 sadly, sorrowfully, woefully
② allow [əˈlaʊ] *v*. 承认 accept, admit, acknowledge, grant
③ shed [ʃed] *v*. 流(泪) cry
④ awhile [əˈwaɪl] *adv*. 片刻;一会儿 for a short time
⑤ yon [jɒn] *det*. 〈古〉(=yonder) 那个 that
⑥ flesh [fleʃ] *n*. (人或动物的)肉 skin, meat
⑦ slide off: 滑落 fall, drop, slip
⑧ accustomed to: 习惯于 used to
⑨ obedience [əˈbiːdiəns] *n*. 顺从 compliance, submission
⑩ ailing [ˈeɪlɪŋ] *adj*. 处境困难的 suffering, troubled, afflicted
⑪ nugget of gold: 天然金块
⑫ patronize [ˈpætrənaɪz] *v*. 资助 assist, back, support, sponsor
⑬ desert [dɪˈzɜːt] *v*. 抛弃 abandon, forsake, relinquish, give up
⑭ whip [wɪp] *n*. 鞭子 scourge, thong
⑮ jeer [dʒɪə(r)] *v*. 嘲笑 mock, ridicule, taunt, sneer, scoff

rid me of two villains①."

"Name them," said his two visitors in one breath. "Both of you!" answered Timon. Giving the painter a whack② with a big stick, he said, "Put that into your palette③ and make money out of it." Then he gave a whack to the poet, and said, "Make a poem out of that and get paid for it. There's gold for you."

They hurriedly withdrew.

Finally Timon was visited by two senators④ who, now that Athens was threatened by Alcibiades, desired to have on their side this bitter⑤ noble whose gold might help the foe.[xi]

"Forget your injuries," said the first senator. "Athens offers you dignities whereby⑥ you may honorably⑦ live."

"Athens confesses that your merit⑧ was overlooked, and wishes to atone⑨, and more than atone, for her forgetfulness⑩," said the second senator.

"Worthy senators," replied Timon, in his grim⑪ way, "I am almost weeping; you touch me so! All I need are the eyes of a woman and the heart of a fool."

But the senators were patriots⑫. They believed that this bitter man could save Athens, and they would not quarrel with him. "Be our captain," they said, "and lead Athens against Alcibiades, who threatens to destroy her."

"Let him destroy the Athenians too, for all I care," said Timon. And seeing an evil despair in his face, they left him.

The senators returned to Athens, and soon afterwards trumpets⑬ were blown before its walls. Upon the walls they stood and listened to Alcibiades, who told them that wrongdoers should quake⑭ in their easy chairs. They looked at his confident army, and were convinced that Athens must yield if he assaulted⑮ it, therefore they used the voice that strikes deeper than arrows.[xii]

"These walls of ours were built by the hands of men who never wronged you, Alcibiades," said the first senator.

---

① rid sb./sth. of sb./sth.：去除；摆脱
② whack [wæk] *n*. 重击 blow, thump
③ palette ['pælət] *n*. 调色板
④ senator ['senətə(r)] *n*. 元老 statesman
⑤ bitter ['bɪtə(r)] *adj*. 愤愤不平的 resentful, embittered
⑥ whereby [weə'baɪ] *adv*. 凭此，借以 by which
⑦ honorably ['ɒnərəbli] *adj*. 体面地；值得尊敬地 decently, respectably
⑧ merit ['merɪt] *n*. 价值 strength, value, worth
⑨ atone [ə'təʊn] *v*. 赎罪 make amends/reparation
⑩ forgetfulness [fə'getflnəs] *n*. 健忘 poor memory
⑪ grim [grɪm] *adj*. 冷酷无情的 cruel, heartless, merciless
⑫ patriot ['pætriət] *n*. 爱国者 nationalist, loyalist
⑬ trumpet ['trʌmpɪt] *n*. 小号；喇叭 horn
⑭ quake [kweɪk] *v*. 颤抖 shake, tremble, quiver, shiver, shudder
⑮ assault [ə'sɔːlt] *v*. 袭击 attack, assail

"Enter," said the second senator, "and slay every tenth man, if your revenge needs human flesh."

"Spare the cradle[1]," said the first senator.

"I ask only justice," said Alcibiades. "If you admit my army, I will inflict[2] the penalty of your own laws upon any soldier who breaks them."

At that moment a soldier approached Alcibiades, and said, "My noble general, Timon is dead." He handed Alcibiades a sheet of wax, saying, "He is buried by the sea, on the beach, and over his grave is a stone with letters on it which I cannot read, and therefore I have impressed[3] them on wax."

Alcibiades read from the sheet of wax this couplet[4]—

"Here lie I, Timon, who, alive, all living men did hate.

Pass by and say your worst; but pass, and stay not here your gait[5]."[xiii]

"Dead, then, is noble Timon," said Alcibiades. And he entered Athens with an olive branch instead of a sword.

So it was one of Timon's friends who was generous in a greater matter than Timon's need; yet are the sorrow and rage of Timon remembered as a warning lest[6] another ingratitude should arise to turn love into hate.[xiv]

① cradle [ˈkreɪdl] *n*. 摇篮 bassinet
② inflict [ɪnˈflɪkt] *v*. 使遭受 impose
③ impress [ɪmˈpres] *v*. 压印 imprint
④ couplet [ˈkʌplət] *n*. (押韵等长)对句 two lines of poetry
⑤ gait [geɪt] *n*. 步法,步态 a way of walking
⑥ lest [lest] *conj*. 以免,唯恐 in case, for fear that, in order to avoid

ⅰ In this mixed world anyone with a number of acquaintances knows a person who talks bitterly of men, but does not shun them, and boasts that he is never deceived by their fine speeches, and is inwardly cheerful and proud. 大千世界，任何一个拥有很多泛泛之交的人都认识一两个总是说些瞧不起他人的话的人，但是他并不避开这些人，而是吹嘘自己绝不会被他们的花言巧语所蒙蔽，然后暗自得意。

ⅱ "You could have spent the price of the world if you had possessed it," said Flavius. "要是您拥有整个世界的财富，您也能把它糟蹋精光。"弗莱维斯说。（could have done...if...had done...：与过去事实相反的虚拟语气）

ⅲ But not for all; so much did he owe! 但解决不了所有的问题，他欠了太多的钱。（部分倒装）

ⅳ "La! La! La!" said Lucullus, who could not pretend to mean, "Ha! Ha! Ha!" "呀！呀！呀！"路库勒斯说。他无法违心说出"哈！哈！哈！"。

ⅴ "If he had sent to me at first, I would gladly have lent him money, but I'm not going to be such a fool as to lend him any now." "如果他一开始就来找我，我会很高兴地借钱给他，但是现在我一个子儿也不会借给他，因为那样做就像个傻子。"（if...had done..., ...would have done...：与过去事实相反的虚拟语气）

ⅵ "Give each man enough," he said, "for if you, who are our gods, were to borrow of men they would cease to adore you. Let men love the joint more than the host. Let every score of guests contain twenty villains. Bless my friends as much as they have blessed me. Uncover the dishes, dogs, and lap!" 他说："让每个人都心满意足吧，因为如果你们——我们的神——也要向人类借钱，他们就会舍弃你们。让人们喜爱肉食，更甚于把肉食赏给他们的人。让二十个客人身边聚集二十个恶棍。祝福我的朋友们，就像他们祝福我那样。揭开盖子吧，狗子们，去舔吧！"

ⅶ "I wash off the flatteries with which you plastered me and sprinkle you with your villainy." "我被你们的谄媚蒙住了心窍，我要把它清洗干净，把你们的丑恶卑劣洒还给你们。"

ⅷ If he had been a wise man, he would have enriched himself quickly, and returned to Athens to live in comfort. 如果他是一个聪明人，他会立即发财致富，然后回到雅典，过上舒适的生活。（if... had done..., ...would have done...：与过去事实相反的虚拟语气）

ⅸ "If I were like you," said Timon, "I should throw myself away." "要是我像你，我情愿丢掉自己。"泰门说。（if... were..., ...should do...：与现在事实相反的虚拟语气）

ⅹ I will make you very rich if you promise me that you will see the flesh slide off the beggar's bones before you feed him, and let the debtor die in jail before you pay his debt. 我可以让你非常富裕，只要你答应我，你能做到眼睁睁看着乞丐被饿得形销骨立，也不给他们吃的；让借债的人死在监狱里，也不帮他们还债。

ⅹⅰ Finally Timon was visited by two senators who, now that Athens was threatened by Alcibiades, desired to have on their side this bitter noble whose gold might help the foe. 最后，两位元老来拜访泰门。当时，雅典受到了艾西巴第斯的威胁，那两位元老希望这位心怀怨恨的贵族——他的金子可能帮助到敌方——能站在他们这边。

ⅹⅱ They looked at his confident army, and were convinced that Athens must yield if he assaulted it, therefore they used the voice that strikes deeper than arrows. 他们看着那支信心满满的军队，都认为如果他进攻雅典，他们就不得不投降，因此他们拼命高喊——他们的声音比弓箭的穿透力还强。

ⅹⅲ "Here lie I, Timon, who, alive, all living men did hate. Pass by and say your worst; but pass, and stay not here your gait." "我泰门睡在这里；生时人人厌恶。走过去，尽你骂；但莫停留你的脚步。"

ⅹⅳ So it was one of Timon's friends who was generous in a greater matter than Timon's need; yet are the sorrow and rage of Timon remembered as a warning lest another ingratitude should arise to turn love into hate. 这就是泰门的一个朋友，他慷慨的给予远多于泰门的所需。但是，泰门的悲伤和愤怒如警示永留人间，以免再出现背信弃义的事，让爱成仇。（it was...who...：强调句型；yet are...：yet 放在句首用于倒装句，表示弱转折，意思是"可是，然而"；lest...should...："以免……"，目的状语从句中的虚拟语气）

苔丝狄蒙娜《奥瑟罗》

That I did love the Moor to live with him,
My downright violence and storm of fortunes,
May trumpet to the world. My heart's subdued
Even to the very quality of My Lord.
I saw Othello's visage in his mind,
And to his honors and his valiant parts,
Did I my soul and fortunes consecrate.

我不顾一切跟命运对抗的行动可以代我
向世人宣告,我因为爱这摩尔人,
所以愿意和他过共同的生活;
我的心灵完全为他的高贵的德性所征服;
我先认识他那颗心,
然后认识他那奇伟的仪表;
我已经把我的灵魂和命运一起呈献给他了。

奥瑟罗
Othello

主要人物

Othello [əʊ'θeləʊ] 奥瑟罗(摩尔族贵裔,供职威尼斯政府)

Brabantio [brə'bænʃɪəʊ] 勃拉班修(元老)

Desdemona [ˌdezdɪ'məʊnə] 苔丝狄蒙娜(勃拉班修之女,奥瑟罗之妻)

Cassio ['kæsɪəʊ] 凯西奥(奥瑟罗的副将)

Bianca [bɪ'æŋkə] 比恩卡(凯西奥的情妇)

Iago [ɪ'ɑːgəʊ] 伊阿古(奥瑟罗的旗官)

Emilia [ɪ'mɪlɪə] 爱米利娅(伊阿古之妻)

Roderigo [ˌrɒdə'riːgəʊ] 罗德利哥(威尼斯绅士)

Duke [djuːk] of Venice ['venɪs] 威尼斯公爵

Montano [mɒn'tænəʊ] 蒙太诺(塞浦路斯前总督)

Lodovico [ˌlɒdəʊ'viːkəʊ] 罗多维科(勃拉班修的亲戚)

Four hundred years ago there lived in Venice an ensign① named Iago, who hated his general, Othello, for not making him a lieutenant②. Instead of Iago, who was strongly recommended, Othello had chosen Michael Cassio, whose smooth tongue had helped him to win the heart of Desdemona. Iago had a friend called Roderigo, who supplied him with money and felt he could not be happy unless Desdemona was his wife.

Othello was a Moor③, but of so dark a complexion that his enemies called him a Blackamoor④. His life had been hard and exciting. He had been vanquished⑤ in battle and sold into slavery⑥; and he had been a great traveler and seen men whose shoulders were higher than their heads. Brave as a lion, he had one great fault—jealousy. His love was a terrible selfishness. To love a woman meant with him to possess her as absolutely as he possessed something that did not live and think.[1] The story of Othello is a story of jealousy.

One night Iago told Roderigo that Othello had carried off Desdemona without the knowledge⑦ of her father, Brabantio. He persuaded Roderigo to arouse⑧ Brabantio, and when

---

① ensign ['ensən] *n*.(旧时团或连队的)掌旗官

② lieutenant [lef'tenənt] *n*. 副官

③ Moor [mɔː(r)] *n*. 摩尔人(居住在非洲西北部的穆斯林,曾于 8 世纪侵占西班牙部分地区)

④ Blackamoor ['blækəmɔː(r)] *n*.(含冒犯意)黑人,黑鬼

⑤ vanquish ['væŋkwɪʃ] *v*. 完全征服 beat, defeat, conquer

⑥ be sold into slavery: 被卖为奴

⑦ knowledge ['nɒlɪdʒ] *n*. 知晓 awareness

⑧ arouse [ə'raʊz] *v*. 叫醒 rouse, (a)waken, wake up

that senator appeared Iago told him of Desdemona's elopement① in the most unpleasant way. Though he was Othello's officer, he termed② him a thief and a Barbary③ horse.

Brabantio accused④ Othello before the Duke of Venice of using sorcery⑤ to fascinate⑥ his daughter, but Othello said that the only sorcery he used was his voice, which told Desdemona his adventures and hairbreadth escapes⑦. Desdemona was led into the council chamber⑧, and she explained how she could love Othello despite his almost black face by saying, "I saw Othello's visage⑨ in his mind." [ii]

As Othello had married Desdemona, and she was glad to be his wife, there was no more to be said against him, especially as the Duke wished him to go to Cyprus⑩ to defend it against the Turks⑪. Othello was quite ready to go, and Desdemona, who pleaded to go with him, was permitted to join him at Cyprus.

Othello's feelings on landing in this island were intensely⑫ joyful. "Oh, my sweet," he said to Desdemona, who arrived with Iago, his wife, and Roderigo before him, "I hardly know what I say to you. I am in love with my own happiness." [iii]

News coming presently that the Turkish fleet⑬ was out of action⑭, he proclaimed a festival in Cyprus from five to eleven at night.

Cassio was on duty in the Castle where Othello ruled Cyprus, so Iago decided to make the lieutenant drink too much. He had some difficulty, as Cassio knew that wine soon went to his head, but servants brought wine into the room where Cassio was, and Iago sang a drinking song, and so Cassio lifted a glass too often to the health of the general. [iv]

When Cassio was inclined to be quarrelsome⑮, Iago told Roderigo to say something

---

① elopement [ɪ'ləʊpmənt] *n*. 私奔 the act of running away with a lover
② term [tɜːm] *v*. 把……称为 call, name, label, describe as
③ Barbary ['bɑːbəri]: 巴巴里(北非伊斯兰教区)
④ accuse [ə'kjuːz] *v*. 控诉 charge, indict, arraign
⑤ sorcery ['sɔːsəri] *n*. 巫术 witchcraft, black magic
⑥ fascinate ['fæsɪneɪt] *v*. 迷住 charm, enchant, captivate
⑦ hairbreadth escape: 死里逃生 narrow escape
⑧ council chamber: 会议厅
⑨ visage ['vɪzɪdʒ] *n*. 容貌 face, feature, countenance
⑩ Cyprus ['saɪprəs]: 塞浦路斯(地中海东部岛国)
⑪ Turk [tɜːk] *n*. 土耳其人
⑫ intensely [ɪn'tensli] *adv*. 强烈地 highly, extremely
⑬ fleet [fliːt] *n*. 舰队 military ships
⑭ out of action: 不能工作,失去作用
⑮ quarrelsome ['kwɒrəlsəm] *adj*. 爱争吵的 argumentative

unpleasant to him. Cassio cudgeled① Roderigo, who ran into the presence of Montano, the ex-governor②. Montano civilly③ interceded④ for Roderigo, but received so rude an answer from Cassio that he said, "Come, come, you're drunk!" Cassio then wounded him, and Iago sent Roderigo out to scare the town with a cry of mutiny⑤.

The uproar⑥ aroused Othello, who, on learning its cause, said, "Cassio, I love thee, but never more be officer of mine."

On Cassio and Iago being alone together, the disgraced⑦ man moaned⑧ about his reputation.[v] Iago said reputation and humbug⑨ were the same thing. "O God," exclaimed Cassio, without heeding⑩ him, "that men should put an enemy in their mouths to steal away their brains!"[vi]

Iago advised him to beg Desdemona to ask Othello to pardon him. Cassio was pleased with the advice, and next morning made his request to Desdemona in the garden of the castle. She was kindness itself, and said, "Be merry, Cassio, for I would rather die than forsake⑪ your cause."

Cassio at that moment saw Othello advancing⑫ with Iago, and retired⑬ hurriedly.

Iago said, "I don't like that."

"What did you say?" asked Othello, who felt that he had meant something unpleasant, but Iago pretended he had said nothing. "Was not that Cassio who went from my wife?" asked Othello, and Iago, who knew that it was Cassio and why it was Cassio, said, "I cannot think it was Cassio who stole⑭ away in that guilty manner."

Desdemona told Othello that it was grief and humility⑮ which made Cassio retreat at his approach.[vii] She reminded him how Cassio had taken his part when she was still heart-free⑯, and found fault with⑰ her Moorish lover. Othello was melted, and said, "I will deny thee nothing." But Desdemona told him that what she asked was as much for his good as dining.

---

① cudgel [ˈkʌdʒl] *v*. 用短棒打 club, fustigate
② ex-governor [ˌeksˈgʌvənə(r)] *n*. 前总督 former governor
③ civilly [ˈsɪvəli] *adv*. 有礼貌地 politely, courteously
④ intercede [ˌɪntəˈsiːd] *v*. 说情 intervene
⑤ mutiny [ˈmjuːtəni] *n*. 叛乱 rebellion, revolt, insurrection, uprising
⑥ uproar [ˈʌprɔː(r)] *n*. 喧嚣 noise
⑦ disgraced [dɪsˈgreɪst] *adj*. 遭贬谪的 degraded
⑧ moan [məʊn] *v*. 抱怨 complain, grumble, groan, grouse
⑨ humbug [ˈhʌmbʌg] *n*. 谎话 lie
⑩ heed [hiːd] *v*. 注意,留心 pay attention to
⑪ forsake [fəˈseɪk] *v*. (forsook, forsaken)遗弃 desert, abandon
⑫ advance [ədˈvɑːns] *v*. 向前走动 go/come/move forward
⑬ retire [rɪˈtaɪə] *v*. 离去 leave
⑭ steal [stiːl] *v*. 偷偷地走 sneak, creep, slink, tiptoe
⑮ humility [hjuːˈmɪləti] *n*. 谦恭 modesty, humbleness
⑯ heart-free [ˈhɑːt friː] *adj*. 心无所属的,不为爱情所困的
⑰ find fault with: 挑剔 criticize, complain about, pick holes in

Desdemona left the garden, and Iago asked if it was really true that Cassio had known Desdemona before her marriage.

"Yes," said Othello.

"Indeed," said Iago, as though something that had mystified① him was now very clear.

"Is he not honest?" demanded Othello, and Iago repeated the adjective inquiringly②, as though he were afraid to say "No."

"What do you mean?" insisted Othello.

To this Iago would only say the flat③ opposite④ of what he said to Cassio. He had told Cassio that reputation was humbug. To Othello he said, "Who steals my purse steals trash, but he who filches⑤ from me my good name ruins me."[viii]

At this Othello almost leapt into the air, and Iago was so confident of his jealousy that he ventured to warn him against it. Yes, it was no other than⑥ Iago who called jealousy "the green-eyed monster which doth mock⑦ the meat it feeds on."[ix]

Iago having given jealousy one blow, proceeded⑧ to feed⑨ it with the remark that Desdemona deceived her father when she eloped⑩ with Othello.[x] "If she deceived him, why not you?" was his meaning.

Presently Desdemona reentered to tell Othello that dinner was ready. She saw that he was ill at ease⑪. He explained it by a pain in his forehead. Desdemona then produced a handkerchief, which Othello had given her. A prophetess⑫, two hundred years old, had made this handkerchief from the silk of sacred silkworms, dyed⑬ it in a liquid prepared from the hearts of maidens, and embroidered⑭ it with strawberries.[xi] Gentle Desdemona thought of it simply as a cool, soft thing for a throbbing⑮ brow; she knew of no spell upon it that would work destruction for her who lost it.[xii] "Let me tie it round your head," she said to Othello; "you will be well in an hour." But Othello pettishly⑯ said it was too small, and let it fall. Desdemona and he then went indoors to dinner, and

---

① mystify [ˈmɪstɪfaɪ] *v*. 使困惑 puzzle, confuse, bewilder

② inquiringly [ɪnˈkwaɪərɪŋli] *adv*. 好奇地;探询地 curiously, inquisitively

③ flat [flæt] *adj*. 断然的;绝对的 direct, definite

④ opposite [ˈɒpəzɪt] *n*. 对立面 contrary, converse, reverse

⑤ filch [fɪltʃ] *v*. 偷窃 steal, take, thieve, pilfer, pinch, lift

⑥ no other than: 正是 exactly, precisely, accurately, literally

⑦ mock [mɒk] *v*. 嘲弄 tease, ridicule, laugh at, make fun of

⑧ proceed [prəˈsiːd] *v*. 继续做 continue, go on

⑨ feed [fiːd] *v*. 加深,强化 fuel, encourage, strengthen, boost

⑩ elope [ɪˈləʊp] *v*. 私奔 run off

⑪ ill at ease: 心神不宁 uneasy, nervous, uncomfortable

⑫ prophetess [ˌprɒfɪˈtes] *n*. 女先知 soothsayer

⑬ dye [daɪ] *v*. 给……染色 color, stain, tint, tinge

⑭ embroider [ɪmˈbrɔɪdə(r)] *v*. 刺绣 sew, stitch

⑮ throb [θrɒb] *v*. 抽动 beat, pulsate

⑯ pettishly [ˈpetɪʃli] *adv*. 怒气冲冲地 peevishly, sulkily

Emilia picked up the handkerchief which Iago had often asked her to steal.

She was looking at it when Iago came in. After a few words about it he snatched① it from her, and bade her leave him.

In the garden he was joined by Othello, who seemed hungry for the worst lies he could offer.[xiii] He therefore told Othello that he had seen Cassio wipe his mouth with a handkerchief, which, because it was spotted with② strawberries, he guessed to be one that Othello had given his wife.

The unhappy Moor went mad with fury, and Iago bade the heavens witness that he devoted his hand and heart and brain to Othello's service. "I accept your love," said Othello. "Within three days let me hear that Cassio is dead."

Iago's next step was to leave Desdemona's handkerchief in Cassio's room. Cassio saw it, and knew it was not his, but he liked the strawberry pattern③ on it, and he gave it to his sweetheart Bianca and asked her to copy it for him.

Iago's next move was to induce Othello, who had been bullying④ Desdemona about the handkerchief, to play the eavesdropper⑤ to a conversation between Cassio and himself. His intention was to talk about Cassio's sweetheart, and allow Othello to suppose that the lady spoken of was Desdemona.

"How are you, lieutenant?" asked Iago when Cassio appeared.

"The worse for being called what I am not," replied Cassio, gloomily⑥.

"Keep on reminding Desdemona, and you'll soon be restored," said Iago, adding, in a tone too low for Othello to hear, "If Bianca could set the matter right, how quickly it would mend⑦!"[xiv]

"Alas! Poor rogue⑧," said Cassio, "I really think she loves me." And like the talkative coxcomb he was, Cassio was led on to boast of Bianca's fondness for him, while Othello imagined, with choked⑨ rage, that he prattled⑩ of Desdemona, and thought, "I see your nose, Cassio, but not the dog I shall throw it to."

Othello was still spying when Bianca entered, boiling over⑪ with the idea that Cassio, whom she considered her property, had asked her to copy the embroidery⑫ on the handkerchief of a new sweetheart. She tossed⑬ him the handkerchief with scornful⑭ words, and Cassio departed with her.

---

① snatch [snætʃ] *v*. 夺取 grab, seize
② be spotted with：满是……斑点 be dotted with
③ pattern ['pætn] *n*. 图案 design
④ bully ['bʊli] *v*. 恐吓 terrorize, intimidate
⑤ eavesdropper ['iːvzdrɒpə(r)] *n*. 偷听者
⑥ gloomily ['gluːmɪli] *adv*. 沮丧地 despondently, dejectedly
⑦ mend [mend] *v*. 解决 settle, resolve
⑧ rogue [rəʊg] *n*. 调皮鬼；骗子 rascal, deceiver
⑨ choked [tʃəʊkt] *adj*. 生气(而难以说出话来)的 angry, upset
⑩ prattle ['prætl] *v*. 闲聊 chat
⑪ boil over：大怒 fly into a rage
⑫ embroidery [ɪm'brɔɪdəri] *n*. 刺绣 needlework
⑬ toss [tɒs] *v*. 扔，抛，掷 throw, cast
⑭ scornful ['skɔːnfl] *adj*. 轻蔑的 mocking, contemptuous

Othello had seen Bianca, who was in station[1] lower, in beauty and speech inferior[2] far, to Desdemona and he began in spite of himself[3] to praise his wife to the villain before him. He praised her skill with the needle, her voice that could "sing the savageness[4] out of a bear," her wit, her sweetness, the fairness of her skin. Every time he praised her Iago said something that made him remember his anger and utter it foully[5], and yet he must needs[6] praise her, and say, "The pity of it, Iago! O Iago, the pity of it, Iago!"

There was never in all Iago's villainy one moment of wavering[7]. If there had been he might have wavered then.

"Strangle[8] her," he said; and "Good, good!" said his miserable dupe[9].

The pair were still talking murder when Desdemona appeared with a relative of Desdemona's father, called Lodovico, who bore a letter for Othello from the Duke of Venice. The letter recalled[10] Othello from Cyprus, and gave the governorship[11] to Cassio.

Luckless Desdemona seized this unhappy moment to urge once more the suit of Cassio.

"Fire and brimstone[12]!" shouted Othello.

"It may be the letter agitates[13] him[xv]," explained Lodovico to Desdemona, and he told her what it contained.

"I am glad," said Desdemona. It was the first bitter speech that Othello's unkindness had wrung out of her[14].

"I am glad to see you lose your temper," said Othello.

"Why, sweet Othello?" she asked, sarcastically[15]; and Othello slapped[16] her face.

Now was the time for Desdemona to have saved her life by separation, but she knew not her peril—only that her love was wounded to the core. "I have not deserved this," she said, and the tears rolled slowly down her face.

Lodovico was shocked and disgusted. "My Lord," he said, "this would not be believed in Venice. Make her amends[17]." But, like a madman talking in his nightmare[18], Othello poured out

---

① station [ˈsteɪʃn] *n*. 身份 position, status, standing
② inferior [ɪnˈfɪəriə(r)] *adj*. 较差的 poorer, worse
③ in spite of oneself: 不由自主地
④ savageness [ˈsævɪdʒnəs] *n*. 凶残;野蛮 brutality, barbarity
⑤ foully [ˈfaʊlli] *adv*. 充满脏话地;很令人不快地 offensively, unpleasantly
⑥ must needs: 必须
⑦ waver [ˈweɪvə(r)] *v*. 踌躇 hesitate, vacillate
⑧ strangle [ˈstræŋgl] *v*. 勒死 throttle
⑨ dupe [djuːp] *n*. 上当受骗者 gull, victim, simpleton
⑩ recall [rɪˈkɔːl] *v*. 召回 order sb. to return
⑪ governorship [ˈgʌvənəʃɪp] *n*. 总督职位
⑫ brimstone [ˈbrɪmstəʊn] *n*. 硫黄 sulphur
⑬ agitate [ˈædʒɪteɪt] *v*. 使焦虑 upset, worry, disturb
⑭ wring sth. out of sb.: 从……处费力弄到;从……压榨出
⑮ sarcastically [sɑːˈkæstɪkli] *adv*. 讽刺地 ironically, satirically
⑯ slap [slæp] *v*. (用手掌)打,掴 smack
⑰ make amends: (因某事向某人)赔偿 make up for sth.
⑱ nightmare [ˈnaɪtmeə(r)] *n*. 噩梦 bad dream

his foul① thought in ugly speech, and roared②, "Out of my sight!"

"I will not stay to offend you," said his wife, but she lingered even in going, and only when he shouted "Avaunt!" did she leave her husband and his guests.

Othello then invited Lodovico to supper, adding, "You are welcome, sir, to Cyprus. Goats and monkeys![xvi]" Without waiting for a reply he left the company.

Distinguished③ visitors detest④ being obliged to look on at family quarrels, and dislike being called either goats or monkeys, and Lodovico asked Iago for an explanation.

True to himself, Iago, in a roundabout⑤ way, said that Othello was worse than he seemed, and advised them to study his behavior and save him from the discomfort⑥ of answering any more questions.[xvii]

He proceeded to tell Roderigo to murder Cassio. Roderigo was out of tune⑦ with his friend. He had given Iago quantities of jewels for Desdemona without effect; Desdemona had seen none of them, for Iago was a thief.

Iago smoothed⑧ him with a lie, and when Cassio was leaving Bianca's house, Roderigo wounded him, and was wounded in return. Cassio shouted, and Lodovico and a friend came running up. Cassio pointed out Roderigo as his assailant⑨, and Iago, hoping to rid himself of an inconvenient⑩ friend, called him "Villain!" and stabbed him, but not to death. At the Castle, Desdemona was in a sad mood. She told Emilia that she must leave her; her husband wished it. "Dismiss⑪ me!" exclaimed Emilia. "It was his bidding," said Desdemona. "We must not displease him now."

She sang a song which a girl had sung whose lover had been base to her—a song of a maiden crying by that tree whose boughs droop⑫ as though it weeps, and she went to bed and slept.

She woke with her husband's wild eyes upon her. "Have you prayed tonight?" he asked. And he told this blameless and sweet woman to ask God's pardon for any sin she might have on her conscience⑬. "I would not kill thy soul," he said.

He told her that Cassio had confessed, but she knew Cassio had nought to confess that concerned her. She said that Cassio could not say anything that would damage her. Othello said his mouth was stopped.

Then Desdemona wept, but with violent⑭ words, in spite of all her pleading, Othello pressed

---

① foul [faʊl] *adj*. 充满脏话的 offensive
② roar [rɔː(r)] *v*. 吼叫 cry, shout, yell, howl, bellow, bawl
③ distinguished [dɪˈstɪŋgwɪʃt] *adj*. 尊贵的 respectable, noble
④ detest [dɪˈtest] *v*. 憎恨 hate, loathe, abominate
⑤ roundabout [ˈraʊndəbaʊt] *adj*. 迂回的 indirect, devious
⑥ discomfort [dɪsˈkʌmfət] *n*. 苦事;不自在 trouble, inconvenience
⑦ out of tune: (与……)不协调/一致/融洽 be at odds, in disagreement
⑧ smooth [smuːð] *v*. 安抚 calm, soften, appease, assuage
⑨ assailant [əˈseɪlənt] *n*. 攻击者 attacker, assaulter
⑩ inconvenient [ˌɪnkənˈviːniənt] *adj*. 引起麻烦的 troublesome
⑪ dismiss [dɪsˈmɪs] *v*. 让(某人)离开 send sb. away
⑫ droop [druːp] *v*. 低垂 hang
⑬ conscience [ˈkɒnʃəns] *n*. 良心 scruples
⑭ violent [ˈvaɪələnt] *adj*. 强烈的 wild, fierce, powerful

upon her throat and mortally① hurt her.

Then with boding② heart came Emilia, and besought entrance at the door, and Othello unlocked it, and a voice came from the bed saying, "A guiltless③ death I die."

"Who did it?" cried Emilia. And the voice said, "Nobody—I myself. Farewell!"

" 'Twas I that killed her," said Othello.

He poured out his evidence by that sad bed to the people who came running in, Iago among them. But when he spoke of the handkerchief, Emilia told the truth.

And Othello knew. "Are there no stones in heaven but thunderbolts④?" he exclaimed, and ran at Iago, who gave Emilia her death blow⑤ and fled.

But they brought him back, and the death that came to him later on was a relief from torture⑥.

They would have taken Othello back to Venice to try him there, but he escaped them on his sword.[xviii] "A word or two before you go," he said to the Venetians in the chamber. "Speak of me as I was—no better, no worse. Say I cast away the pearl of pearls, and wept with these hard eyes. And say that, when in Aleppo⑦ years ago I saw a Turk beating a Venetian, I took him by the throat and smote⑧ him thus."[xix]

With his own hand he stabbed himself to the heart. And ere he died his lips touched the face of Desdemona with despairing⑨ love.

① mortally [ˈmɔːtəli] *adv*. 致命地 fatally
② boding [ˈbəʊdɪŋ] *adj*. 凶兆的 ominous, inauspicious
③ guiltless [ˈɡɪltləs] *adj*. 无辜的 innocent, blameless
④ thunderbolt [ˈθʌndəbəʊlt] *n*. 霹雳,雷电 thunderclap
⑤ death blow: 致命的一击 finishing stroke
⑥ torture [ˈtɔːtʃə] *n*. 折磨 torment, suffering
⑦ Aleppo [əˈlepəʊ]: 阿勒颇(叙利亚的一个城市)
⑧ smite [smaɪt] *v*. (smote, smitten)重击 thump, whack
⑨ despairing [dɪˈspeərɪŋ] *adj*. 绝望的 hopeless, desperate

ⅰ To love a woman meant with him to possess her as absolutely as he possessed something that did not live and think. 对他而言，爱上一个女人意味着完全占有她，就好像完全占有某些没有生命、不会思考的东西。

ⅱ "I saw Othello's visage in his mind." "我在奥瑟罗高贵的心灵里看到了他的模样。"

ⅲ "I hardly know what I say to you. I am in love with my own happiness." "我几乎不知道跟你说什么，我沉醉在我的幸福当中。"

ⅳ He had some difficulty, as Cassio knew that wine soon went to his head, but servants brought wine into the room where Cassio was, and Iago sang a drinking song, and so Cassio lifted a glass too often to the health of the general. 最初他没有得逞，因为凯西奥知道酒很快会让他失去理智，可是仆人们带着酒进入凯西奥的房间，伊阿古还唱起了祝酒歌，凯西奥忍不住端起一杯又一杯酒为元帅的健康干杯。

ⅴ On Cassio and Iago being alone together, the disgraced man moaned about his reputation. 凯西奥和伊阿古两人独处的时候，这个遭贬黜的男人感叹自己名誉尽毁。(on...being..., ...:"一……就……")

ⅵ "O God," exclaimed Cassio, without heeding him, "that men should put an enemy in their mouths to steal away their brains!" 凯西奥没有留意到他，感叹道："哦，神哪！人们竟然会把一个仇敌放进他们的嘴里，让它偷去他们的头脑！"

ⅶ Desdemona told Othello that it was grief and humility which made Cassio retreat at his approach. 苔丝狄蒙娜对奥瑟罗说，凯西奥是因为悲伤和谦恭才会以那种方式告退。(it was...which...:强调句型，现代英语中多用 that 而不用 which)

ⅷ "Who steals my purse steals trash, but he who filches from me my good name ruins me." "谁偷我的钱包，也就只能偷到一些垃圾；可若是谁偷去了我的名誉，就会让我遭遇灭顶之灾。"

ⅸ Yes, it was no other than Iago who called jealousy "the green-eyed monster which doth mock the meat it feeds on." 没错，恰如伊阿古所说，嫉妒是"一个绿眼妖魔，它吃下谁，就会愚弄谁"。(it was...who...:强调句型；no other than:"只有")

ⅹ Iago having given jealousy one blow, proceeded to feed it with the remark that Desdemona deceived her father when she eloped with Othello. 伊阿古继续添油加醋，让奥瑟罗加重嫉妒，他说苔丝狄蒙娜和奥瑟罗私奔的时候欺骗了她的父亲。

ⅺ A prophetess, two hundred years old, had made this handkerchief from the silk of sacred silkworms, dyed it in a liquid prepared from the hearts of maidens, and embroidered it with strawberries. 一名两百岁的女巫缝出了这块手帕，她用的原料是神圣的蚕丝。这块手帕曾浸泡在少女心炼成的溶液里，还绣上了草莓花样。

ⅻ Gentle Desdemona thought of it simply as a cool, soft thing for a throbbing brow; she knew of no spell upon it that would work destruction for her who lost it. 温柔的苔丝狄蒙娜以为那不过是一件柔软凉爽的东西，刚好可以用来盖在作痛的额头上；她不知道它还附着一个咒语，会令失去它的人，也就是她，遭遇灾祸。

xiii In the garden he was joined by Othello, who seemed hungry for the worst lies he could offer. 奥瑟罗又来到花园找伊阿古，他似乎很渴望从伊阿古嘴里听到最恶毒的谎言。

xiv "If Bianca could set the matter right, how quickly it would mend!" "如果是比恩卡来处理这个问题，早就解决了！"(if...could done..., ...would do...:与现在事实相反的虚拟语气)

xv It may be the letter agitates him... 也许是那封信刺激到了他……(it may be... that...:强调句型中省略了 that，为过时用法，现代英语中不能省略 that)

xvi Goats and monkeys! 畜生兽行！(在西方文化中，"山羊和猴子"都被认为是淫兽)

xvii True to himself, Iago, in a roundabout way, said that Othello was worse than he seemed, and advised them to study his behavior and save him from the discomfort of answering any more questions. 作恶到底的伊阿古拐弯抹角地说，奥瑟罗比他看起来要坏，并建议他们留心他的行动，用不着他多说。

xviii They would have taken Othello back to Venice to try him there, but he escaped them on his sword. 他们本来要把奥瑟罗带回威尼斯接受审判，可是他仗着剑逃脱了。(would have done...:与过去事实相反的虚拟语气)

xix "Speak of me as I was—no better, no worse. Say I cast away the pearl of pearls, and wept with these hard eyes. And say that, when in Aleppo years ago I saw a Turk beating a Venetian, I took him by the throat and smote him thus." "你们照我本来的样子叙述——不要美言，也不要诬陷。你们可说我随手抛弃了一颗珍珠中的珍珠，我哭瞎了眼睛；你们还可以说，多年前在阿勒坡，我曾经见到一个土耳其人殴打一个威尼斯人，我就一把抓住他的咽喉，把他杀了。"

凯瑟丽娜《驯悍记》

What, will you not suffer me? Nay, now I see	啊！你不让我打她吗？好，我知道了，
She is your treasure; she must have a husband.	她是你的宝贝，她一定要嫁个好丈夫；
I must dance barefoot on her wedding day,	我就只好在她结婚的那一天光着脚跳舞，
And for your love to her, lead apes in hell.	因为你偏爱她的缘故，我一辈子也嫁不出去，死了在地狱里也只能陪猴子玩。
Talk not to me. I will go sit and weep,	不要跟我说话，我要去找个地方坐下来痛哭一场。
Till I can find occasion of revenge.	你看着吧，我总有一天要报仇的。

比恩卡《驯悍记》

Good sister, wrong me not, nor wrong yourself,
To make a bondmaid and a slave of me—
That I disdain; but for these other goods—
Unbind my hands; I'll pull them off myself,
Yea, all my raiment to my petticoat,
Or what you will command me will I do,
So well I know my duty to my elders.

好姐姐,我是你的亲妹妹,
不要把我当作婢子奴才一样看待。
你要是不喜欢我身上穿戴的东西,
那么请你松开我手上的捆缚,我会自己把它们拿下来的;
只要你吩咐我,我把裙子脱下来都可以;
你要我怎么做,我就怎么做,
因为你是姐姐,我是应该服从你的。

驯悍记
The Taming of the Shrew

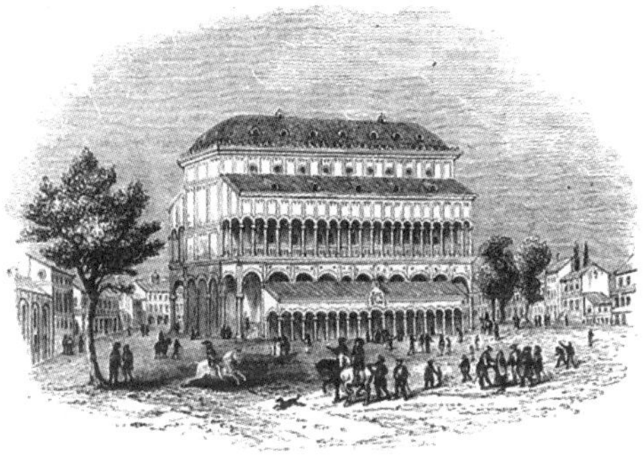

主要人物

Baptista [bæpˈtɪstə] 巴普提斯塔（帕度亚的富翁）

Katharina [ˌkæθəˈriːnə] 凯瑟丽娜（悍妇，巴普提斯塔的女儿）

Petruchio [pɪˈtruːkɪəʊ] 彼特鲁乔（维洛那的绅士，凯瑟丽娜的求婚者）

Bianca [bɪˈæŋkə] 比恩卡（巴普提斯塔的女儿）

Lucentio [luːˈsenʃɪəʊ] 路森修（爱恋比恩卡者）

Hortensio [hɔːˈtensɪəʊ] 霍坦西奥（比恩卡的求婚者）

There lived in Padua[1] a gentleman named Baptista, who had two fair daughters. The eldest, Katharina, was so very cross[2] and ill-tempered[3], and unmannerly[4], that no one ever dreamed of marrying her, while her sister, Bianca, was so sweet and pretty, and pleasant-spoken[5], that more than one suitor asked her father for her hand.[i] But Baptista said the elder daughter must marry first.

So Bianca's suitors decided among themselves to try and get some one to marry Katharina—and then the father could at least be got to listen to their suit for Bianca.

A gentleman from Verona, named Petruchio, was the one they thought of, and, half in jest[6], they asked him if he would marry Katharina, the disagreeable[7] scold[8]. Much to their surprise he said yes, that was just the sort of wife for him, and if Katharina were handsome and rich, he himself would undertake soon to make her good-tempered.

Petruchio began by asking Baptista's permission to pay court to[9] his gentle daughter Katharina—and Baptista was obliged to own[10] that she was anything but[11] gentle. And just then her

---

① Padua [ˈpædjʊə]：帕多瓦（意大利北部城市，朱生豪译本中译为“帕度亚”）
② cross [krɒs] *adj*. 易怒的 angry, short, irascible, bad-tempered
③ ill-tempered [ˌɪl ˈtempəd] *adj*. 脾气坏的 bad-tempered, touchy, irritable
④ unmannerly [ʌnˈmænəli] *adj*. 无礼的 impolite, disrespectful
⑤ pleasant-spoken [ˌplezntˈspəʊkən] *adj*. 谈吐谦和的
⑥ in jest：开玩笑地 jokingly, in fun, as a joke
⑦ disagreeable [ˌdɪsəˈgriːəbl] *adj*. 不友善的，难相处的 unfriendly, unpleasant
⑧ scold [skəʊld] *n*. 泼妇 shrew, termagant, vixen
⑨ pay court to：向……献殷勤 court, woo, make love to
⑩ own [əʊn] *v*. 承认 acknowledge, admit, confess, disclose
⑪ anything but：根本不 never, not at all, not in the least

music master rushed in, complaining that the naughty girl had broken her lute① over his head, because he told her she was not playing correctly.

"Never mind," said Petruchio, "I love her better than ever, and long to have some chat with her."

When Katharina came, he said, "Good morrow, Kate—for that, I hear, is your name."

"You've only heard half," said Katharina, rudely.

"Oh, no," said Petruchio, "they call you plain② Kate, and bonny③ Kate, and sometimes Kate the shrew, and so, hearing your mildness④ praised in every town, and your beauty too, I ask you for my wife."

"Your wife!" cried Kate. "Never!" She said some extremely disagreeable things to him, and, I am sorry to say, ended by boxing his ears⑤.

"If you do that again, I'll cuff⑥ you," he said quietly. And still protested, with many compliments, that he would marry none but her.

When Baptista came back, he asked at once—

"How speed⑦ you with my daughter?"

"How should I speed but well," replied Petruchio—"how, but well?"

"How now, daughter Katharina?" the father went on.

"I don't think," said Katharina, angrily, "you are acting a father's part in wishing me to marry this madcap⑧ ruffian⑨."

"Ah!" said Petruchio, "You and all the world would talk amiss⑩ of her. You should see how kind she is to me when we are alone. In short, I will go off to Venice to buy fine things for our wedding—for—kiss me, Kate! We will be married on Sunday."

With that, Katharina flounced⑪ out of the room by one door in a violent temper, and he, laughing, went out by the other. But whether she fell in love with Petruchio, or whether she was only glad to meet a man who was not afraid of

---

① lute [luːt] *n*. 诗琴
② plain [pleɪn] *adj*. 直率的 frank, outspoken, straightforward
③ bonny ['bɒni] *adj*. 漂亮的 beautiful, pretty, fair, lovely
④ mildness ['maɪldnəs] *n*. 温和 tenderness
⑤ box one's ears: 打某人耳光 slap one's face
⑥ cuff [kʌf] *v*. 用巴掌拍打 smack, slap
⑦ speed [spiːd] *v*. 相处得好;进展 get along, fare
⑧ madcap ['mædkæp] *adj*. 鲁莽的 rash, hotheaded, reckless
⑨ ruffian ['rʌfiən] *n*. 恶棍 thug, villain, rogue, rascal, scoundrel
⑩ amiss [ə'mɪs] *adv*. 错误地 wrongly, incorrectly, mistakenly
⑪ flounce [flaʊns] *v*. (因愤怒或烦躁等而)走动 storm

her, or whether she was flattered that, in spite of her rough① words and spiteful② usage③, he still desired her for his wife—she did indeed marry him on Sunday, as he had sworn she should.[ii]

To vex and humble④ Katharina's naughty, proud spirit, he was late at the wedding, and when he came, came wearing such shabby⑤ clothes that she was ashamed to be seen with him. His servant was dressed in the same shabby way, and the horses they rode were the sport of everyone they passed.

And, after the marriage, when should have been the wedding breakfast, Petruchio carried his wife away, not allowing her to eat or drink—saying that she was his now, and he could do as he liked with her.[iii]

And his manner was so violent, and he behaved all through his wedding in so mad and dreadful a manner, that Katharina trembled and went with him. He mounted⑥ her on a stumbling⑦, lean⑧, old horse, and they journeyed by rough muddy ways to Petruchio's house, he scolding and snarling⑨ all the way.[iv]

She was terribly tired when she reached her new home, but Petruchio was determined that she should neither eat nor sleep that night, for he had made up his mind to teach his bad-tempered wife a lesson she would never forget.

So he welcomed her kindly to his house, but when supper was served he found fault with everything—the meat was burnt, he said, and ill-served, and he loved her far too much to let her eat anything but the best. At last Katharina, tired out with her journey, went supperless to bed. Then her husband, still telling her how he loved her, and how anxious he was that she should have slept well, pulled her bed to pieces, throwing the pillows and bedclothes on the floor, so that she could not go to bed at all, and still kept growling⑩ and scolding at the servants so that Kate might see how unbeautiful a thing ill-temper was.[v]

---

① rough [rʌf] *adj*. 粗野的 rude, impolite, coarse, unpolished

② spiteful ['spaɪtfl] *adj*. 恶意的 malicious, ill-natured

③ usage ['juːsɪdʒ] *n*. 对待 treatment

④ humble ['hʌmbl] *v*. 使感到惭愧 shame

⑤ shabby ['ʃæbi] *adj*. 破旧的 tatty, worn, ragged, tattered

⑥ mount [maʊnt] *v*. 使骑上 get on, bestride

⑦ stumbling ['stʌmblɪŋ] *adj*. 蹒跚的 tottering, staggering, faltering

⑧ lean [liːn] *adj*. 瘦的 thin, slim, slender

⑨ snarl [snɑːl] *v*. 吼叫 growl

⑩ growl [graʊl] *v*. 怒吼 howl, bellow, snarl

The next day, too, Katharina's food was all found fault with, and caught away before she could touch a mouthful, and she was sick and giddy① for want of sleep②. Then she said to one of the servants—

"I pray thee go and get me some repast③. I care not what."

"What say you to a neat's foot④?" said the servant.

Katharina said "Yes" eagerly, but the servant, who was in his master's secret, said he feared it was not good for hasty-tempered⑤ people. Would she like tripe⑥?

"Bring it me," said Katharina.

"I don't think that is good for hasty-tempered people," said the servant. "What do you say to a dish of beef and mustard⑦?"

"I love it," said Kate.

"But mustard is too hot."

"Why, then, the beef, and let the mustard go," cried Katharina, who was getting hungrier and hungrier.

"No," said the servant, "you must have the mustard, or you get no beef from me."

"Then," cried Katharina, losing patience, "let it be both, or one, or anything thou wilt."

"Why, then," said the servant, "the mustard without the beef!"

Then Katharina saw he was making fun of her, and boxed his ears.

Just then Petruchio brought her some food—but she had scarcely begun to satisfy her hunger, before he called for the tailor to bring her new clothes, and the table was cleared, leaving her still hungry.[vi] Katharina was pleased with the pretty new dress and cap that the tailor had made for her, but Petruchio found fault with everything, flung the cap and gown on the floor vowing his dear wife should not wear any such foolish things.

"I will have them," cried Katharina. "All gentlewomen wear such caps as these—"

"When you are gentle you shall have one too," he answered, "and not till then." When he had driven away the tailor with angry words—but privately asking his

① giddy [ˈgɪdi] *adj*. 头晕眼花 dizzy, light-headed
② want of sth.: 缺少 lack of sth.
③ repast [rɪˈpɑːst] *n*. 饭菜 food, meal
④ neat's foot: 牛蹄
⑤ hasty-tempered [heɪstiˈtempəd] *adj*. 性急的 quick-tempered
⑥ tripe [traɪp] *n*. 牛肚 the lining of a cow's stomach
⑦ mustard [ˈmʌstəd] *n*. 芥末酱

friend to see him paid—Petruchio said—

"Come, Kate, let's go to your father's, shabby as we are, for as the sun breaks through the darkest clouds, so honor peereth① in the meanest② habit.[vii] It is about seven o'clock now. We shall easily get there by dinner time."

"It's nearly two," said Kate, but civilly enough, for she had grown to see that she could not bully her husband, as she had done her father and her sister. "It's nearly two, and it will be supper time before we get there."

"It shall be seven," said Petruchio, obstinately③, "before I start. Why, whatever I say or do, or think, you do nothing but contradict. I won't go today, and before I do go, it shall be what o'clock I say it is."

At last they started for her father's house.

"Look at the moon," he said.

"It's the sun," said Katharina, and indeed it was.

"I say it is the moon. Contradicting again! It shall be sun or moon, or whatever I choose, or I won't take you to your father's."

Then Katharina gave in, once and for all④. "What you will have it named," she said, "it is, and so it shall be so for Katharina."[viii] And so it was, for from that moment Katharina felt that she had met her master, and never again showed her naughty tempers to him, or anyone else.

So they journeyed on to Baptista's house, and arriving there, they found all folks keeping Bianca's wedding feast, and that of another newly married couple, Hortensio and his wife. They were made welcome, and sat down to the feast, and all was merry, save that Hortensio's wife, seeing Katharina subdued⑤ to her husband, thought she could safely say many disagreeable things, that in the old days, when Katharina was free and froward⑥, she would not have dared to say.[ix] But Katharina answered with such spirit and such moderation⑦, that she turned the laugh against the new bride.[x]

After dinner, when the ladies had retired, Baptista joined in a laugh against Petruchio, saying "Now in good sadness, son Petruchio, I fear you have got the veriest⑧ shrew of all."

"You are wrong," said Petruchio. "Let me prove it to you. Each of us shall send a message to his wife, desiring her to come to him, and the one whose wife comes most readily shall win a wager which we will agree on."

The others said yes readily enough, for each thought his own wife the most dutiful⑨, and each thought he was quite sure to win the wager.

---

① peer [pɪə(r)] *v*. 隐现 appear, emerge, become visible, peep out

② mean [miːn] *adj*. 破旧的 ragged, shabby, tattered, worn out

③ obstinately [ˈɒbstɪnətli] *adv*. 固执地 stubbornly

④ once and for all: 彻底地 finally, completely, for good

⑤ subdue [səbˈdjuː] *v*. 制服;克制 defeat, master, conquer

⑥ froward [ˈfrəʊ(w)əd] *adj*. 顽固的 obstinate, contrary

⑦ moderation [ˌmɒdəˈreɪʃn] *n*. 温和 mildness

⑧ very [ˈveri] *adj*. 完全的,十足的 real, actual

⑨ dutiful [ˈdjuːtɪfl] *adj*. 顺从的 obedient, compliant

They proposed a wager of twenty crowns[①].

"Twenty crowns," said Petruchio. "I'll venture so much on my hawk or hound, but twenty times as much upon my wife."

"A hundred then," cried Lucentio, Bianca's husband.

"Content," cried the others.

Then Lucentio sent a message to the fair Bianca bidding her to come to him. And Baptista said he was certain his daughter would come. But the servant coming back, said—

"Sir, my mistress is busy, and she cannot come."

"There's an answer for you," said Petruchio.

"You may think yourself fortunate if your wife does not send you a worse."

"I hope, better," Petruchio answered. Then Hortensio said—

"Go and entreat my wife to come to me at once."

"Oh—if you entreat her," said Petruchio.

"I am afraid," answered Hortensio, sharply, "do what you can. Yours will not be entreated."

But now the servant came in, and said—

"She says you are playing some jest[②]. She will not come."

"Better and better," cried Petruchio. "Now go to your mistress and say I command her to come to me."

They all began to laugh, saying they knew what her answer would be, and that she would not come.

Then suddenly Baptista cried—

"Here comes Katharina!" And sure enough—there she was.

"What do you wish, sir?" she asked her husband.

"Where are your sister and Hortensio's wife?"

"Talking by the parlor fire."

"Fetch them here."

When she was gone to fetch them, Lucentio said—

"Here is a wonder!"

"I wonder what it means," said Hortensio.

"It means peace," said Petruchio, "and love, and quiet life."

"Well," said Baptista, "you have won the wager, and I will add another twenty thousand crowns to her dowry[③]—another dowry for another daughter—for she is as changed as if she were someone else."[xi]

So Petruchio won his wager, and had in Katharina always a loving wife and true, and now he had broken her proud and angry spirit he loved her well, and there was nothing ever but love between those two. And so they lived happy ever afterwards.

---

① crown [kraʊn] *n*. 克朗(欧洲一些国家的货币单位)

② jest [dʒest] *n*. 玩笑 joke, crack, banter, prank

③ dowry [ˈdaʊəri] *n*. 嫁妆 dower

ⅰ The eldest, Katharina, was so very cross and ill-tempered, and unmannerly, that no one ever dreamed of marrying her, while her sister, Bianca, was so sweet and pretty, and pleasant-spoken, that more than one suitor asked her father for her hand. 大女儿凯瑟丽娜脾气暴躁，待人非常凶狠、粗鲁，没有一个人愿意娶她；小女儿比恩卡性格温柔、甜美，说话柔声细语，不止一个人向她父亲提出想娶她为妻。

ⅱ But whether she fell in love with Petruchio, or whether she was only glad to meet a man who was not afraid of her, or whether she was flattered that, in spite of her rough words and spiteful usage, he still desired her for his wife—she did indeed marry him on Sunday, as he had sworn she should. 也不知凯瑟丽娜是因为爱上了彼特鲁乔呢，还是因为高兴自己终于碰到一个不怕她的男人，又或是因为就算她说话难听、态度粗暴，但彼特鲁乔仍愿意娶她做妻子，这让她多少有点儿受宠若惊——总之，她真的在星期天跟他举办了婚礼——彼特鲁乔早就一口咬定她会同意的。

ⅲ And, after the marriage, when should have been the wedding breakfast, Petruchio carried his wife away, not allowing her to eat or drink—saying that she was his now, and he could do as he liked with her. 就在举行完婚礼，应当享用喜宴的时候，彼特鲁乔却带走了他的妻子，不允许她吃吃喝喝，还说她现在是他的了，他可以对她做任何他想做的事情。

ⅳ He mounted her on a stumbling, lean, old horse, and they journeyed by rough muddy ways to Petruchio's house, he scolding and snarling all the way. 他让凯瑟丽娜骑一匹皮包骨头、走路磕磕绊绊的老马，前往彼特鲁乔家的宅子。他们一路走的都是坑坑洼洼的烂泥路，彼特鲁乔还不停地骂骂咧咧，大声吼叫。

ⅴ Then her husband, still telling her how he loved her, and how anxious he was that she should have slept well, pulled her bed to pieces, throwing the pillows and bedclothes on the floor, so that she could not go to bed at all, and still kept growling and scolding at the servants so that Kate might see how unbeautiful a thing ill-temper was. 她的丈夫仍然在口口声声地说着自己多么爱她，多么担心她睡不好觉，但同时却把她的床砸烂了，把她的枕头和床单都扔在地上，使她根本无法安睡；他还不停地大声咆哮，恶声恶气地骂那些仆人，就为了让凯德看到一个坏脾气的人是多么丑陋。

ⅵ Just then Petruchio brought her some food—but she had scarcely begun to satisfy her hunger, before he called for the tailor to bring her new clothes, and the table was cleared, leaving her still hungry. 就在这个时候，彼特鲁乔给她端来了食物，她正要大快朵颐时，他却叫来裁缝给她看新衣服。桌子收拾干净了，她还没有吃饱。（scarcely...before...：“刚一……就……”）

ⅶ Come, Kate, let's go to your father's, shabby as we are, for as the sun breaks through the darkest clouds, so honor peereth in the meanest habit. 走吧，凯德，我们就穿着这身破烂衣服到你爸爸家里去吧，就像太阳会穿透最黑暗的乌云，粗布衣服可以格外显出一个人的品格。

viii "What you will have it named," she said, "it is, and so it shall be so for Katharina." 她说:"随你叫它什么名字吧,你叫它什么,凯瑟丽娜也叫它什么就是了。"

ix They were made welcome, and sat down to the feast, and all was merry, save that Hortensio's wife, seeing Katharina subdued to her husband, thought she could safely say many disagreeable things, that in the old days, when Katharina was free and froward, she would not have dared to say. 凯瑟丽娜和彼特鲁乔受到大家的欢迎,他们坐下享用盛宴,周围一片其乐融融。不过霍坦西奥的妻子看见凯瑟丽娜温柔地对她丈夫说话,还以为她可以放心地说些不友善的话,而她以前是不敢在随心所欲又倔强固执的凯瑟丽娜面前说这些话的。

x But Katharina answered with such spirit and such moderation, that she turned the laugh against the new bride. 没想到,凯瑟丽娜的回答温和有礼,弄得那位新娘搬起石头砸了自己的脚。

xi "Well," said Baptista, "you have won the wager, and I will add another twenty thousand crowns to her dowry — another dowry for another daughter—for she is as changed as if she were someone else." 巴普提斯塔说:"好吧,你已经赢得了赌注,而且我还要额外给你两万克朗作为我"另外一个女儿"的嫁妆,因为她好像完全变了一个人。"

依莎贝拉《一报还一报》

As much for my poor brother as myself:	为了我可怜的弟弟，也为了我自己，
That is, were I under the terms of death,	我宁愿接受死刑的宣判，
The impression of keen whips I'ld wear as rubies,	让无情的皮鞭在我身上留下斑斑的血迹，我会把它当作鲜明的红玉；
And strip myself to death, as to a bed	即使把我粉身碎骨，我也会从容就死，
That longing have been sick for, ere I'ld yield	像一个疲倦的旅人奔赴他的渴慕的安息，
My body up to shame.	我却不愿让我的身体蒙上羞辱。

玛利安娜《一报还一报》

Isabel,	依莎贝拉,
Sweet Isabel, do yet but kneel by me;	好依莎贝拉,你只要在我一旁跪下,
Hold up your hands, say nothing; I'll speak all.	把你的手举起,不用说一句话,一切由我来说。
They say, best men are moulded out of faults;	人家说,最好的好人,都是犯过错误的过来人;
And, for the most, become much more the better	一个人往往因为有一点小小的缺点,将来会变得更好。
For being a little bad: so may my husband.	那么我的丈夫为什么不会也是这样?
O Isabel, will you not lend a knee?	啊,依莎贝拉,你愿意陪着我下跪吗?

一报还一报
Measure for Measure

主要人物

Vincentio [vɪnˈsenʃɪəʊ] 文森修(公爵)

Angelo [ˈændʒɪləʊ] 安哲鲁(公爵在假期中的摄政)

Escalus [ˈeskələs] 爱斯卡勒斯(辅佐安哲鲁的老臣)

Claudio [ˈklɔːdɪəʊ] 克劳狄奥(少年绅士)

Lucio [ˈluːsɪəʊ] 路西奥(纨绔子)

Isabella [ˌɪzəˈbelə] 依莎贝拉(克劳狄奥的姐姐)

Mariana [ˌmeərɪˈænə] 玛利安娜(安哲鲁的未婚妻)

More centuries ago than I care to say, the people of Vienna[1] were governed[2] too mildly. The reason was that the reigning Duke Vincentio was excessively good-natured[3], and disliked to see offenders[4] made unhappy.

The consequence was that the number of ill-behaved[5] persons in Vienna was enough to make the Duke shake his head in sorrow when his chief secretary showed him it at the end of a list. He decided, therefore, that wrongdoers must be punished. But popularity was dear to him. He knew that, if he were suddenly strict after being lax[6], he would cause people to call him a tyrant.[i] For this reason he told his Privy Council[7] that he must go to Poland[8] on important business of state. "I have chosen Angelo to rule in my absence," he said.

Now this Angelo, although he appeared to be noble, was really a mean man. He had promised to marry a girl called Mariana, and now would have nothing to say to her, because her dowry had been lost. So poor Mariana lived forlornly[9], waiting every day for the footstep of her stingy lover, and loving him still.

Having appointed Angelo his deputy[10], the Duke went to a friar[11] called Thomas and asked him for a friar's dress and instruction in the art of giving religious counsel[12], for he did not intend to go to Poland, but to stay at home and see how Angelo governed.[ii]

---

① Vienna [vɪˈenə]: 维也纳(奥地利首都)

② govern [ˈgʌvn] *v*. 统治,管理 rule, manage, administer

③ good-natured [ˌgʊd ˈneɪtʃəd] *adj*. 本性善良的

④ offender [əˈfendə(r)] *n*. 违法者 criminal, lawbreaker

⑤ ill-behaved [ˌɪl bɪˈheɪvd] *adj*. 行为不端的 misbehaving

⑥ lax [læks] *adj*. 不严格的 slack, casual, careless

⑦ Privy Council [ˌprɪvi ˈkaʊnsl]: 枢密院

⑧ Poland [ˈpəʊlənd]: 波兰(欧洲国名)

⑨ forlornly [fəˈlɔːnli] *adv*. 孤苦伶仃地 lonelily

⑩ deputy [ˈdepjuti] *n*. 副手;代理 lieutenant

⑪ friar [ˈfraɪə(r)] *n*. 男修道士 monk, brother

⑫ counsel [ˈkaʊnsl] *n*. 建议 advice, suggestion

Angelo had not been a day in office when he condemned① to death a young man named Claudio for an act of rash selfishness which nowadays would only be punished by severe reproof②.[iii]

Claudio had a queer③ friend called Lucio, and Lucio saw a chance of freedom for Claudio if Claudio's beautiful sister Isabella would plead with Angelo.

Isabella was at that time living in a nunnery④. Nobody had won her heart, and she thought she would like to become a sister⑤, or nun.

Meanwhile Claudio did not lack an advocate⑥.

An ancient lord, Escalus, was for leniency⑦. "Let us cut a little, but not kill," he said. "This gentleman had a most noble father."

Angelo was unmoved. "If twelve men find me guilty, I ask no more mercy than is in the law."

Angelo then ordered the Provost⑧ to see that Claudio was executed⑨ at nine the next morning.

After the issue of this order Angelo was told that the sister of the condemned man desired to see him.

"Admit her," said Angelo.

On entering with Lucio, the beautiful girl said, "I am a woeful suitor⑩ to Your Honor⑪."

"Well?" said Angelo.

She colored⑫ at his chill monosyllable⑬ and the ascending red increased the beauty of her face. "I have a brother who is condemned to die," she continued. "Condemn⑭ the fault, I pray you, and spare my brother."

"Every fault," said Angelo, "is condemned before it is committed⑮. A fault cannot suffer. Justice would be void⑯ if the committer⑰ of a fault went free."[iv]

---

① condemn [kən'dem] *v*. 判处 sentence, judge
② reproof [rɪ'pruːf] *n*. 责备 blame, scolding, chiding, criticism
③ queer [kwɪə(r)] *adj*. 古怪的 strange, odd, funny
④ nunnery ['nʌnəri] *n*. 女修道院 convent
⑤ sister ['sɪstə(r)] *n*. 修女 nun
⑥ advocate ['ædvəkət] *n*. 拥护者 backer, supporter, defender
⑦ leniency ['liːniənsi] *n*. 仁慈 mercy, tolerance, clemency
⑧ provost ['prɒvəst] *n*. 监狱看守 jailer
⑨ execute ['eksɪkjuːt] *v*. 处决 kill, put to death
⑩ suitor ['suːtə(r)] *n*. 请愿者 supplicant
⑪ Your Honor：阁下 Your Lordship/Excellency
⑫ color ['kʌlə(r)] *v*. 脸红 blush, flush, redden
⑬ monosyllable ['mɒnəsɪləbl] *n*. 单音节词
⑭ condemn [kən'dem] *v*. 谴责 blame, criticize, denounce
⑮ commit [kə'mɪt] *v*. 犯(错) do sth. wrong or illegal
⑯ void [vɔɪd] *adj*. 无效的 useless, invalid, ineffective
⑰ committer [kə'mɪtə(r)] *n*. 犯错者 bumbler

She would have left the court if Lucio had not whispered to her, "You are too cold; you could not speak more tamely① if you wanted a pin."[v]

So Isabella attacked② Angelo again, and when he said, "I will not pardon him," she was not discouraged, and when he said, "He's sentenced; 'tis too late," she returned to the assault③. But all her fighting was with reasons, and with reasons she could not prevail④ over the Deputy.[vi]

She told him that nothing becomes power like mercy. She told him that humanity⑤ receives and requires mercy from Heaven, that it was good to have gigantic⑥ strength, and had to use it like a giant.[vii] She told him that lightning rives⑦ the oak and spares the myrtle⑧. She bade him look for fault in his own breast, and if he found one, to refrain⑨ from making it an argument against her brother's life.

Angelo found a fault in his breast at that moment. He loved Isabella's beauty, and was tempted to do for her beauty what he would not do for the love of man.

He appeared to relent⑩, for he said, "Come to me tomorrow before noon."

She had, at any rate⑪, succeeded in prolonging⑫ her brother's life for a few hours.

In her absence Angelo's conscience rebuked⑬ him for trifling with his judicial⑭ duty.

When Isabella called on him the second time, he said, "Your brother cannot live."

Isabella was painfully astonished, but all she said was, "Even so, Heaven keep Your Honor."

But as she turned to go, Angelo felt that his duty and honor were slight in comparison with⑮ the loss of her.

"Give me your love," he said, "and Claudio shall be freed."

"Before I would marry you, he should die if he had twenty heads to lay upon the block⑯[viii]," said Isabella, for she saw then that he was not the just⑰ man he pretended to be.

So she went to her brother in prison, to inform him that he must die. At first he was boastful⑱, and promised to hug the darkness of death. But when he clearly understood that his sister could buy his life by marrying Angelo, he felt his life more valuable than her happiness, and he exclaimed, "Sweet sister, let me live."

---

① tamely [ˈteɪmli] *adv*. 温顺地 docilely, obediently, submissively
② attack [əˈtæk] *v*. 全力应对 tackle, deal with
③ assault [əˈsɔːlt] *n*. 抨击 attack, blame, criticism
④ prevail [prɪˈveɪl] *v*. 胜过 win, triumph
⑤ humanity [hjuːˈmænəti] *n*. 人类 mankind, humankind
⑥ gigantic [dʒaɪˈgæntɪk] *adj*. 巨大的 huge, massive, enormous
⑦ rive [raɪv] *v*. 劈开 cleave
⑧ myrtle [ˈmɜːtl] *n*. 桃金娘;桃金娘科植物
⑨ refrain [rɪˈfreɪn] *v*. 克制 stop, avoid, give up, cease, abstain
⑩ relent [rɪˈlent] *v*. 变温和;终于答应 soften, give in
⑪ at any rate: 无论如何 anyway, in any case, at all events
⑫ prolong [prəˈlɒŋ] *v*. 延长 lengthen, extend
⑬ rebuke [rɪˈbjuːk] *v*. 谴责 blame, reproach, reprimand
⑭ judicial [dʒuˈdɪʃl] *adj*. 司法的 legal, juridical
⑮ in comparison with: 与……相比较
⑯ block [blɒk] *n*. (古代斩首用)垫头木
⑰ just [dʒʌst] *adj*. 正直的,公正的 upright, fair
⑱ boastful [ˈbəʊstfl] *adj*. 自夸的 vain, bragging, conceited

"O faithless[1] coward! O dishonest wretch[2]!" she cried.

At this moment the Duke came forward, in the habit of a friar, to request some speech with Isabella. He called himself Friar Lodowick.

The Duke then told her that Angelo was affianced[3] to Mariana, whose love story he related[4]. He then asked her to consider this plan. Let Mariana, in the dress of Isabella, go closely veiled[5] to Angelo, and say, in a voice resembling[6] Isabella's, that if Claudio were spared she would marry him. Let her take the ring from Angelo's little finger, that it might be afterwards proved that his visitor was Mariana.

Isabella had, of course, a great respect for friars, who are as nearly like nuns as men can be. She agreed, therefore, to the Duke's plan. They were to meet again at the moated[7] grange[8], Mariana's house.

In the street the Duke saw Lucio, who, seeing a man dressed like a friar, called out, "What news of the Duke, friar?" "I have none," said the Duke.

Lucio then told the Duke some stories about Angelo. Then he told one about the Duke. The Duke contradicted him. Lucio was provoked[9], and called the Duke "a shallow[10], ignorant fool," though he pretended to love him. "The Duke shall know you better if I live to report you," said the Duke, grimly[11]. Then he asked Escalus, whom he saw in the street, what he thought of his ducal[12] master. Escalus, who imagined he was speaking to a friar, replied, "The Duke is a very temperate[13] gentleman, who prefers to see another merry to being merry himself."

---

① faithless [ˈfeɪθləs] *adj*. 不忠诚的 disloyal, unfaithful
② wretch [retʃ] *n*. 坏蛋 villain, rogue, ruffian, bad egg
③ affiance [əˈfaɪəns] *v*. 订婚 engage, betroth
④ relate [rɪˈleɪt] *v*. 讲述 tell, narrate
⑤ veil [veɪl] *v*. 戴面纱;遮掩 cover, screen, mask, hide, conceal
⑥ resemble [rɪˈzembl] *v*. 与……相像 similar to, look like, take after
⑦ moated [ˈməʊtɪd] *adj*. 有护城河围绕的;围有壕沟的
⑧ grange [greɪndʒ] *n*. 庄园,农场 country house, farm
⑨ provoke [prəˈvəʊk] *v*. 激怒 goad, anger, irritate
⑩ shallow [ˈʃæləʊ] *adj*. 浅薄的 superficial, skin-deep
⑪ grimly [ˈgrɪmli] *adv*. 严肃地 seriously, severely, gravely
⑫ ducal [ˈdjuːkl] *adj*. 公爵的;公爵领地的
⑬ temperate [ˈtempərət] *adj*. 温和的 gentle, mild

The Duke then proceeded to call on Mariana.

Isabella arrived immediately afterwards, and the Duke introduced the two girls to one another, both of whom thought he was a friar. They went into a chamber apart from him to discuss the saving of Claudio, and while they talked in low and earnest tones, the Duke looked out of the window and saw the broken sheds① and flower beds black with moss, which betrayed Mariana's indifference to her country dwelling.[ix] Some women would have beautified their garden: not she. She was for the town; she neglected the joys of the country. He was sure that Angelo would not make her unhappier.

"We are agreed, Father," said Isabella, as she returned with Mariana.

So Angelo was deceived by the girl whom he had dismissed from② his love, and put on her finger a ring he wore, in which was set a milky stone which flashed in the light with secret colors.[x]

Hearing of her success, the Duke went next day to the prison prepared to learn that an order had arrived for Claudio's release. It had not, however, but a letter was handed to the Provost while he waited. His amazement was great when the Provost read aloud these words, "Whatsoever you may hear to the contrary, let Claudio be executed by four of the clock. Let me have his head sent me by five."

But the Duke said to the Provost, "You must show the Deputy another head," and he held out a letter and a signet③. "Here," he said, "are the hand and seal④ of the Duke. He is to return, I tell you, and Angelo knows it not. Give Angelo another head."

The Provost thought, "This friar speaks with power. I know the Duke's signet and I know his hand."

He said at length⑤, "A man died in prison this morning, a pirate of the age of Claudio, with a beard of his color. I will show his head."

The pirate's head was duly⑥ shown to Angelo, who was deceived by its resemblance⑦ to Claudio's.

The Duke's return was so popular that the citizens removed the city gates from their hinges⑧ to assist his entry into Vienna. Angelo and Escalus duly presented themselves, and were profusely⑨ praised for their conduct of affairs in the Duke's absence.

---

① shed [ʃed] *n*. 棚屋,小屋 hut, shack, lean-to

② dismiss from: 摒除(思想、感情等) put thoughts or feelings out of one's mind

③ signet [ˈsɪgnət] *n*. 小图章 mark, seal, stamp

④ seal [siːl] *n*. 印章 mark, stamp, emblem

⑤ at length: 最终 finally, eventually, at last, in the end

⑥ duly [ˈdjuːli] *adv*. 按时地 on time, promptly, punctually

⑦ resemblance [rɪˈzembləns] *n*. 相似 similarity, likeness

⑧ hinge [hɪndʒ] *n*. 铰链,合页

⑨ profusely [prəˈfjuːsli] *adv*. 大量地 plentifully, abundantly, lavishly

It was, therefore, the more unpleasant for Angelo when Isabella, passionately angered by his treachery, knelt before the Duke, and cried for justice.

When her story was told, the Duke cried, "To prison with her for a slanderer① of our right hand②! But stay, who persuaded you to come here?"

"Friar Lodowick,"she said.

"Who knows him?" inquired the Duke.

"I do, My Lord," replied Lucio. "I beat him because he spake③ against Your Grace."

A friar called Peter here said, "Friar Lodowick is a holy man."

Isabella was removed by an officer, and Mariana came forward. She took off her veil④, and said to Angelo, "This is the face you once swore was worth looking on."

Bravely he faced her as she put out her hand and said, "This is the hand which wears the ring you thought to give another."

"I know the woman," said Angelo. "Once there was talk of marriage between us, but I found her frivolous⑤."

Mariana here burst out that they were affianced by the strongest vows. Angelo replied by asking the Duke to insist on the production of Friar Lodowick.

"He shall appear," promised the Duke, and bade Escalus examine the missing witness⑥ thoroughly while he was elsewhere.

Presently the Duke reappeared in the character of Friar Lodowick, and accompanied by Isabella and the Provost. He was not so much examined as abused⑦ and threatened by Escalus.[xi] Lucio asked him to deny, if he dared, that he called the Duke a fool and a coward, and had had his nose pulled for his impudence.[xii]

"To prison with him!" shouted Escalus, but as hands were laid upon him, the Duke pulled off his friar's hood⑧, and was a Duke before them all.

"Now," he said to Angelo, "if you have any impudence that can yet serve you, work it for all it's worth."

"Immediate sentence⑨ and death is all I beg," was the reply.

"Were you affianced to Mariana?" asked the Duke.

"I was," said Angelo.

"Then marry her instantly," said his master. "Marry them," he said to Friar Peter, "and return with them here."

"Come hither, Isabel," said the Duke, in tender tones. "Your friar is now your Prince, and

---

① slanderer [ˈslɑːndərə(r)] *n*. 诽谤者 defamer, libeler

② right hand: 得力助手 right-hand man

③ spake [speɪk] *v*. 〈古〉(=spoke) speak 的过去式,为过时用法

④ veil [veɪl] *n*. 面纱,面罩 mask, covering

⑤ frivolous [ˈfrɪvələs] *adj*. 愚蠢轻浮的 flippant, foolish

⑥ witness [ˈwɪtnəs] *n*. 见证人 observer, eyewitness

⑦ abuse [əˈbjuːs] *v*. 辱骂 insult, curse, swear

⑧ hood [hʊd] *n*. 兜帽

⑨ sentence [ˈsentəns] *n*. 判决 verdict, ruling, judgment

grieves he was too late to save your brother." But well the roguish[①] Duke knew he had saved him.

"O pardon me," she cried, "that I employed my Sovereign[②] in my trouble."

"You are pardoned," he said, gaily.

At that moment Angelo and his wife reentered. "And now, Angelo," said the Duke, gravely, "we condemn thee to the block on which Claudio laid his head!"

"O my most gracious Lord," cried Mariana, "mock me not!"

"You shall buy a better husband," said the Duke.

"O my dear Lord," she said, "I crave[③] no better man."

Isabella nobly added her prayer to Mariana's, but the Duke feigned[④] inflexibility[⑤].

"Provost," he said, "how came it that Claudio was executed at an unusual hour?"

Afraid to confess the lie he had imposed upon[⑥] Angelo, the Provost said, "I had a private message."

"You are discharged[⑦] from your office," said the Duke. The Provost then departed. Angelo said, "I am sorry to have caused such sorrow. I prefer death to mercy." Soon there was a motion[⑧] in the crowd. The Provost reappeared with Claudio. Like a big child the Provost said, "I saved this man; he is like Claudio." The Duke was amused, and said to Isabella, "I pardon him because he is like your brother. He is like my brother, too, if you, dear Isabel, will be mine."

She was his with a smile, and the Duke forgave Angelo, and promoted the Provost.

Lucio he condemned to marry a stout[⑨] woman with a bitter tongue.

① roguish [ˈrəʊgɪʃ] *adj*. 淘气的 naughty, mischievous
② sovereign [ˈsɒvrɪn] *n*. 君主 monarch, king/queen
③ crave [kreɪv] *v*. 渴望 want, desire, long/thirst for
④ feign [feɪn] *v*. 假装 pretend, affect
⑤ inflexibility [ɪnˌfleksəˈbɪləti] *n*. 顽固不变 rigidness, stubborness
⑥ impose upon: 欺骗 cheat, deceive, take advantage of
⑦ discharge [dɪsˈtʃɑːdʒ] *v*. 解雇 fire, sack, dismiss, remove
⑧ motion [ˈməʊʃn] *n*. 运动;骚动 movement, commotion
⑨ stout [staʊt] *adj*. 肥壮的 strong, plump

ⅰ He knew that, if he were suddenly strict after being lax, he would cause people to call him a tyrant. 他知道如果他突然从过去的宽容变得严厉,子民们也许会把他看成暴君。

ⅱ Having appointed Angelo his deputy, the Duke went to a friar called Thomas and asked him for a friar's dress and instruction in the art of giving religious counsel, for he did not intend to go to Poland, but to stay at home and see how Angelo governed. 任命安哲鲁代行职权之后,公爵去见了一个名叫托马斯的修士,找他要了一套修士服,并请他传授一个修士传道时所应有的举止。因为公爵不打算去波兰,而是要留在城里看看安哲鲁是如何治理城邦的。

ⅲ Angelo had not been a day in office when he condemned to death a young man named Claudio for an act of rash selfishness which nowadays would only be punished by severe reproof. 安哲鲁上任还不到一天,就下令处死一个叫克劳狄奥的年轻人,因为他做了鲁莽自私的事。而这种行为在今天一般只会受到强烈的谴责而已。

ⅳ "Every fault," said Angelo, "is condemned before it is committed. A fault cannot suffer. Justice would be void if the committer of a fault went free." 安哲鲁说:"所有的过失在未犯以前,应处的惩罚就已经定下。过失本身不能代表惩罚,但如果犯下过错的人逍遥法外,正义不就成了一句空话?"

ⅴ She would have left the court if Lucio had not whispered to her, "You are too cold; you could not speak more tamely if you wanted a pin." 她刚要离开宫里,路西奥悄声对她说:"你太冷淡了。你就是向人讨一枚针,也得说得低声下气一点啊。"

ⅵ But all her fighting was with reasons, and with reasons she could not prevail over the Deputy. 她的回击都是有理有据的,却不能说服摄政官。

ⅶ She told him that humanity receives and requires mercy from Heaven, that it was good to have gigantic strength, and had to use it like a giant. 她告诉他,世人都蒙受、祈求过上天的恩惠,有着巨人一样的力量是一件好事,要像一个巨人那样把它使用出来。

ⅷ Before I would marry you, he should die if he had twenty heads to lay upon the block... 即使他长了二十颗脑袋,他宁愿让这二十颗脑袋在断头台被人砍落,也不愿让我嫁给你……

ⅸ They went into a chamber apart from him to discuss the saving of Claudio, and while they talked in low and earnest tones, the Duke looked out of the window and saw the broken sheds and flower beds black with moss, which betrayed Mariana's indifference to her country dwelling. 她们走进室内讨论如何营救克劳狄奥,公爵留在室外。她们轻声、恳切地交谈着,公爵往窗外望去,瞧见破破烂烂的棚屋和长满黑苔的花坛,可见玛利安娜对她的乡下生活并不上心。

ⅹ So Angelo was deceived by the girl whom he had dismissed from his love, and put on her finger a ring he wore, in which was set a milky stone which flashed in the light with secret colors. 就那样,安哲鲁被他所抛弃的女孩骗了,他取下自己的戒指给她戴上,戒指上镶嵌着一颗乳白色宝石,在阳光下闪耀着神秘的色彩。

ⅺ He was not so much examined as abused and threatened by Escalus. 他与其说是被爱斯卡勒斯盘问,不如说是被他辱骂和威胁。

ⅻ Lucio asked him to deny, if he dared, that he called the Duke a fool and a coward, and had had his nose pulled for his impudence. 路西奥问他是否有胆量否认曾经骂公爵是一个蠢货、一个懦夫,还曾说要扯下公爵的鼻子以惩戒他的桀骜不驯。

朱利娅《维洛那二绅士》

And yet I would I had o'erlooked the letter:
It were a shame to call her back again
And pray her to a fault for which I chid her.
What a fool is she, that knows I am a maid,
And would not force the letter to my view!
Since maids, in modesty, say "no" to that
Which they would have the profferer construe "ay."

可是我希望我曾经窥见这信的内容。
我把她这样责骂过了,现在又不好意思
叫她回来,反过来恳求她。这傻丫头明知
我是一个闺女,偏不把信硬塞给我看。
一个温淑的姑娘嘴里尽管说不,
她却要人家解释作是的。唉!唉!
这一段痴愚的恋情是多么颠倒,

Fie, fie, how wayward is this foolish love
That, like a testy babe, will scratch the nurse
And presently all humbled kiss the rod!

正像一个坏脾气的婴孩一样，
一会儿在他保姆身上乱抓乱打，
一会儿又服服帖帖地甘心受责。

西尔维娅《维洛那二绅士》

Who is Silvia? What is she,	西尔维娅伊何人，
That all our swains commend her?	乃能颠倒众生心？
Holy, fair and wise is she;	神圣娇丽且聪明，
The heaven such grace did lend her,	天赋诸美萃一身，
That she might admired be.	俾令举世诵其名。
Is she kind as she is fair?	伊人颜色如花浓，
For beauty lives with kindness.	伊人宅心如春柔；

Love doth to her eyes repair，	盈盈妙目启瞽矇，
To help him of his blindness；	创平痍复相思瘳，
And，being help'd，inhabits there.	寸心永驻眼梢头。
Then to Silvia let us sing，	弹琴为伊歌一曲，
That Silvia is excelling；	伊人美好世无伦；
She excels each mortal thing	尘世萧条苦寂寞，
Upon the dull earth dwelling；	唯伊灿耀如星辰；
To her let us garlands bring.	穿花为束献佳人。

维洛那二绅士
The Two Gentlemen of Verona

主要人物

Duke [djuːk] of Milan [mɪˈlæn] 米兰公爵(西尔维娅的父亲)

Valentine [ˈvæləntaɪn] 凡伦丁(二绅士之一)

Proteus [ˈprəʊtɪəs] 普洛丢斯(二绅士之一)

Antonio [ænˈtəʊnɪəʊ] 安东尼奥(普洛丢斯的父亲)

Julia [ˈdʒuːljə] 朱利娅(普洛丢斯的恋人)

Lucetta [luːˈsetə] 露西塔(朱利娅的女仆)

Silvia [ˈsɪlvɪə] 西尔维娅(凡伦丁的恋人)

Speed [spiːd] 史比德(凡伦丁的傻仆)

Only one of them was really a gentleman, as you will discover later. Their names were Valentine and Proteus. They were friends, and lived at Verona, a town in northern Italy. Valentine was happy in his name because it was that of the patron saint① of lovers; it is hard for a Valentine to be fickle or mean.[i] Proteus was unhappy in his name, because it was that of a famous shape-changer②, and therefore it encouraged him to be a lover at one time and a traitor at another.[ii]

One day, Valentine told his friend that he was going to Milan. "I'm not in love like you," he said, "and therefore I don't want to stay at home."

Proteus was in love with a beautiful yellow-haired girl called Julia, who was rich, and had no one to order her about. He was, however, sorry to part from Valentine, and he said, "If ever you are in danger tell me, and I will pray for you." Valentine then went to Milan with a servant called Speed, and at Milan he fell in love with the Duke of Milan's daughter, Silvia.

When Proteus and Valentine parted Julia had not acknowledged that she loved Proteus. Indeed, she had actually torn up one of his letters in the presence of her maid, Lucetta. Lucetta, however, was no simpleton③, for when she saw the pieces she said to herself, "All

---

① patron saint: 守护神 guardian angel

② shape-changer [ˈʃeɪp tʃeɪndʒə(r)] *n.* 变化无常者

③ simpleton [ˈsɪmpltən] *n.* 傻瓜 fool, idiot, halfwit, blockhead

she wants is to be annoyed by another letter." Indeed, no sooner had Lucetta left her alone than Julia repented of her tearing, and placed between her dress and her heart the torn piece of paper on which Proteus had signed his name.[iii] So by tearing a letter written by Proteus she discovered that she loved him. Then, like a brave, sweet girl, she wrote to Proteus, "Be patient, and you shall marry me."

Delighted with these words Proteus walked about, flourishing① Julia's letter and talking to himself.

"What have you got there?" asked his father, Antonio.

"A letter from Valentine," fibbed Proteus.

"Let me read it," said Antonio.

"There is no news," said deceitful② Proteus. "He only says that he is very happy, and the Duke of Milan is kind to him, and that he wishes I were with him."

This fib③ had the effect of making Antonio think that his son should go to Milan and enjoy the favors in which Valentine basked④. "You must go tomorrow," he decreed⑤. Proteus was dismayed⑥. "Give me time to get my outfit ready." He was met with the promise, "What you need shall be sent after you."

It grieved Julia to part from her lover before their engagement was two days' old. She gave him a ring, and said, "Keep this for my sake." And he gave her a ring, and they kissed like two who intend to be true till death. Then Proteus departed for Milan.

Meanwhile Valentine was amusing Silvia, whose gray eyes, laughing at him under auburn⑦ hair, had drowned him in love. One day she told him that she wanted to write a pretty letter to a gentleman whom she thought well of, but had no time: would he write it? Very much did Valentine dislike writing that letter, but he did write it, and gave it to her coldly.[iv] "Take it back," she said. "You did it unwillingly."

"Madam," he said, "it was difficult to write such a letter for you."

"Take it back," she commanded. "You did not write tenderly enough."

Valentine was left with the letter, and condemned to write another; but his servant Speed saw that, in effect⑧, the Lady Silvia had allowed Valentine to write for her a love letter to

① flourish [ˈflʌrɪʃ] *v*. 挥舞 wave, flutter
② deceitful [dɪˈsiːtfl] *adj*. 骗人的 false, dishonest, deceiving
③ fib [fɪb] *n*. 无伤大雅的谎言,小谎 small/unimportant lie
④ bask [bɑːsk] *v*. 沐浴于 enjoy, indulge
⑤ decree [dɪˈkriː] *v*. 命令 order, demand, command
⑥ dismayed [dɪsˈmeɪd] *adj*. 惊慌的 afraid, worried
⑦ auburn [ˈɔːbən] *adj*. 红褐色的 russet, reddish-brown
⑧ in effect: 事实上 in fact

Valentine's own self.[v] "The joke," he said, "is as invisible as a weathercock① on a steeple②." He meant that it was very plain; and he went on to say exactly what it was: "If master will write her love letters, he must answer them."

On the arrival of Proteus, he was introduced by Valentine to Silvia and afterwards, when they were alone, Valentine asked Proteus how his love for Julia was prospering.

"Why," said Proteus, "you used to get weary when I spoke of her."

"Aye," confessed Valentine, "but it's different now. I can eat and drink all day with nothing but love on my plate and love in my cup."

"You idolize③ Silvia," said Proteus.

"She is divine," said Valentine.

"Come, come!" remonstrated④ Proteus.

"Well, if she's not divine," said Valentine, "she is the queen of all women on earth."

"Except Julia," said Proteus.

"Dear boy," said Valentine, "Julia is not excepted, but I will grant⑤ that she alone is worthy to bear my lady's train⑥."

"Your bragging⑦ astounds⑧ me," said Proteus.

But he had seen Silvia, and he felt suddenly that the yellow-haired Julia was black in comparison. He became in thought a villain without delay, and said to himself what he had never said before—"I to myself am dearer than my friend."

It would have been convenient for Valentine if Proteus had changed, by the power of the god whose name he bore, the shape of his body at the evil moment when he despised Julia in admiring Silvia.[vi] But his body did not change, his smile was still affectionate⑨, and Valentine confided⑩ to him the great secret that Silvia had now promised to run away with him. "In the pocket of this cloak," said Valentine, "I have a silken rope ladder, with hooks which will clasp the window bar of her room."

Proteus knew the reason why Silvia and her lover were bent on⑪ flight. The Duke intended her to wed Sir Thurio, a gentlemanly noodle⑫ for whom she did not care a straw⑬.

Proteus thought that if he could get rid of Valentine he might make Silvia fond of him,

---

① weathercock ['weðəkɒk] n.(公鸡形)风向标,风信鸡
② steeple ['stiːpl] n.(教堂的)尖塔 spire
③ idolize ['aɪdəlaɪz] v.崇拜 love, adore, admire, worship
④ remonstrate ['remənstreɪt] v.抗议 protest, object
⑤ grant [grɑːnt] v.同意 agree, allow, permit
⑥ train [treɪn] n.裙裾 tail, trail
⑦ brag [bræg] v.夸耀 boast, flaunt, vaunt, show off
⑧ astound [ə'staʊnd] v.使震惊 astonish
⑨ affectionate [ə'fekʃənət] adj.深情的 fond, loving, tender
⑩ confide [kən'faɪd] v.吐露 reveal, disclose
⑪ be bent on:决心要做,一心想做(通常指坏事) be insistent on, be determined to do
⑫ noodle ['nuːdl] n.(=noddle)笨蛋 fool, idiot, blockhead
⑬ not care a straw:毫不在乎 not care a snap/pin/dime

especially if the Duke insisted on her enduring① Sir Thurio's tiresome② chatter③. He therefore went to the Duke, and said, "Duty before friendship! It grieves me to thwart④ my friend Valentine, but Your Grace should know that he intends tonight to elope with Your Grace's daughter." He begged the Duke not to tell Valentine the giver of this information, and the Duke assured⑤ him that his name would not be divulged⑥.

Early that evening the Duke summoned Valentine, who came to him wearing a large cloak with a bulging⑦ pocket.

"You know," said the Duke, "my desire to marry my daughter to Sir Thurio?"

"I do," replied Valentine. "He is virtuous⑧ and generous, as befits⑨ a man so honored in Your Grace's thoughts."

"Nevertheless she dislikes him," said the Duke. "She is a peevish⑩, proud, disobedient⑪ girl, and I should be sorry to leave her a penny. I intend, therefore, to marry again."

Valentine bowed.

"I hardly know how the young people of today make love," continued the Duke, "and I thought that you would be just the man to teach me how to win the lady of my choice."

"Jewels have been known to plead rather well," said Valentine.

"I have tried them," said the Duke.

"The habit of liking the giver may grow if Your Grace gives her some more."[vii]

"The chief difficulty," pursued⑫ the Duke, "is this. The lady is promised to a young gentleman, and it is hard to have a word with her. She is, in fact, locked up."

"Then Your Grace should propose an elopement," said Valentine. "Try a rope ladder."

"But how should I carry it?" asked the Duke.

"A rope ladder is light," said Valentine. "You can carry it in a cloak."

"Like yours?"

"Yes, Your Grace."

"Then yours will do. Kindly lend it to me."

Valentine had talked himself into a trap. He could not refuse to lend his cloak, and when the Duke had donned⑬ it, His Grace drew from the pocket a sealed⑭ missive⑮ addressed⑯ to Silvia. He

---

① endure [ɪn'djʊə(r)] *v*. 忍耐 stand, bear, tolerate, put up with
② tiresome ['taɪəsəm] *adj*. 烦人的 annoying, irritating
③ chatter ['tʃætə(r)] *n*. 唠叨的话
④ thwart [θwɔːt] *v*. 阻挠，挫败 frustrate, stop, foil, defeat
⑤ assure [ə'ʃʊə(r)] *v*. 使确信 convince, persuade
⑥ divulge [daɪ'vʌldʒ] *v*. 透露 reveal, disclose
⑦ bulge [bʌldʒ] *v*. 鼓起 swell, project, protrude, stick out
⑧ virtuous ['vɜːtʃuəs] *adj*. 品行端正的 moral, honorable, irreproachable
⑨ befit [bɪ'fɪt] *v*. 适合 suit, match, agree with
⑩ peevish ['piːvɪʃ] *adj*. 易怒的 irritable, touchy, short-tempered
⑪ disobedient [ˌdɪsə'biːdiənt] *adj*. 不顺从 defiant, noncompliant
⑫ pursue [pə'sjuː] *v*. 继续探讨 continue, carry on
⑬ don [dɒn] *v*. 穿上，披上 put/pull on, get into, dress in
⑭ seal [siːl] *v*. 密封 close
⑮ missive ['mɪsɪv] *n*. 信件 letter
⑯ address [ə'dres] *v*. 致函 direct, send, post, mail

coolly opened it, and read these words: "Silvia, you shall be free tonight."

"Indeed," he said, "and here's the rope ladder. Prettily contrived①, but not perfectly.[viii] I give you, sir, a day to leave my dominions. If you are in Milan by this time tomorrow, you die."

Poor Valentine was saddened to the core. "Unless I look on Silvia in the day," he said, "there is no day for me to look upon."[ix]

Before he went he took farewell of Proteus, who proved a hypocrite② of the first order. "Hope is a lover's staff③," said Valentine's betrayer④. "Walk hence⑤ with that."

After leaving Milan, Valentine and his servant wandered into a forest near Mantua where the great poet Virgil⑥ lived. In the forest, however, the poets (if any) were brigands⑦, who bade the travelers stand. They obeyed, and Valentine made so good an impression⑧ upon his captors⑨ that they offered him his life on condition that he became their captain.

"I accept," said Valentine, "provided⑩ you release my servant, and are not violent to women or the poor."

The reply was worthy of Virgil, and Valentine became a brigand chief.

We return now to Julia, who found Verona too dull to live in since Proteus had gone. She begged her maid Lucetta to devise⑪ a way by which she could see him. "Better wait for him to return," said Lucetta, and she talked so sensibly⑫ that Julia saw it was idle⑬ to hope that Lucetta would bear the blame of any rash and interesting adventure. Julia therefore said that she intended to go to Milan and dressed like a page.

"You must cut off your hair then," said Lucetta, who thought that at this announcement Julia would immediately abandon her scheme.

"I shall knot it up," was the disappointing rejoinder.

---

① contrive [kən'traɪv] *v*. 巧妙地策划 plan, plot, design, devise
② hypocrite ['hɪpəkrɪt] *n*. 伪君子 dissembler, dissimulator
③ staff [stɑːf] *n*. 手杖,拐杖 walking stick
④ betrayer [bɪ'treɪə(r)] *n*. 告密者 traitor, informer
⑤ hence [hens] *adv*. 从今以后 later, hereafter, from now on
⑥ Virgil ['vɜːdʒɪl]: 维吉尔(普布留斯·维吉留斯·马罗,意大利诗人,70BC—19 BC)
⑦ brigand ['brɪgənd] *n*. 强盗 robber, bandit
⑧ impression [ɪm'preʃn] *n*. 影响 effect, influence, impact
⑨ captor ['kæptə(r)] *n*. 捕捉者 capturer, detainer
⑩ provided [prə'vaɪdɪd] *conj*. 假如 if, providing
⑪ devise [dɪ'vaɪz] *v*. 设计,想出 plan, design, think up
⑫ sensibly ['sensəbli] *adv*. 明智地 wisely
⑬ idle ['aɪdl] *adj*. 毫无意义的 useless, pointless, vain, futile

Lucetta then tried to make the scheme seem foolish to Julia, but Julia had made up her mind and was not to be put off by ridicule①. And when her toilet② was completed, she looked as comely③ a page as one could wish to see.

Julia assumed④ the male name Sebastian, and arrived in Milan in time to hear music being performed outside the Duke's palace.

"They are serenading⑤ the Lady Silvia," said a man to her.

Suddenly she heard a voice lifted in song, and she knew that voice. It was the voice of Proteus. But what was he singing?

"Who is Silvia? What is she,
That all our swains⑥ commend⑦ her?
Holy, fair, and wise is she;
The heaven such grace did lend her,
That she might admired be."

Julia tried not to hear the rest, but these two lines somehow thundered into her mind—

"Then to Silvia let us sing;
She excels each mortal⑧ thing."[x]

Then Proteus thought Silvia excelled Julia. And since he sang so beautifully for all the world to hear, it seemed that he was not only false to Julia, but had forgotten her. Yet Julia still loved him. She even went to him, and asked to be his page, and Proteus engaged⑨ her.

One day, he handed to her the ring which she had given him, and said, "Sebastian, take that to the Lady Silvia, and say that I should like the picture of her she promised me."

Silvia had promised the picture, but she disliked Proteus. She was obliged to talk to him because he was high in the favor of her father, who thought he pleaded with her on behalf of⑩ Sir Thurio. Silvia had learned from Valentine that Proteus was pledged⑪ to a sweetheart in Verona; and when he said tender things to her, she felt that he was disloyal in friendship as well as love.

Julia bore the ring to Silvia, but Silvia said, "I will not wrong the woman who gave it him by wearing it."

"She thanks you," said Julia.

"You know her, then?" said Silvia, and Julia spoke so tenderly of herself that Silvia wished that Sebastian would marry Julia.

Silvia gave Julia her portrait for Proteus, who would have received it the worse for extra touches on the nose and eyes if Julia had not made up her mind that she was as pretty as Silvia.[xi]

---

① ridicule [ˈrɪdɪkjuːl] *n*. 嘲笑 mockery, scorn, derision
② toilet [ˈtɔɪlət] *n*. 梳洗,打扮 freshening up
③ comely [ˈkʌmli] *adj*. 清秀的 fair, pretty, good-looking
④ assume [əˈsjuːm] *v*. 装出 put on, pretend
⑤ serenade [ˌserəˈneɪd] *v*. 唱小夜曲 sing or play music for sb.
⑥ swain [sweɪn] *n*. 情郎 boyfriend, lover, sweetheart
⑦ commend [kəˈmend] *v*. 赞扬 praise, applaud, speak highly of
⑧ mortal [ˈmɔːtl] *adj*. 终有一死的
⑨ engage [ɪnˈgeɪdʒ] *v*. 雇用 hire, employ
⑩ on behalf of sb.: 代表某人 as the representative of sb.
⑪ pledged [pledʒd] *adj*. 订婚的 engaged, plighted, betrothed

Soon there was an uproar in the palace. Silvia had fled.

The Duke was certain that her intention was to join the exiled① Valentine, and he was not wrong.

Without delay he started in pursuit, with Sir Thurio, Proteus, and some servants.

The members of the pursuing party got separated, and Proteus and Julia (in her page's dress) were by themselves when they saw Silvia, who had been taken prisoner by outlaws② and was now being led to their Captain. Proteus rescued her, and then said, "I have saved you from death; give me one kind look."

"O misery, to be helped by you!" cried Silvia. "I would rather be a lion's breakfast."

Julia was silent, but cheerful. Proteus was so much annoyed with Silvia that he threatened her, and seized her by the waist.

"O heaven!" cried Silvia.

At that instant there was a noise of crackling③ branches. Valentine came crashing through the Mantuan forest to the rescue of his beloved. Julia feared he would slay Proteus, and hurried to help her false lover. But he struck no blow, he only said, "Proteus, I am sorry I must never trust you more."

Thereat④ Proteus felt his guilt, and fell on his knees, saying, "Forgive me! I grieve! I suffer!"

"Then you are my friend once more," said the generous Valentine. "If Silvia, that is lost to me, will look on you with favor, I promise that I will stand aside and bless you both."

These words were terrible to Julia, and she swooned. Valentine revived her, and said, "What was the matter, boy?"

"I remembered," fibbed Julia, "that I was charged to give a ring to the Lady Silvia, and that

① exiled ['eksaɪld] *adj*. 被流放的 banished, expelled
② outlaw ['aʊtlɔː] *n*. 逃犯 criminal, fugitive
③ crackle ['krækl] *v*. 噼啪作响
④ thereat [ˌðeər'æt] *adv*. 因此,于是 therefore, thus

I did not."

"Well, give it to me," said Proteus.

She handed him a ring, but it was the ring that Proteus gave to Julia before he left Verona.

Proteus looked at her hand, and crimsoned to the roots of his hair.

"I changed my shape when you changed your mind," she said.

"But I love you again," he said.

Just then outlaws entered, bringing two prizes—the Duke and Sir Thurio.

"Forbear①!" cried Valentine, sternly. "The Duke is sacred."

Sir Thurio exclaimed, "There's Silvia; she's mine!"

"Touch her, and you die!" said Valentine.

"I should be a fool to risk anything for her," said Sir Thurio.

"Then you are base," said the Duke. "Valentine, you are a brave man. Your banishment② is over. I recall you. You may marry Silvia. You deserve her."

"I thank Your Grace," said Valentine, deeply moved, "and yet must ask you one more boon."

"I grant it," said the Duke.

"Pardon these men, Your Grace, and give them employment. They are better than their calling③.[xii]"

"I pardon them and you," said the Duke. "Their work henceforth shall be for wages."

"What think you of this page, Your Grace?" asked Valentine, indicating④ Julia.

The Duke glanced at⑤ her, and said, "I think the boy has grace in him."

"More grace than boy, say I," laughed Valentine, and the only punishment which Proteus had to bear for his treacheries against love and friendship was the recital⑥ in his presence of the adventures of Julia—Sebastian of Verona.[xiii]

① forbear [fɔːˈbeə(r)] v. 克制 refrain, restrain, stop from
② banishment [ˈbænɪʃmənt] n. 放逐 expulsion, deportation
③ calling [ˈkɔːlɪŋ] n. 行业,职业 career, profession
④ indicate [ˈɪndɪkeɪt] v. 暗示 hint, imply, suggest
⑤ glance at: 瞥视 glimpse at
⑥ recital [rɪˈsaɪtl] n. 叙说 tale, account, relation, narration

i Valentine was happy in his name because it was that of the patron saint of lovers; it is hard for a Valentine to be fickle or mean. 凡伦丁很中意自己的名字，因为它是爱的守护神的名字，而爱的守护神很难做到喜新厌旧或吝啬小气。

ii Proteus was unhappy in his name, because it was that of a famous shape-changer, and therefore it encouraged him to be a lover at one time and a traitor at another. 普洛丢斯却很不满意自己的名字，因为那是变幻无常的海神的名字，所以他深得名字的鼓励，时而是情人时而是叛徒。（Proteus是古希腊神话中能改变外形的神）

iii Indeed, no sooner had Lucetta left her alone than Julia repented of her tearing, and placed between her dress and her heart the torn piece of paper on which Proteus had signed his name. 没错，露西塔刚走开，朱利娅就后悔撕掉信，她把纸片捧在胸口，那上面签着普洛丢斯的名字。（no sooner...than...："一……就……"）

iv Very much did Valentine dislike writing that letter, but he did write it, and gave it to her coldly. 凡伦丁非常厌恶写这封信，但还是写了，他冷冰冰地把信交给她。

v Valentine was left with the letter, and condemned to write another; but his servant Speed saw that, in effect, the Lady Silvia had allowed Valentine to write for her a love letter to Valentine's own self. 凡伦丁拿着信走了，他被罚着要写另一封信。他的仆人史比德目睹了这一幕。事实上，西尔维娅小姐是叫凡伦丁替她写一封给凡伦丁本人的情书。

vi It would have been convenient for Valentine if Proteus had changed, by the power of the god whose name he bore, the shape of his body at the evil moment when he despised Julia in admiring Silvia. 于是，普洛丢斯开始嫌弃朱利娅，转而追求西尔维娅。如果此时他的身形能像与他同名的海神那样有所改变，凡伦丁就好办了。

vii "The habit of liking the giver may grow if Your Grace gives her some more." "阁下，要是您再给她多送点礼物，她对您的喜爱会与日俱增。"

viii Prettily contrived , but not perfectly. 好一场精心策划的计谋，却不够完美啊。

ix "Unless I look on Silvia in the day," he said, "there is no day for me to look upon." 他说："除非白天能见到西尔维娅，否则我的生命将不见天日。"

x

"Who is Silvia? What is she,	"西尔维娅伊何人，
That all our swains commend her?	乃能颠倒众生心？
Holy, fair, and wise is she;	神圣娇丽且聪明，
The heaven such grace did lend her,	天赋诸美萃一身，
That she might admired be.	俾令举世诵其名。
Then to Silvia let us sing;	弹琴为伊歌一曲，
She excels each mortal thing."	伊人美好世无伦。"

xi Silvia gave Julia her portrait for Proteus, who would have received it the worse for extra touches on the nose and eyes if Julia had not made up her mind that she was as pretty as Silvia. 西尔维娅把送给普洛丢斯的画像交给朱利娅。要不是朱利娅打心眼里觉得自己和西尔维娅一样美丽，普洛丢斯收到的画像就有可能被动过鼻子和眼睛了。

xii They are better than their calling. 他们名声不好，但品性都很好。

xiii ...the only punishment which Proteus had to bear for his treacheries against love and friendship was the recital in his presence of the adventures of Julia—Sebastian of Verona. ……普洛丢斯遭受的唯一惩罚就是，他不得不听人当着他的面，讲述他如何背叛维洛那的朱利娅，即西巴斯辛，以及他如何欺骗他朋友的故事。

海丽娜《终成眷属》

I know I love in vain, strive against hope;
Yet in this captious and intenible sieve
I still pour in the waters of my love
And lack not to lose still: thus, Indian-like,
Religious in mine error, I adore
The sun, that looks upon his worshipper,
But knows of him no more.

我知道我的爱是没有希望的徒劳，
可是在这罗网一样千孔万眼的筛子里，
依然把我如水的深情灌注下去，
永远不感到干涸。我正像印度人一样
虔信而执迷，我崇拜着太阳，
它的光辉虽然也照到它的信徒的身上，
却根本不知道有这样一个人存在。

终成眷属
All's Well That Ends Well

主要人物

King of France　法国国王

Countess [ˈkaʊntəs] of Rousillon [ˌruːsiːˈjɒn] 罗西昂伯爵夫人

Bertram [ˈbɜːtrəm] 勃特拉姆(罗西昂伯爵)

Lafeu [ləˈfjuː] 拉佛(法国宫廷中的老臣)

Parolles [pəˈrɒlɪz] 帕洛(勃特拉姆的侍从)

Helena [ˈhelɪnə] 海丽娜(寄养于伯爵夫人府中的少女)

Diana [daɪˈænə] 狄安娜(寡妇之女)

In the year thirteen hundred and something, the Countess of Rousillon[1] was unhappy in her palace near the Pyrenees[2]. She had lost her husband, and the King of France had summoned her son Bertram to Paris, hundreds of miles away.

Bertram was a pretty youth with curling hair, finely arched[3] eyebrows, and eyes as keen[4] as a hawk's. He was as proud as ignorance[5] could make him, and would lie with a face like truth itself to gain a selfish end.[i] But a pretty youth is a pretty youth, and Helena was in love with him.

Helena was the daughter of a great doctor who had died in the service of the Count of Rousillon. Her sole[6] fortune consisted in[7] a few of her father's prescriptions[8].

When Bertram had gone, Helena's forlorn[9] look was noticed by the Countess, who told her that she was exactly the same to her as her own child. Tears then gathered in Helena's eyes, for she felt that the Countess made Bertram seem like a brother whom she could never marry. The Countess guessed her secret forthwith, and Helena confessed that Bertram was to her as the sun is to the day.

She hoped, however, to win this sun by earning the gratitude of the King of France, who

---

① Rousillon [ˌruːsiːˈjɒn] 鲁西永(法国东南部比利牛斯山脉北麓一地区,朱生豪译本中译为"罗西昂")

② Pyrenees [ˌpɪrəˈniːz]:比利牛斯山(欧洲西南部山脉)

③ arched [ɑːtʃt] *adj*. 拱形的,弧形的 curved

④ keen [kiːn] *adj*. 锐利的 sharp, piercing

⑤ ignorance [ˈɪgnərəns] *n*. 无知 stupidity, foolishness

⑥ sole [səʊl] *adj*. 唯一的,仅有的 only, single

⑦ consist in:在于,存在于 involve, lie/reside in

⑧ prescription [prɪˈskrɪpʃn] *n*. 药方 medicine, drug, cure

⑨ forlorn [fəˈlɔːn] *adj*. 孤苦伶仃的 lonely, desolate

suffered from a lingering[1] illness, which made him lame[2]. The great doctors attached[3] to the Court despaired of curing him, but Helena had confidence[4] in a prescription which her father had used with success.

Taking an affectionate leave of the Countess, she went to Paris, and was allowed to see the King.

He was very polite, but it was plain he thought her a quack[5]. "It would not become me," he said, "to apply to a simple maiden for the relief which all the learned doctors cannot give me."

"Heaven uses weak instruments[6] sometimes[ii]," said Helena, and she declared that she would forfeit her life if she failed to make him well.

"And if you succeed?" questioned the King.

"Then I will ask Your Majesty to give me for a husband the man whom I choose!"

So earnest a young lady could not be resisted forever by a suffering king. Helena, therefore, became the King's doctor, and in two days the royal cripple[7] could skip.

He summoned his courtiers, and they made a glittering[8] throng[9] in the throne room of his palace. Well might the country girl have been dazzled[10], and seen a dozen husbands worth dreaming of among the handsome young noblemen before her. But her eyes only wandered till they found Bertram. Then she went up to him, and said, "I dare not say I take you, but I am yours!" Raising her voice that the King might hear, she added, "This is the Man!"

"Bertram," said the King, "take her; she's your wife!"

"My wife, my liege[11]?" said Bertram. "I beg Your Majesty to permit me to choose a wife."

"Do you know, Bertram, what she has done for your King?" asked the monarch[12], who had treated Bertram like a son.

"Yes, Your Majesty," replied Bertram, "but why should I marry a girl who owes her

---

① lingering [ˈlɪŋgərɪŋ] *adj*. 拖延的 slow, prolonged, dragging
② lame [leɪm] *adj*. 瘸的,跛的 crippled, limping, hobbling
③ attached to: 为……工作 working for
④ confidence [ˈkɒnfɪdəns] *n*. 信赖 trust, belief, faith, reliance
⑤ quack [kwæk] *n*. 江湖郎中 charlatan, pretender, impostor
⑥ instrument [ˈɪnstrəmənt] *n*. 促成某事的人
⑦ cripple [ˈkrɪpl] *n*. 瘸子 lameter, a lame person
⑧ glitter [ˈglɪtə(r)] *v*. 闪亮 gleam, glisten, sparkle
⑨ throng [θrɒŋ] *n*. 人群 crowd, multitude
⑩ dazzle [ˈdæzl] *v*. 使眼花 blind, bedazzle
⑪ liege [liːdʒ] *n*. 君主;领主 lord, king
⑫ monarch [ˈmɒnək] *n*. 君主 king/queen, emperor, sovereign

breeding[①] to[②] my father's charity?"

"You disdain her for lacking a title, but I can give her a title," said the King. And as he looked at the sulky[③] youth a thought came to him, and he added, "Strange that you think so much of blood when you could not distinguish your own from a beggar's if you saw them mixed together in a bowl."[iii]

"I cannot love her," asserted[④] Bertram. And Helena said gently, "Urge him not, Your Majesty. I am glad to have cured my King for my country's sake."

"My honor requires that scornful boy's obedience," said the King. "Bertram, make up your mind to this. You marry this lady, of whom you are so unworthy, or you learn how a king can hate. Your answer?"

Bertram bowed low and said, "Your Majesty has ennobled[⑤] the lady by your interest in her. I submit."

"Take her by the hand," said the King, "and tell her she is yours."

Bertram obeyed, and with little delay he was married to Helena.

Fear of the King, however, could not make him a lover. Ridicule helped to sour[⑥] him. A base soldier named Parolles told him to his face that now he had a "kicky-wicky[⑦]" his business was not to fight but to stay at home. "Kicky-wicky" was only a silly epithet[⑧] for a wife, but it made Bertram feel he could not bear having a wife, and that he must go to the war in Italy, though the King had forbidden him.

Helena he ordered to take leave of the King and return to Rousillon, giving her letters for his mother and herself. He then rode off, bidding her a cold goodbye.

She opened the letter addressed to herself, and read, "When you can get the ring from my finger you can call me husband, but against that 'when' I write 'never.'"[iv]

Dry-eyed had Helena been when she entered the King's presence and said farewell, but he was uneasy on her account[⑨], and gave her a ring from his own finger, saying, "If you send this to me, I shall know you are in trouble, and help you."

She did not show him Bertram's letter to his wife; it would have made him wish to kill the truant Count; but she went back to Rousillon and handed her mother-in-law the second letter.[v] It was short and bitter. "I have run away," it said. "If the world be broad enough, I will be always far away from her."

"Cheer up," said the noble widow to the deserted wife. "I wash his name out of my blood, and you alone are my child."[vi]

---

① breeding [ˈbriːdɪŋ] *n*. 抚养 educating, nurturing
② owe to：归因于，归功于 attribute to, ascribe to
③ sulky [ˈsʌlki] *adj*. 愠怒的 cross, moody, sullen, ill-humored
④ assert [əˈsɜːt] *v*. 坚称 maintain, declare, affirm
⑤ ennoble [ɪˈnəʊbl] *v*. 使高贵 dignify
⑥ sour [ˈsaʊə(r)] *v*. 使变得不愉快 become less pleasant or friendly
⑦ kicky-wicky [ˌkɪki ˈwɪki] *n*. 河东狮，悍妇 shrew
⑧ epithet [ˈepɪθet] *n*. 绰号 tag, nickname
⑨ on one's account：为了某人 on sb.'s behalf

The Dowager① Countess, however, was still mother enough to Bertram to lay the blame of his conduct on Parolles②, whom she called "a very tainted③ fellow."vii

Helena did not stay long at Rousillon. She clad herself as a pilgrim④, and, leaving a letter for her mother-in-law, secretly set out for Florence⑤.

On entering that city she inquired of a woman the way to the Pilgrims' House of Rest, but the woman begged "the holy pilgrim" to lodge⑥ with her.

Helena found that her hostess was a widow, who had a beautiful daughter named Diana.

When Diana heard that Helena came from France, she said, "A countryman of yours, Count Rousillon, has done worthy service for Florence." But after a time, Diana had something to tell which was not at all worthy of Helena's husband. Bertram was making love to Diana. He did not hide the fact that he was married, but Diana heard from Parolles that his wife was not worth caring for.

The widow was anxious for Diana's sake, and Helena decided to inform her that she was the Countess Rousillon.

"He keeps asking Diana for a lock⑦ of her hair," said the widow.

Helena smiled mournfully, for her hair was as fine as Diana's and of the same color. Then an idea struck her, and she said, "Take this purse of gold for yourself. I will give Diana three thousand crowns if she will help me to carry out this plan. Let her promise to give a lock of her hair to my husband if he will give her the ring which he wears on his finger. It is an ancestral⑧ ring. Five Counts of Rousillon have worn it, yet he will yield⑨ it up for a lock of your daughter's hair. Let your daughter insist that he shall cut the lock of hair from her in a dark room, and agree in advance that she shall not speak a single word."

The widow listened attentively⑩, with the purse of gold in her lap. She said at last, "I consent, if Diana is willing."

Diana was willing, and, strange to say, the prospect⑪ of cutting off a lock of hair from a silent girl in a dark room was so pleasing to Bertram that he handed Diana his ring, and was told when to follow her into the dark room. At the time appointed he came with a sharp knife, and felt a sweet face touch his as he cut off the lock of hair, and he left the room satisfied, like a man who is filled with renown⑫, and on his finger was a ring which the girl in the dark room had given him.

The war was nearly over, but one of its concluding chapters taught Bertram that the soldier

---

① dowager [ˈdaʊədʒə(r)] *n*. 贵妇;继承亡夫爵位的遗孀 lady, widow
② lay the blame on sb.: 归咎于某人,责怪某人 pin sth. on sb.
③ tainted [teɪntɪd] *adj*. 受玷污的 besmirched
④ pilgrim [ˈpɪlgrɪm] *n*. 朝圣者
⑤ Florence: 佛罗伦萨(意大利中部城市)
⑥ lodge [lɒdʒ] *v*. 寄住 stay, board, sojourn
⑦ lock [lɒk] *n*. 一绺头发 strand, curl, tuft, tress
⑧ ancestral [ænˈsestrəl] *adj*. 祖传的 inherited, patrimonial
⑨ yield up: 缴出 relinquish, surrender, deliver up
⑩ attentively [əˈtentɪvli] *adv*. 专心地 heedful, intently
⑪ prospect [ˈprɒspekt] *n*. 景象 view, sight, outlook
⑫ renown [rɪˈnaʊn] *n*. 名誉 fame, repute, reputation

who had been impudent enough to call Helena his "kicky-wicky" was far less courageous[1] than a wife.[viii] Parolles was such a boaster[2], and so fond of trimmings[3] to his clothes, that the French officers played him a trick to discover what he was made of.[ix] He had lost his drum, and had said that he would regain it unless he was killed in the attempt. His attempt was a very poor one, and he was inventing the story of a heroic failure, when he was surrounded and disarmed[4].

"Portotartarossa," said a French lord.

"What horrible lingo[5] is this?" thought Parolles, who had been blindfolded[6].

"He's calling for the tortures," said a French man, affecting to act as interpreter[7]. "What will you say without 'em?"

"As much," replied Parolles, "as I could possibly say if you pinched[8] me like a pasty." He was as good as his word[9]. He told them how many there were in each regiment[10] of the Florentine[11] army, and he refreshed[12] them with spicy[13] anecdotes[14] of the officers commanding it.[x]

Bertram was present, and heard a letter read, in which Parolles told Diana that he was a fool.

"This is your devoted friend," said a French lord.

"He is a cat to me now," said Bertram, who detested our hearthrug[15] pets.

Parolles was finally let go, but henceforth he felt like a sneak[16], and was not addicted to[17] boasting.

We now return to France with Helena, who had spread a report of her death, which was conveyed[18] to the Dowager Countess at Rousillon by Lafeu, a lord who wished to marry his daughter Magdalen to Bertram.

---

① courageous [kəˈreɪdʒəs] *adj*. 勇敢的 brave, bold, daring, heroic
② boaster [ˈbəʊstə(r)] *n*. 自夸的人，吹牛者 braggart, blowhard
③ trimming [ˈtrɪmɪŋ] *n*. (衣服)装饰 decoration, adornment
④ disarm [dɪsˈɑːm] *v*. 解除武装 take away weapons
⑤ lingo [ˈlɪŋgəʊ] *n*. 行话 jargon
⑥ blindfold [ˈblaɪndfəʊld] *v*. 蒙住眼睛 cover, cloak
⑦ interpreter [ɪnˈtɜːprɪtə(r)] *n*. 译员
⑧ pinch [pɪntʃ] *v*. 捏，拧，掐 nip, squeeze
⑨ as good as one's word：说话算数，言行一致，守信用
⑩ regiment [ˈredʒɪmənt] *n*. (军队)团 battalion
⑪ Florentine [ˈflɒrəntaɪn] *adj*. 佛罗伦萨的
⑫ refresh [rɪˈfreʃ] *v*. 更新 freshen, update
⑬ spicy [ˈspaɪsi] *adj*. 刺激的；粗俗的 exciting, shocking
⑭ anecdote [ˈænɪkdəʊt] *n*. 轶事 story, ana
⑮ hearthrug [ˈhɑːθrʌg] *n*. 壁炉前的地毯
⑯ sneak [sniːk] *n*. 鬼鬼祟祟的人；打小报告的人
⑰ addicted to：沉迷于 obsessed with
⑱ convey [kənˈveɪ] *v*. 传达 impart

The King mourned for Helena, but he approved of the marriage proposed for Bertram, and paid a visit to Rousillon in order to see it accomplished.

"His great offence is dead①," he said. "Let Bertram approach me."

Then Bertram, scarred② in the cheek, knelt before his Sovereign, and said that if he had not loved Lafeu's daughter before he married Helena, he would have prized his wife, whom he now loved when it was too late.[xi]

"Love that is late offends the Great Sender," said the King.[xii] "Forget sweet Helena, and give a ring to Magdalen."

Bertram immediately gave a ring to Lafeu, who said indignantly③, "It's Helena's!"

"It's not!" said Bertram.

Hereupon the King asked to look at the ring, and said, "This is the ring I gave to Helena, and bade her send to me if ever she needed help. So you had the cunning④ to get from her what could help her most."

Bertram denied again that the ring was Helena's, but even his mother said it was.

"You lie!" exclaimed the King. "Seize him, guards!" But even while they were seizing him, Bertram wondered how the ring, which he thought Diana had given him, came to be so like Helena's. A gentleman now entered, craving permission to deliver a petition⑤ to the King. It was a petition signed Diana Capulet, and it begged that the King would order Bertram to marry her whom he had deserted after winning her love.

"I'd sooner buy a son-in-law at a fair than take Bertram now," said Lafeu.

"Admit the petitioner⑥," said the King.

Bertram found himself confronted⑦ by Diana and her mother. He denied that Diana had any claim⑧ on him, and spoke of her as though her life was spent in the gutter⑨.[xiii] But she asked him what sort of gentlewoman it was to whom he gave, as to her he gave, the ring of his ancestors now missing from his finger?[xiv]

Bertram was ready to sink into the earth, but fate had one crowning⑩ generosity reserved for him. Helena entered.

"Do I see reality?" asked the King.

"O pardon! Pardon!" cried Bertram.

She held up his ancestral ring. "Now that I have this," she said, "will you love me, Bertram?"

"To the end of my life," he cried.

"My eyes smell onions," said Lafeu. Tears for Helena were twinkling⑪ in them.

---

① dead [ded] *adj*. 过时的，不再相关的 outdated, unrelated
② scarred [skɑːd] *adj*. 有疤痕的
③ indignantly [ɪnˈdɪgnəntli] *adv*. 愤怒地 angrily, madly, furiously
④ cunning [ˈkʌnɪŋ] *n*. 狡诈 craftiness, guile
⑤ petition [pəˈtɪʃn] *n*. 请愿书
⑥ petitioner [pəˈtɪʃənə(r)] *n*. 请愿者 suitor
⑦ confront [kənˈfrʌnt] *v*. 面对；与(某人)对峙 face, challenge
⑧ claim [kleɪm] *n*. 权利 right, entitlement
⑨ gutter [ˈgʌtə(r)] *n*. 排水沟 drain, channel, ditch, trench
⑩ crowning [ˈkraʊnɪŋ] *adj*. 最高的 supreme
⑪ twinkle [ˈtwɪŋkl] *v*. 闪烁 shine, sparkle, glitter, gleam

The King praised Diana when he was fully informed by that not very shy young lady of the meaning of her conduct. For Helena's sake she had wished to expose Bertram's meanness, not only to the King, but to himself. His pride was now in shreds①, and it is believed that he made a husband of some sort② after all.[xv]

ⅰ Bertram was a pretty youth with curling hair, finely arched eyebrows, and eyes as keen as a hawk's. He was as proud as ignorance could make him, and would lie with a face like truth itself to gain a selfish end. 勃特拉姆是个英俊的小伙子,长着一头鬈发,有两道漂亮的弯眉以及鹰一样的眼睛。他无知而傲慢,还会为一己之利而堂而皇之地撒谎。

ⅱ Heaven uses weak instruments sometimes... 上天常常借助于微弱者之手……

ⅲ Strange that you think so much of blood when you could not distinguish your own from a beggar's if you saw them mixed together in a bowl. 你这么看重血统真奇怪。要是把人们的血液混在一个大碗里,你也不能区分出你的血和乞丐的血有什么不同。

ⅳ "When you can get the ring from my finger you can call me husband, but against that 'when' I write 'never.'" "什么时候你能得到我手指上的这枚指环,你就能管我叫丈夫,但'那一天'是'永远不会'到来的。"

ⅴ She did not show him Bertram's letter to his wife; it would have made him wish to kill the truant Count; but she went back to Rousillon and handed her mother-in-law the second letter. 她没有把勃特拉姆写给她的信给国王看,因为它会让国王恨不得杀死这个不负责的伯爵;但是她回到罗西昂以后,把第二封信交给了她的婆婆。

ⅵ "I wash his name out of my blood, and you alone are my child." "只要我和他断绝母子情分,你就是我唯一的孩子了。"

ⅶ The Dowager Countess, however, was still mother enough to Bertram to lay the blame of his conduct on Parolles, whom she called "a very tainted fellow." 无论如何,伯爵遗孀依然是勃特拉姆的母亲,她把他的行为都归咎于帕洛,她称帕洛是"一个满身污点的家伙"。

ⅷ The war was nearly over, but one of its concluding chapters taught Bertram that the soldier who had been impudent enough to call Helena his "kicky-wicky" was far less courageous than a wife. 战争接近尾声,但最后时分勃特拉姆才领教

① shred [ʃred] *n*. 碎片 bit, piece, scrap, fragment

② of some sort: 某种程度上的 to some extent

到，那个轻薄无耻的士兵，也就是管海丽娜叫“河东狮”的人，其实远远不及一个女人勇敢。

ⅸ Parolles was such a boaster, and so fond of trimmings to his clothes, that the French officers played him a trick to discover what he was made of. 帕洛太爱吹牛，还十分爱惜自己衣服上的装饰；法兰西军官们耍了他一把，看清了他的真面目。

ⅹ He told them how many there were in each regiment of the Florentine army, and he refreshed them with spicy anecdotes of the officers commanding it. 他告诉他们佛罗伦萨军队的每个团里有多少人马，还说了许多叫他们吃惊的沙场军官们的奇闻逸事。

ⅺ ...if he had not loved Lafeu's daughter before he married Helena, he would have prized his wife, whom he now loved when it was too late. ……他要不是在娶海丽娜以前就爱上了拉佛的女儿，他肯定会珍惜他的妻子，而不是等到一切都已经太迟了的时候才爱她。(if...had done..., ...would have done...：与过去事实相反的虚拟语气)

ⅻ “Love that is late offends the Great Sender,” said the King. “迟来的爱情，是对爱人的冒犯。”国王说道。

xiii He denied that Diana had any claim on him, and spoke of her as though her life was spent in the gutter. 他不肯承认他和狄安娜有什么约定，他说起她就好像她是个沦落街头的人。

xiv But she asked him what sort of gentlewoman it was to whom he gave, as to her he gave, the ring of his ancestors now missing from his finger? 然而她问他，他把祖先留下的指环——他手指上没有戴那个指环——给了哪位高贵的女人？是不是给了她？

xv The King praised Diana when he was fully informed by that not very shy young lady of the meaning of her conduct. For Helena's sake she had wished to expose Bertram's meanness, not only to the King, but to himself. His pride was now in shreds, and it is believed that he made a husband of some sort after all. 国王得知这位胆大心细的年轻姑娘上诉的意图以后，对她称赞不已。狄安娜为了海丽娜，不仅向国王揭露了勃特拉姆的卑劣行为，还希望勃特拉姆好好反省。勃特拉姆一改往日的傲慢，在世人看来，他最后变成了一个名副其实的好丈夫。

附录
Appendix

莎士比亚经典语录(节选)

ACTION 行动

Action is eloquence, and the eyes of the ignorant
More learned than their ears. *Coriolanus*
行为往往胜于雄辩,愚人的眼睛是比他们的耳朵聪明得多的。 ——《科利奥兰纳斯》

ADVERSITY 逆境

Sweet are the uses of adversity,
Which, like the toad, ugly and venomous,
Wears yet a precious jewel in his head. *As You Like It*
逆运也有它的好处,就像丑陋而有毒的蟾蜍,它的头上却顶着一颗珍贵的宝石。
——《皆大欢喜》

That sir, which serves and seeks for gain,
And follows but for form,
Will pack when it begins to rain
And leave thee in the storm. *King Lear*
他为了自己的利益,向你屈节卑躬,天色一变就要告别,留下你在雨中。 ——《李尔王》

Ah, when the means are gone, that buy this praise,
The breath is gone whereof this praise is made:
Feast-won, fast-lost; one cloud of winter showers,
These flies are couch'd. *Timon of Athens*
唉!花费了无数的钱财,买到人家一声赞美,钱财一旦去手,赞美的声音也寂灭了。酒食上得来的朋友,等到酒尽樽空,转眼成为路人;一片冬天的乌云刚刚出现,这些飞虫们早就躲得不知去向了。
——《雅典的泰门》

ADVICE TO A SON LEAVING HOME 给离家之子的忠告

Give thy thoughts no tongue,
Nor any unproportioned thought his act.
Be thou familiar but by no means vulgar.
Those friends thou hast, and their adoption tried,

Grapple them unto thy soul with hoops of steel,
But do not dull thy palm with entertainment
Of each new-hatched, unfledged comrade. Beware
Of entrance to a quarrel, but, being in,
Bear 't, that th' opposed may beware of thee.
Give every man thy ear but few thy voice.
Take each man's censure but reserve thy judgment.
Costly thy habit as thy purse can buy,
But not expressed in fancy—rich, not gaudy,
For the apparel oft proclaims the man,
And they in France of the best rank and station
Are of a most select and generous, chief in that.
Neither a borrower nor a lender be,
For loan oft loses both itself and friend,
And borrowing dulls the edge of husbandry.
This above all: to thine own self be true,
And it must follow, as the night the day,
Thou canst not then be false to any man. *Hamlet*

不要想到什么就说什么,凡事必须三思而行。对人要和气,可是不要过分狎昵。相知有素的朋友,应该用钢圈箍在你的灵魂上,可是不要对每一个泛泛的新知滥施你的交情。留心避免和人家争吵;可是万一争端已起,就应该让对方知道你不是可以轻侮的。倾听每一个人的意见,可是只对极少数人发表你的意见;接受每一个人的批评,可是保留你自己的判断。尽你的财力购置贵重的衣服,可是不要炫新立异,必须富丽而不浮艳,因为服装往往可以表现人格;法国的名流要人,在这一点上是特别注重的,不要向人告贷,也不要借钱给人;因为债款放了出去,往往不但丢了本钱,而且还失去了朋友;向人告贷的结果,容易养成因循懒惰的习惯。尤其要紧的,你必须对你自己忠实,正像有了白昼才有黑夜一样,对自己忠实,才不会对别人欺诈。 ——《哈姆莱特》

AGE 晚年

My way of life
Is fall'n into the sere, the yellow leaf,
And that which should accompany old age,
As honor, love, obedience, troops of friends,
I must not look to have, but, in their stead,
Curses, not loud but deep, mouth-honor, breath,
Which the poor heart would fain deny and dare not. *Macbeth*

我的生命已经日就枯萎,像一片凋谢的黄叶;凡是老年人所应该享有的尊荣、敬爱、服从和一大群的朋友,我是没有希望再得到的了;代替这一切的,只有低声而深刻的诅咒,口头上的恭维和一些违心的假话。 ——《麦克白》

AMBITION 野心

Truly, and I hold ambition of so airy and light a quality that it is but a shadow's shadow.

Hamlet

不错,因为野心是那么空虚轻浮的东西,所以我认为它不过是影子的影子。 ——《哈姆莱特》

I charge thee, fling away ambition:
By that sin fell the angels; how can man, then,
The image of his Maker, hope to win by it?
Love thyself last: cherish those hearts that hate thee;
Corruption wins not more than honesty.
Still in thy right hand carry gentle peace,
To silence envious tongues. Be just, and fear not:
Let all the ends thou aim'st at be thy country's,
Thy God's, and truth's. *Henry VIII*

你一定要听我的嘱咐,把野心抛掉,天使们就是因为犯了野心的罪而堕落的,而人不过是他的创造主的影像,岂能希望通过野心而得到胜利?爱你自己要爱在最后,珍爱那些恨你的人,诚实比起腐败会给你赢得更多的好处。在你的右手里永远举着温顺的和平枝,免得嫉妒之徒说闲话。做人要公正,不要怕;你所要达到的一切目的应该是你的国家、上帝和真理所要达到的目的。

——《亨利八世》

ANGER 愤怒

Anger is like
A full-hot horse, who being allow'd his way,
Self-mettle tires him. *Henry VIII*

怒气就像一匹烈性的马,如果由它的性子,就会使它自己筋疲力尽。 ——《亨利八世》

ARROGANCE 傲慢

There are a sort of men, whose visages
Do cream and mantle like a standing pond,
And do a willful stillness entertain,
With purpose to be dressed in an opinion
Of wisdom, gravity, profound conceit,
As who should say, "I am Sir Oracle,
And when I ope my lips, let no dog bark!"
O my Antonio, I do know of these
That therefore only are reputed wise
For saying nothing, when I am very sure
If they should speak, would almost damn those ears
Which, hearing them, would call their brothers fools. *The Merchant of Venice*

世界上有一种人,他们的脸上装出一副心如止水的神气,故意表示他们的冷静,好让人家称赞他们一声智慧深沉，思想渊博；他们的神气之间，好像说，“我的说话都是纶音天语，我要是一张开嘴唇来，不许有一头狗乱叫！”啊，我的安东尼奥，我看透这一种人，他们只是因为不说话，博得了智慧的名声；可是我可以确定说一句，要是他们说起话来，听见的人，谁都会骂他们是傻瓜的。

——《威尼斯商人》

AUTHORITY 威权

Thou hast seen a farmer's dog bark at a beggar?
And the creature run from the cur?
There thou mightst behold the great image of authority: a dog's obeyed in office. *King Lear*

你见过农夫的一条狗向一个乞丐乱吠吗？你还看见那家伙怎样给那条狗赶走吗？从这一件事情上面，你就可以看到威权的伟大的影子：一条得势的狗，也可以使人家唯命是从。

——《李尔王》

Could great men thunder
As Jove himself does, Jove would ne'er be quiet,
For every pelting, petty officer
Would use his heaven for thunder;
Nothing but thunder! Merciful heaven,
Thou rather with thy sharp and sulphurous bolt
Split'st the unwedgeable and gnarled oak
Than the soft myrtle: but man, proud man,
Drest in a little brief authority,
Most ignorant of what he's most assured,
His glassy essence, like an angry ape,
Plays such fantastic tricks before high heaven
As make the angels weep. *Measure for Measure*

世上的大人先生们倘使都能够兴雷作电，那么天上的神明将永远得不到安静，因为每一个微僚末吏都要卖弄他的威风，让天空中充满了雷声。上天是慈悲的，它宁愿把雷霆的火力，去劈碎一株槎枒壮硕的橡树，却不去损坏柔弱的郁金香；可是骄傲的世人掌握到暂时的权力，却会忘记了自己琉璃易碎的本来面目，像一头盛怒的猴子一样，装扮出种种丑恶的怪相，使天上的神明们因为怜悯他们的痴愚而流泪。

——《一报还一报》

BEAUTY 美貌

The hand that hath made you fair hath made you good; the goodness that is cheap in beauty makes beauty brief in goodness; but grace, being the soul of your complexion, shall keep the body of it ever fair. *Measure for Measure*

造物给你美貌，也给你美好的德性；没有德性的美貌，是转瞬即逝的；可是因为在你的美貌之中，有一颗美好的灵魂，所以你的美貌是永存的。

——《一报还一报》

BLESSINGS UNDERVALUED 被低估的恩典

For it so falls out
That what we have we prize not to the worth
Whiles we enjoy it, but being lacked and lost,
Why then we rack the value, then we find
The virtue that possession would not show us
Whiles it was ours. *Much Ado About Nothing*

我们往往在享有某一件东西的时候,一点不看重它的好处;等到失掉它以后,却会格外夸张它的价值,发现当它还在我们手里的时候所看不出来的优点。——《无事生非》

BRAGGARTS 狂妄的人

Who knows himself a braggart,
Let him fear this, for it will come to pass
That every braggart shall be found an ass. *All's Well That Ends Well*

可是我要警告那些喜欢吹牛的朋友们,不要太吹过了头,有一天你会发现自己是一头驴子的。
——《终成眷属》

They that have the voice of lions, and the act of bares, are they not monsters?
Troilus and Cressida

这种声音像狮子、行动像兔子一样的家伙,可不是怪物吗? ——《特洛伊罗斯与克瑞西达》

CALUMNY 诽谤

Be thou as chaste as ice, as pure as snow,
Thou shalt not escape calumny. *Hamlet*

尽管你像冰一样坚贞,像雪一样纯洁,你还是逃不过谗人的诽谤。 ——《哈姆莱特》

No might nor greatness in mortality
Can censure 'scape; back-wounding calumny
The whitest virtue strikes. What king so strong
Can tie the gall up in the slanderous tongue? *Measure for Measure*

人间的权力尊荣,总是逃不过他人的讥弹;最纯洁的德性,也免不了背后的诽谤。哪一个国王有力量堵塞住谗言的唇舌呢? ——《一报还一报》

CEREMONY 礼仪

Ceremony was but devised at first
To set a gloss on faint deeds, hollow welcomes,
Recanting goodness, sorry ere 'tis shown;
But where there is true friendship, there needs none. *Timon of Athens*

一切礼仪,都是为了文饰那些虚应故事的行为、言不由衷的欢迎、出尔反尔的殷勤而设立的;如果有真实的友谊,这些虚伪的形式就该一律摈弃。 ——《雅典的泰门》

COMFORT 慰藉

For, brother, men
Can counsel, and speak comfort to that grief
Which they themselves not feel, but, tasting it,
Their counsel turns to passion, which before
Would give preceptial medicine to rage,
Fetter strong madness in a silken thread,
Charm ache with air and agony with words.
No, no, 'tis all men's office to speak patience
To those that wring under the load of sorrow,
But no man's virtue nor sufficiency,
To be so moral when he shall endure
The like himself. *Much Ado About Nothing*

因为,兄弟,人们对于自己并不感觉到的痛苦,是会用空洞的话来劝告慰藉的,可是他们要是自己尝到了这种痛苦的滋味,他们的理性就会让感情来主宰了,他们就会觉得他们给人家服用的药饵,对自己也不会发生效力;极度的疯狂,是不能用一根丝线把它拴住的,就像空话不能止痛一样。不,不,谁都会劝一个在悲哀的重压下辗转呻吟的人安心忍耐,可是谁也没有那样的修养和勇气,能够叫自己忍受同样的痛苦。——《无事生非》

COMPARISON 比较

When the moon shone, we did not see the candle.
So doth the greater glory dim the less.
A substitute shines brightly as a king
Until a king be by, and then his state
Empties itself, as doth an inland brook
Into the main of waters. *The Merchant of Venice*

月光明亮的时候,我们就瞧不见灯光。小小的荣耀也正是这样给更大的光荣所掩。国王出巡的时候摄政的威权未尝不就像一个君主,可是一到国王回来,他的威权就归于乌有,正像溪涧中的细流注入大海一样。

——《威尼斯商人》

CONSCIENCE 顾虑

Thus conscience does make cowards of us all,
And thus the native hue of resolution
Is sicklied o'er with the pale cast of thought,
And enterprises of great pitch and moment,
With this regard their currents turn awry,
And lose the name of action. *Hamlet*

这样,重重的顾虑使我们全变成了懦夫,决心的赤热的光彩,被审慎的思维盖上了一层灰色。伟大的事业在这一种考虑之下,也会逆流而退,失去了行动的意义。——《哈姆莱特》

CONTENT 听天由命

My crown is in my heart, not on my head;
Not decked with diamonds and Indian stones,
Nor to be seen: my crown is called content:
A crown it is that seldom kings enjoy. *Henry VI*, Part 3

我的王冠不戴在头上,是藏在心里。我的王冠不镶珠宝,肉眼看不见它;我的王冠就是"听天由命",这是许多国王享受不到的一顶王冠。 ——《亨利六世》(下篇)

CONTENTION 争夺

How, in one house,
Should many people, under two commands
Hold amity? *King Lear*

一间屋子里养了这许多人,受着两个主人支配,怎么不会发生争闹? ——《李尔王》

When two authorities are up,
Neither supreme, how soon confusion
May enter 'twixt the gap of both and take
The one by the other. *Coriolanus*

当两种权力彼此对峙的时候,混乱就会乘机而起。 ——《科利奥兰纳斯》

CONTENTMENT 知足常乐

'Tis better to be lowly born,
And range with humble livers in content,
Than to be perk'd up in a glistering grief,
And wear a golden sorrow. *Henry VIII*

与其绫罗绸缎、珠光宝影,生活在忧愁痛苦之中,不如出身清寒,和贫贱人来往。
——《亨利八世》

COWARDS 懦夫

Cowards die many times before their deaths.
The valiant never taste of death but once. *Julius Caesar*

懦夫在未死以前,就已经死过好多次;勇士一生只死一次。 ——《裘力斯·凯撒》

CUSTOM 习惯

That monster, custom, who all sense doth eat,
Of habits devil, is angel yet in this:
That to the use of actions fair and good
He likewise gives a frock or livery
That aptly is put on. Refrain tonight,
And that shall lend a kind of easiness

To the next abstinence, the next more easy.
For use almost can change the stamp of nature,
And either rein the devil or throw him out
With wondrous potency. *Hamlet*

习惯虽然是一个可以使人失去羞耻的魔鬼,但是它也可以做一个天使,对于勉力为善的人,它会用潜移默化的手段,使他弃恶从善。您要是今天晚上自加抑制,下一次就会觉得这种自制的功夫并不怎样为难,慢慢地就可以习以为常了;因为习惯简直有一种改变气质的神奇的力量,它可以制服魔鬼,并且把他从人们心里驱逐出去。 ——《哈姆莱特》

But to my mind, though I am native here
And to the manner born, it is a custom
More honored in the breach then the observance. *Hamlet*

可是我虽然从小就熟习这种风俗,我却以为把它破坏了倒比遵守它还体面些。
——《哈姆莱特》

DEATH 死亡

But Kings and mightiest potentates must die,
For that's the end of human misery. *Henry VI*, Part 1

可是王侯将相总不免一死,悲惨的人生,总是如此结局的呵。 ——《亨利六世》(上篇)

Of all the wonders that I yet have heard,
It seems to me most strange that men should fear,
Seeing that death, a necessary end,
Will come when it will come. *Julius Caesar*

在我所听到过的一切怪事之中,人们的贪生怕死是一件最奇怪的事情,因为死本来是一个人免不了的结局,它要来的时候谁也不能叫它不来。 ——《裘力斯·凯撒》

The sense of death is most in apprehension. *Measure for Measure*

死的惨痛大部分是心理上造成的恐怖。 ——《一报还一报》

By medicine life may be prolong'd, yet death
Will seize the doctor too. *Cymbeline*

可是我想医药虽然可以延长生命,毕竟医生也是不免一死的。 ——《辛白林》

DECEPTION 欺骗

The devil can cite Scripture for his purpose.
An evil soul producing holy witness
Is like a villain with a smiling cheek,
A goodly apple rotten at the heart.
O, what a goodly outside falsehood hath! *The Merchant of Venice*

魔鬼也会引证《圣经》来替自己辩护哩。一个指着神圣的名字作证的恶人，就像一个脸带笑容的奸徒，又像一只外表光鲜、心中腐烂的苹果。唉，奸伪的表面是多么动人！ ——《威尼斯商人》

DEEDS 罪行

Foul deeds will rise,
Though all the earth o'erwhelm them, to men's eyes. *Hamlet*
罪恶的行为总有一天会发现，虽然地上所有的泥土把它们遮掩。 ——《哈姆莱特》

How oft the sight of means to do ill deeds
Make deeds ill done! *King John*
看见了罪恶的工具，多么容易使人造成罪恶！ ——《约翰王》

DELAY 迟延

That we would do,
We should do when we would; for this "would" changes,
And hath abatements and delays as many
As there are tongues, are hands, are accidents.
And then this "should" is like a spendthrift sigh
That hurts by easing. *Hamlet*
我们所要做的事，应该一想到就做；因为人的想法是会变化的，有多少舌头、多少手、多少意外，就会有多少犹豫、多少迟延；那时候再空谈该做什么，只不过等于聊以自慰的长吁短叹，只能伤害自己的身体罢了。 ——《哈姆莱特》

DELUSION 妄想

Mother, for love of grace,
Lay not that flattering unction to your soul
That not your trespass but my madness speaks.
It will but skin and film the ulcerous place
Whiles rank corruption, mining all within,
Infects unseen. *Hamlet*
母亲，为了上帝的慈悲，不要自己安慰自己，以为我这一番说话，只是出于疯狂，不是真的对您的过失而发；那样的思想不过是骗人的油膏，只能使您溃烂的良心上结起一层薄膜，那内部的毒疮却在底下愈长愈大。 ——《哈姆莱特》

DISCRETION 谨慎

Let's teach ourselves that honorable stop
Not to outsport discretion. *Othello*
我们必须随时谨慎，免得因为纵乐无度而肇成意外。 ——《奥瑟罗》

DOUBTS AND FEARS 疑惑与恐惧

But now I am cabined, cribbed, confined, bound in
To saucy doubts and fears. *Macbeth*

现在我却被恼人的疑惑和恐惧所包围拘束。 ——《麦克白》

INTEMPERANCE 纵欲

Boundless intemperance
In nature is a tyranny. It hath been
The untimely emptying of the happy throne
And fall of many kings. *Macbeth*

从人的生理来说,无限制的纵欲是一种"虐政",它曾经推翻了无数君主,使他们不能长久地坐在王位上。 ——《麦克白》

DUTY OWING TO OURSELVES AND OTHERS 对自己和对他人的责任

Love all, trust a few,
Do wrong to none: be able for thine enemy
Rather in power than use, and keep thy friend
Under thy own life's key: be cheque'd for silence,
But never tax'd for speech. *All's Well That Ends Well*

对众人一视同仁,对少数人推心置腹,对任何人不要亏负;在能力上你应当能和你的敌人抗衡,但不要因为争强好胜而炫耀你的才干;对于你的朋友,你应该开诚相与;宁可被人责备你木讷寡言,不要让人嗔怪你多言偾事。 ——《终成眷属》

EQUIVOCATION 含糊其辞

I do not like "but yet." It does allay
The good precedence. Fie upon "But yet."
"But yet" is as a jailer to bring forth
Some monstrous malefactor. *Antony and Cleopatra*

我不爱听"可是",它会推翻先前所说的那些好消息;呸,"可是"!"可是"就像一个狱卒,它会带上一个大奸巨恶的罪犯。 ——《安东尼与克莉奥佩特拉》

EXCESS 过度

For as a surfeit of the sweetest things
The deepest loathing to the stomach brings. *A Midsummer Night's Dream*

一个人吃饱了太多的甜食,能使胸胃中发生强烈的厌恶。 ——《仲夏夜之梦》

Every inordinate cup is unblest,
and the ingredient is a devil. *Othello*

每一杯过量的酒都是魔鬼酿成的毒汁。 ——《奥瑟罗》

FALSEHOOD 虚伪

The best way is to slander Valentine
With falsehood, cowardice, and poor descent,
Three things that women highly hold in hate. *The Two Gentlemen of Verona*

最好的法子是散播关于凡伦丁的坏话，说他心思不正、行为懦弱、出身贫贱，这三件是女人家听见了最恨的事情。 ——《维洛那二绅士》

FEAR 恐惧

Fear frames disorder, and disorder wounds
Where it should guard. *Henry VI*, Part 2

由于害怕，就产生混乱，一混乱，就挺不下去了。 ——《亨利六世》(中篇)

Fear and be slain; no worse can come to fight:
And fight and die is death destroying death;
Where fearing dying pays death servile breath. *Richard II*

畏惧并不能免于一死，战争的结果大不了也不过一死。奋战而死，是以死亡摧毁死亡；畏怯而死，却做了死亡的奴隶。 ——《理查二世》

FEASTS 欢宴

Small cheer and great welcome makes a merry feast. *The Comedy of Errors*

酒肴即使稀少，只要主人好客，也一样可以尽欢。 ——《错误的喜剧》

FILIAL INGRATITUDE 忘恩负义

More hideous when thou show'st thee in a child
Than the sea monster. *King Lear*

丑恶的海怪也比不上忘恩的儿女那样可怕。 ——《李尔王》

How sharper than a serpent's tooth it is
To have a thankless child. *King Lear*

一个负心的孩子，比毒蛇的牙齿还要多么使人痛入骨髓！ ——《李尔王》

FORETHOUGHT 远见

Determine on some course,
More than a wild exposure to each chance
That starts i' the way before thee. *Coriolanus*

商量一个妥当的方策，不要盲冲瞎撞，去试探前途的危险。 ——《科利奥兰纳斯》

FORTITUDE 刚毅

Yield not thy neck
To fortune's yoke, but let thy dauntless mind

Still ride in triumph over all mischance. *Henry VI*, Part 3
望您不要甘受命运的欺负，要在任何坏运的面前泰然自若。 ——《亨利六世》(下篇)

FORTUNE 命运

When Fortune means to men most good,
She looks upon them with a threatening eye. *King John*
当命运有心眷顾世人的时候，她会故意向他们怒目而视。 ——《约翰王》

GREATNESS 伟大

Farewell, a long farewell, to all my greatness!
This is the state of man: Today he puts forth
The tender leaves of hope; tomorrow blossoms,
And bears his blushing honors thick upon him;
The third day comes a frost, a killing frost,
And when he thinks, good easy man, full surely
His greatness is aripening, nips his root,
And then he falls, as I do. *Henry VIII*

再见？我全部的宏伟事业从此不再见了。人世间的事就是这样。一个人今天生出了希望的嫩叶，第二天开了花，身上开满了红艳艳的荣誉的花朵，第三天致命的霜冻来了，而这位蒙在鼓里的好人还满有把握，以为他的宏伟事业正在成熟呢，想不到霜冻正在咬噬他的根，接着他就倒下了，和我一样。 ——《亨利八世》

Some are born great, some achieve greatness,
and some have greatness thrust upon 'em. *Twelfth Night*
有的人是生来的富贵，有的人是挣来的富贵，有的人是送上来的富贵。 ——《第十二夜》

HAPPINESS 幸福

O, how bitter a thing it is to look into happiness through another man's eyes.
As You Like It
唉！从别人的眼中看见幸福，多么令人烦闷。 ——《皆大欢喜》

HONESTY 诚实

An honest man, sir, is able to speak for himself, when a knave is not. *Henry IV*, Part 2
一个好人，老爷，可以为他自己辩护，坏人可不能。 ——《亨利四世》(下篇)

To be honest, as this world goes, is to be one man picked out of ten thousand. *Hamlet*
在这世上，一万个人中间只不过有一个老实人。 ——《哈姆莱特》

HYPOCRISY 虚伪

Devils soonest tempt, resembling spirits of light. *Love's Labor's Lost*

魔鬼往往化装光明的天使引诱世人。 ——《爱的徒劳》

One may smile, and smile, and be a villain. *Hamlet*
一个人可以尽管满面都是笑，骨子里却是杀人的奸贼。 ——《哈姆莱特》

INNOCENCE 清白

The trust I have is in mine innocence,
And therefore am I bold and resolute. *Henry VI, Part 2*
我唯一的信赖，是我的坦白的胸怀；问心无愧，就能坚强。 ——《亨利六世》(中篇)

INSINUATIONS 奉承

For calumny will sear
Virtue itself: these shrugs, these hums and ha's,
When you have said "she's goodly," come between
Ere you can say "she's honest." *The Winter's Tale*
因为诽谤是会把贞洁都烙伤了的。你们才说了她是美貌的，还来不及说她是贞洁的，这种耸肩、这种哼、这种嘿，就已经跟着来了。 ——《冬天的故事》

JEALOUSY 嫉妒

Trifles light as air,
Are to the jealous confirmations strong
As proofs of holy writ. *Othello*
像空气一样轻的小事，对于一个嫉妒的人，也会变成天书一样坚强的确证。 ——《奥瑟罗》

O, beware, My Lord, of jealousy!
It is the green-eyed monster, which doth mock
The meat it feeds on. *Othello*
啊，主帅，您要留心嫉妒啊；那是一个绿眼的妖魔，谁做了它的牺牲，就要受它的玩弄。
——《奥瑟罗》

JESTS 嘲弄

A jest's prosperity lies in the ear
Of him that hears it, never in the tongue
Of him that makes it. *Love's Labor's Lost*
可笑或不可笑取决于听者的耳朵，而不是说者的舌头。 ——《爱的徒劳》

He jests at scars that never felt a wound. *Romeo and Juliet*
没有受过伤的才会讥笑别人身上的创痕。 ——《罗密欧与朱丽叶》

JUDGMENT 审判

Heaven is above all yet; there sits a judge
That no king can corrupt. *Henry VIII*
我们大家的头上还有青天，在天上还有个审判官，他是任何国王所不能腐蚀的。
——《亨利八世》

LIFE 人生

Life's but a walking shadow, a poor player
That struts and frets his hour upon the stage,
And then is heard no more. It is a tale
Told by an idiot, full of sound and fury,
Signifying nothing. *Macbeth*
人生不过是一个行走的影子，一个在舞台上指手画脚的拙劣的伶人，登场片刻，就在无声无息中悄然退下；它是一个愚人所讲的故事，充满着喧哗和骚动，却找不到一点意义。 ——《麦克白》

We are such stuff
As dreams are made on, and our little life
Is rounded with a sleep. *The Tempest*
构成我们的料子也就是那梦幻的料子；我们的短暂的一生，前后都环绕在酣睡之中。
——《暴风雨》

LOVE 爱

A murderous guilt shows not itself more soon
Than love that would seem hid. Love's night is noon. *Twelfth Night*
爱比杀人重罪更难隐藏，爱的黑夜有中午的阳光。 ——《第十二夜》

Sweet love, I see, changing his property,
Turns to the sourest and most deadly hate. *Richard II*
亲密的情爱一旦受到激动，是会变成最深切的怨恨的。 ——《理查二世》

When love begins to sicken and decay,
It useth an enforced ceremony. *Julius Caesar*
朋友之间用得着不自然的礼貌的时候，就可以知道他们的感情已经在开始衰落了。
——《裘力斯·凯撒》

The course of true love never did run smooth. *A Midsummer Night's Dream*
真正的爱情，所走的道路永远是崎岖多阻。 ——《仲夏夜之梦》

Love looks not with the eyes, but with the mind. *A Midsummer Night's Dream*

爱情是不用眼睛而用心灵看着的。——《仲夏夜之梦》

She never told her love,
But let concealment, like a worm i' the bud,
Feed on her damask check. She pined in thought,
And with a green and yellow melancholy
She sat like patience on a monument,
Smiling at grief. Was not this love indeed? *Twelfth Night*

她从来不向人诉说她的爱情,让隐藏在内心中的抑郁像蓓蕾中的蛀虫一样,侵蚀着她的绯红的脸颊;她因相思而憔悴,疾病和忧愁折磨着她,像是墓碑上刻着的"忍耐"的化身,默坐着向悲哀微笑。这不是真的爱情吗?——《第十二夜》

But love is blind, and lovers cannot see
The pretty follies that themselves commit. *The Merchant of Venice*

可是恋爱是盲目的,恋人们瞧不见他们自己所干的傻事。——《威尼斯商人》

MAN 人类

What a piece of work is a man! How noble in reason! How infinite in faculties! In form and moving how express and admirable! In action how like an angel! In apprehension how like a god! The beauty of the world, the paragon of animals! *Hamlet*

人类是一件多么了不得的杰作!多么高贵的理性!多么伟大的力量!多么优美的仪表!多么文雅的举动!在行为上多么像一个天使!在智慧上多么像一个天神!宇宙的精华!万物的灵长!——《哈姆莱特》

MERCY 慈悲

The quality of mercy is not strained.
It droppeth as the gentle rain from heaven
Upon the place beneath. It is twice blest:
It blesseth him that gives and him that takes.
'Tis mightiest in the mightiest. It becomes
The throned monarch better than his crown.
His scepter shows the force of temporal power
The attribute to awe and majesty
Wherein doth sit the dread and fear of kings,
But mercy is above this sceptered sway.
It is enthroned in the hearts of kings.
It is an attribute to God himself.
And earthly power doth then show likest God's
When mercy seasons justice. Therefore, Jew,
Though justice be thy plea, consider this—

That in the course of justice none of us
Should see salvation. We do pray for mercy,
And that same prayer doth teach us all to render
The deeds of mercy. *The Merchant of Venice*

慈悲不是出于勉强，它是像甘霖一样从天上降下尘世；它不但给幸福于受施的人，也同样给幸福于施与的人；它有超乎一切的无上威力，比皇冠更足以显出一个帝王的高贵：御杖不过象征着俗世的威权，使人民对于君上的尊严凛然生畏；慈悲的力量却高出于权力之上，它深藏在帝王的内心，是一种属于上帝的德性，执法的人倘能把慈悲调剂着公道，人间的权力就和上帝的神力没有差别。所以，犹太人，虽然你所要求的是公道，可是请你想一想，要是真的按照公道执行起赏罚来，谁也没有死后得救的希望；我们既然祈祷着上帝的慈悲，就应该按照祈祷的指点，自己做一些慈悲的事。 ——《威尼斯商人》

MERIT 美德

And well said too—for who shall go about
To cozen fortune and be honorable
Without the stamp of merit? Let none presume
To wear an undeserved dignity. *The Merchant of Venice*

说得好，一个人要是自己没有几分长处，怎么可以妄图非分？尊荣显贵，原来不是无德之人所可以忝窃的。 ——《威尼斯商人》

MODESTY 谦逊

It is the witness still of excellency
To put a strange face on his own perfection. *Much Ado About Nothing*

越是本领超人一等，越是口口声声不满意自己的才能。 ——《无事生非》

MORAL CONQUEST 道德的胜利

Therefore, brave conquerors—for so you are,
That war against your own affections
And the huge army of the world's desires—
Our late edict shall strongly stand in force. *Love's Labor's Lost*

所以，勇敢的战士们——因为你们都是向你们自己的感情和一切俗世的欲望奋勇作战的英雄——我们必须把我们最近的敕令严格实行起来。 ——《爱的徒劳》

MURDER 谋杀

The great King of kings
Hath in the tables of his law commanded
That thou shalt do no murder. Will you then
Spurn at his edict and fulfil a man's?
Take heed, for he holds vengeance in his band
To hurl upon their heads that break his law. *Richard III*

那崇高的万王之王早已在他的法典上训诫过：不可杀人！你们怎敢违背神旨而奉行一个凡夫的意图？当心；那手执惩仇大锤的是真神，谁犯了天条，谁的头上就要遭到袭击。——《理查三世》

Which blood, like sacrificing Abel's, cries,
Even from the tongueless caverns of the earth. *Richard II*

正像被害的亚伯一样，他的血正在从无言的墓穴里向我高声呼喊。——《理查二世》

MUSIC 音乐

The man that hath no music in himself,
Nor is not moved with concord of sweet sounds,
Is fit for treasons, stratagems, and spoils.
The motions of his spirit are dull as night,
And his affections dark as Erebus.
Let no such man be trusted. *The Merchant of Venice*

灵魂里没有音乐，或是听了甜蜜和谐的乐声而不会感动的人，都是擅于为非作恶、使奸弄诈的；他们的灵魂像黑夜一样昏沉，他们的感情像鬼蜮一样幽暗；这种人是不可信任的。

——《威尼斯商人》

NAMES 名字、名声

What's in a name? That which we call a rose
By any other name would smell as sweet. *Romeo and Juliet*

姓名本来是没有意义的；我们叫作玫瑰的这一种花，要是换了个名字，它的香味还是同样的芬芳。

——《罗密欧与朱丽叶》

Good name in man and woman, dear My Lord,
Is the immediate jewel of their souls.
Who steals my purse steals trash; 'Tis something, nothing:
'Twas mine, 'tis his, and has been slave to thousands.
But he that filches from me my good name
Robs me of that which not enriches him
And makes me poor indeed. *Othello*

我的好主帅，无论男人女人，名誉是他们灵魂里面最切身的珍宝。谁偷窃我的钱囊，不过偷窃到一些废物，一些虚无的东西，它只是从我的手里转到他的手里，而它也曾做过千万人的奴隶；可是谁偷去了我的名誉，那么他虽然并不因此而富足，我却因为失去它而成为赤贫了。——《奥瑟罗》

NEWS, GOOD AND BAD 喜讯和噩耗

Though it be honest, it is never good
To bring bad news. Give to a gracious message
An host of tongues, but let ill tidings tell
Themselves, when they be felt. *Antony and Cleopatra*

把坏消息告诉人家，即使诚实不虚，总不是一件好事；悦耳的喜讯不妨极口渲染，不幸的噩耗还是缄口不言，让那身受的人自己感到的好。

——《安东尼与克莉奥佩特拉》

OFFICE 官僚

'Tis the curse of service.
Preferment goes by letter and affection,
And not by the old gradation, where each second
Stood heir to the first.

Othello

说来真叫人恼恨，军队里的升迁可以全然不管古来的定法，按照各人的阶级依次递补，只要谁的脚力大，能够得到上官的欢心，就可以越级躐升。

——《奥瑟罗》

OPPORTUNITY 时机

Who seeks and will not take when once 'tis offered,
Shall never find it more.

Antony and Cleopatra

放着这样大好机会当面错过，以后再找，还找得到吗？

——《安东尼与克莉奥佩特拉》

There is a tide in the affairs of men,
Which, taken at the flood, leads on to fortune;
Omitted, all the voyage of their life
Is bound in shallows and in miseries.
On such a full sea are we now afloat,
And we must take the current when it serves
Or lose our ventures.

Julius Caesar

世事的起伏本来是波浪式的，人们要是能够趁着高潮一往直前，一定可以功成名就；要是不能把握时机，就要终身蹭蹬，一事无成。我们现在正在满潮的海上漂浮，倘不能顺水行舟，我们的事业就会一败涂地。

——《裘力斯·凯撒》

OPPRESSION 压迫

Press not a falling man too far! 'Tis virtue:
His faults lie open to the laws; let them,
Not you, correct him.

Henry VIII

不要把一个即将失败的人逼得太紧，这是不道德的。他的过错难逃法网，让法律来惩罚他，您不必过问了。

——《亨利八世》

PAST AND FUTURE 过去和未来

O thoughts of men accursed!
Past and to come seem best; things present, worst.

Henry IV, Part 2

啊，可诅咒的人们的思想！过去和未来都是好的，现在的一切却为他们所憎恶。

——《亨利四世》(下篇)

PATIENCE 忍耐

How poor are they that have not patience!
What wound did ever heal but by degrees? *Othello*

没有耐性的人是多么可怜！什么伤口不是慢慢地平复起来的？ ——《奥瑟罗》

PEACE 和平

A peace is of the nature of a conquest,
For then both parties nobly are subdued,
And neither party loser. *Henry IV*, Part 2

和平本身就是一种胜利，因为双方都是光荣的屈服者，可是谁也不曾失败。

——《亨利四世》(下篇)

Bring me into your city,
And I will use the olive with my sword
Make war breed peace; make peace stint war; make each
Prescribe to other as each other's leech. *Timon of Athens*

带我到你们的城里去；我要一手执着橄榄枝，一手握着宝剑，使战争孕育和平，使和平酝酿战争，这样才可以安不忘危。 ——《雅典的泰门》

I know myself now, and I feel within me
A peace above all earthly dignities,
A still and quiet conscience. *Henry VII*

我现在了解我自己了，我感到在我内心里有一种平静，远非人间一切尊荣所能比拟，是一种宁静安详的感觉。 ——《亨利八世》

PENITENCE 忏悔

Who by repentance is not satisfied
Is nor of heaven nor earth, for these are pleased.
By penitence the Eternal's wrath's appeased. *The Two Gentlemen of Verona*

能够忏悔的人，无论天上人间都可以不咎既往。上帝的愤怒也会因为忏悔而平息的。

——《维洛那二绅士》

PLAYERS 戏子

All the world's a stage,
And all the men and women merely players.
They have their exits and their entrances,
And one man in his time plays many parts,
His acts being seven ages. *As You Like It*

全世界是一个舞台，所有的男男女女不过是一些演员；他们都有下场的时候，也都有上场的时候。一个人的一生中扮演着好几个角色，他的表演可以分为七个时期。 ——《皆大欢喜》

O! There be players that I have seen play and heard others praise and that highly, not to speak it profanely, that neither having the accent of Christians, nor the gait of Christian, pagan, nor man, have so strutted and bellowed that I have thought some of nature's journeymen had made men, and not made them well, they imitated humanity so abominably. *Hamlet*

啊！我曾经看见有几个伶人演戏，而且也听见有人把他们极口捧场，说一句比喻不伦的话，他们既不会说基督徒的语言，又不会学着基督徒、异教徒或者一般人的样子走路，瞧他们在台上大摇大摆、使劲叫喊的样子，我心里就想一定是什么造化的雇工把他们造了下来；造得这样拙劣，以至于全然失去了人类的面目。——《哈姆莱特》

POMP 浮华

Why, what is pomp, rule, reign, but earth and dust?
And, live we how we can, yet die we must. *Henry VI*, Part 3

唉，什么气派、权势、威风，都算得什么？不过是一抔黄土罢了！不管你活得多么好，你总逃不了死亡。——《亨利六世》(下篇)

PRECEPT AND PRACTICE 说教与实践

If to do were as easy as to know what were good to do, chapels had been churches, and poor men's cottages princes' palaces. It is a good divine that follows his own instructions. I can easier teach twenty what were good to be done than be one of the twenty to follow mine own teaching. The brain may devise laws for the blood, but a hot temper leaps o'er a cold decree. Such a hare is madness the youth—to skip o'er the meshes of good counsel the cripple. *The Merchant of Venice*

倘使做一件事情就跟知道应该做什么事情一样容易，那么小教堂都要变成大礼拜堂，穷人的草屋都要变成王侯的宫殿了。一个好的说教师才会遵从他自己的训诲；我可以教训二十个人，吩咐他们应该做些什么事，可是要我做这二十个人中间的一个，履行我自己的教训，我就要敬谢不敏了。理智可以制定法律来约束感情，可是热情激动起来，就会把冷酷的法令蔑弃不顾；年轻人是一头不受拘束的野兔，会跳过老年人所设立的理智的藩篱。——《威尼斯商人》

PRINCES AND TITLES 贵族与头衔

Princes have but their titles for their glories,
An outward honor for an inward toil,
And, for unfelt imaginations,
They often feel a world of restless cares
So that between their titles and low name,
There's nothing differs but the outward fame. *Richard III*

王公贵人无非把称号头衔当作尊荣，以浮面的声誉换取满心的苦恼；为了虚无缥缈的感受他们往往亲尝无限烦愁：原来在他们的尊号和一些贱名之间，只涌现着浮华虚荣，哪有找得出一条明白的分界线。——《理查三世》

QUARRELS 争吵

In a false quarrel these is no true valor. *Much Ado About Nothing*

强弱异势，胜了也没有光彩。 ——《无事生非》

Thrice is he armed that hath his quarrel just,
And he but naked, though lock'd up in steel,
Whose conscience with injustice is corrupted. *Henry VI*, Part 2

他理直气壮，好比是披着三重盔甲；而那种理不直、气不壮、丧失天良的人，即便穿上钢盔钢甲，也如同赤身裸体一般。 ——《亨利六世》(中篇)

RAGE 愤怒

Men in rage strike those that wish them best. *Othello*

一个人在愤怒之中，就是好朋友也会翻脸不认。 ——《奥瑟罗》

REPENTANCE 追悔

Men shall deal unadvisedly sometimes,
Which after hours give leisure to repent. *Richard III*

人们往往做事不加考虑，事后却有闲空去思索追悔。 ——《理查三世》

REPUTATION 声誉

The purest treasure mortal times afford
Is spotless reputation; that away,
Men are but gilded loam, or painted clay.
A jewel in a ten-times barr'd-up chest
Is a bold spirit in a loyal breast. *Richard II*

无瑕的名誉是世间最纯粹的珍宝；失去了名誉，人类不过是一些镀金的粪土，染色的泥块。忠贞的胸膛里一颗勇敢的心灵，就像藏在十重键锁的箱中的珠玉。 ——《理查二世》

RETRIBUTION 报应

The gods are just, and of our pleasant vices
Make instruments to scourge us. *King Lear*

公正的天神使我们的风流罪过成为惩罚我们的工具。 ——《李尔王》

Now, if these men have defeated the law and outrun native punishment, though they can outstrip men, they have no wings to fly from God. *Henry V*

现在，这班人逃脱了法网，躲过了罪有应得的惩罚——虽然人们是给他瞒过了，他却插翅难逃过上帝的手心！ ——《亨利五世》

SCARS 伤疤

A sear nobly got, or a noble scar, is a good livery of honor. *All's Well That Ends Well*

光荣的疤痕是最好的装饰。 ——《终成眷属》

O, sir, to such as boasting show their scars,
A mock is due. *Troilus and Cressida*

啊,将军!我真像一个向人夸示他的伤疤的人一样,反而遭到您的讥笑了。
——《特洛伊罗斯与克瑞西达》

SELF-CONQUEST 自我征服

Better conquest never canst thou make
Than arm thy constant and thy nobler parts
Against those giddy loose suggestions. *King John*

你应该秉持你忠贞正大的精神,征服那些轻率谬妄的诱惑。 ——《约翰王》

SELF-EXERTION 自强不息

Men at some time are masters of their fates.
The fault, dear Brutus, is not in our stars
But in ourselves that we are underlings. *Julius Caesar*

人们有时可以支配他们自己的命运;要是我们受制于人,亲爱的勃鲁托斯,那错处并不在我们的命运,而在我们自己。 ——《裘力斯·凯撒》

SELF-RELIANCE 自力更生

Our remedies oft in ourselves do lie,
Which we ascribe to heaven. The fated sky
Gives us free scope; only doth backward pull
Our slow designs when we ourselves are dull. *All's Well That Ends Well*

一切办法都在我们自己,虽然我们把它诿之天意;注定人类命运的上天,给我们自由发展的机会,只有当我们自己冥顽不灵、不能利用这种机会的时候,我们的计划才会遭遇挫折。
——《终成眷属》

SILENCE 沉默

Out of this silence yet I picked a welcome,
And in the modesty of fearful duty
I read as much as from the rattling tongue
Of saucy and audacious eloquence. *A Midsummer Night's Dream*

从这种无言中我却领受了他们一片欢迎的诚意;在诚惶诚恐的忠诚的畏怯上表示出来的意味,并不少于一条娓娓动听的辩舌和无所忌惮的口才。 ——《仲夏夜之梦》

The silence often of pure innocence
Persuades, when speaking fails. *The Winter's Tale*

无言的纯洁的天真,往往比说话更能打动人心。 ——《冬天的故事》

Silence is the perfectest herald of joy:

I were but little happy, if I could say how much. *Much Ado About Nothing*

静默是表示快乐的最好方法，要是我能够说出我的心里多么快乐，那么我的快乐只是有限度的。

——《无事生非》

SLANDER 谣言

No, 'tis slander,
Whose edge is sharper than the sword, whose tongue
Outvenoms all the worms of Nile, whose breath
Rides on the posting winds and doth belie
All corners of the world: kings, queens, and states,
Maids, matrons, nay, the secrets of the grave,
This viperous slander enters. *Cymbeline*

不，那是谣言，它的锋刃比刀剑更锐利，它的长舌比尼罗河中所有的毒蛇更毒，它的呼吸驾着疾风，向世界的每一个角落散播它的恶意的诽谤；宫廷之内、政府之中、少女和妇人的心头，以至于幽暗的坟墓，都是这恶毒的谣言伸展它的势力的所在。 ——《辛白林》

SLEEP 睡眠

The innocent sleep,
Sleep that knits up the raveled sleave of care,
The death of each day's life, sore labor's bath,
Balm of hurt minds, great nature's second course,
Chief nourisher in life's feast. *Macbeth*

那清白的睡眠，把忧虑的乱丝编织起来的睡眠，那日常的死亡，疲劳者的沐浴，受伤的心灵的油膏，大自然的最丰盛的菜肴，生命的盛筵上主要的营养。 ——《麦克白》

SUICIDE 自杀

Against self-slaughter
There is a prohibition so divine
That cravens my weak hand. *Cymbeline*

我的软弱的手没有自杀的勇气，因为那是神圣的教条所禁止的。 ——《辛白林》

TEMPERANCE 节制

Though I look old, yet I am strong and lusty,
For in my youth I never did apply
Hot and rebellious liquors in my blood,
Nor did not with unbashful forehead woo
The means of weakness and debility.
Therefore my age is as a lusty winter,
Frosty, but kindly. *As You Like It*

我虽然瞧上去这么老,可是我的气力还不错;因为我在年轻时候从不曾灌下过一滴猛烈的酒,也不曾鲁莽地贪欲伤身,所以我的老年好比生气勃勃的冬天,虽然结着严霜,却并不惨淡。

——《皆大欢喜》

THEORY AND PRACTICE 理论与实践

For there was never yet philosopher
That could endure the toothache patiently,
However they have writ the style of the gods,
And made a push at chance and sufferance. *Much Ado About Nothing*

就是那些写惯洋洋洒洒的大文的哲学家们,尽管他们像天上的神明一样,蔑视着人生的灾难痛苦,一旦他们的牙齿痛起来,也是会忍受不住的。 ——《无事生非》

TREACHERY 背叛

Though those that are betray'd
Do feel the treason sharply, yet the traitor
Stands in worse case of woe. *Cymbeline*

虽然受欺者的心中感到深刻的剧痛,可是欺诈的人也逃不了更痛苦的良心的谴责。

——《辛白林》

VALOR 英勇

The better part of valor is discretion. *Henry IV*, Part 1

智虑是勇敢的最大要素。 ——《亨利四世》(上篇)

When valor preys on reason,
It eats the sword it fights with. *Antony and Cleopatra*

有勇无谋,结果一定失败。 ——《安东尼与克莉奥佩特拉》

What valor were it, when a cur doth grin,
For one to thrust his band between his teeth,
When he might spurn him with his foot away? *Henry VI*, Part 3

如果看到恶狗龇牙,就把手伸到它的嘴里,那算得什么勇敢行为?只需举起脚来把它踢开就完了。 ——《亨利六世》(下篇)

WAR 战争

How you awake our sleeping sword of war.
We charge you in the name of God, take heed. *Henry IV*

你这是要惊起那睡着的干戈。我凭着上帝的名义,命令你郑重考虑。 ——《亨利五世》

Welcome ever smiles,
And farewell goes out sighing. *Troilus and Cressida*

欢迎是永远含笑的，告别总是带着叹息。 ——《特洛伊罗斯与克瑞西达》

WORDS 言语

Words without thoughts never to heaven go. *Hamlet*

没有思想的言语永远不会上升天界。 ——《哈姆莱特》

Few words shall fit the trespass best,
Where no excuse can give the fault amending. *The Rape of Lucrece*

没有什么言语，能形容这种罪恶，也没有任何辩白，能矫饰这桩过错。 ——《鲁克丽丝受辱记》

WORLDLY CARE 世俗的思虑

You have too much respect upon the world;
They lose it that do buy it with much care. *The Merchant of Venice*

您把世间的事情看得太认真了；一个人思虑太多，就会失却做人的乐趣。 ——《威尼斯商人》

WORLDLY HONORS 世俗的尊荣

And not a man, for being simply man,
Hath any honor, but honor for those honors
That are without him, as place, riches, favor,
Prizes of accident as oft as merit:
Which when they fall, as being slippery standers,
The love that lean'd on them as slippery too,
Do one pluck down another and together
Die in the fall. But 'tis not so with me. *Troilus and Cressida*

在他们的俗眼之中，只有富贵尊荣，这一些不一定用才能去博得的身外浮华，才是值得敬重的；当这些不足恃的浮华化为乌有的时候，人们的敬意也就会烟消云散。可是我还没有到这样的地步。 ——《特洛伊罗斯与克瑞西达》

莎士比亚典故(节选)

词句典故

英文	中文	出处
A cat has nine lives.	猫有九命;生命力极强的人	《罗密欧与朱丽叶》
a fool's paradise	黄粱美梦	《罗密欧与朱丽叶》
a laughing stock	笑柄	《温莎的风流娘儿们》
A little pot is soon hot.	小壶易热;小人易怒	《驯悍记》
a man of salt	易于哭泣的人;以泪洗面的人	《李尔王》
a man of wax	蜡人;完美无缺的人;模范人物	《罗密欧与朱丽叶》
a night owl	夜猫子	《鲁克丽丝受辱记》
a pin's fee	一枚针;一文不值;毫无用处	《哈姆莱特》
a pound of flesh	一磅肉;分文不能缺少的债务;合法但不合理的要求;阎王债	《威尼斯商人》
A rose by any other name would smell as sweet.	玫瑰换名也一样芳香;在实不在名	《罗密欧与朱丽叶》
a sorry sight	令人遗憾的一幕;惨不忍睹	《麦克白》
a tower of strength	中流砥柱	《理查三世》
a wild goose chase	白费心机	《罗密欧与朱丽叶》
a word and a blow	一句话不对头就动手;一言不合就拔刀相向;说干就干;翻脸无情	《罗密欧与朱丽叶》
all corners of the world	世界的每个角落;世界各地	《辛白林》
All that glisters is not gold.	发亮的东西不一定都是金子	《威尼斯商人》
All the world's a stage.	全世界是一个大舞台;人生如戏	《皆大欢喜》
All's well that ends well.	凡事结局好则全部都好;终成眷属	《终成眷属》
applaud to the echo	热烈鼓掌;高声喝彩	《麦克白》
as dead as a doornail	死了;死透了;彻底死了;确信无疑地死了	《亨利六世》(中篇)
as full of...as an egg is of meat	充满……;尽是……	《罗密欧与朱丽叶》
as good as one's word	说话算数;说到做到;一诺千金	《第十二夜》
As good luck would have it.	你们三生有幸	《温莎的风流娘儿们》
as like as eggs	完全一样;毫无区别	《冬天的故事》

（续表）

英文	中文	出处
as merry as the day is long	非常愉快；一天到晚非常快乐	《无事生非》
bag and baggage	一个人的所有财产、拥有物；全部财物	《皆大欢喜》
be all eyes	注视；目不转睛	《暴风雨》
be meat and drink to sb.	最好的享受；无上的乐趣；最喜欢的东西；快乐之源	《皆大欢喜》
be out of one's guard	没提防；疏忽大意	《第十二夜》
bite one's thumb at sb.	对……表示侮辱或蔑视；向……挑战	《罗密欧与朱丽叶》
break the ice	破冰；打破僵局；打破冷场	《驯悍记》
Brevity is the soul of wit.	言以简为贵；简洁是智慧的灵魂	《哈姆莱特》
bring to light	揭示；揭露；暴露	《一报还一报》
cakes and ale	蛋糕和麦芽酒；吃喝玩乐；人生乐事	《第十二夜》
Care kills a cat.	忧虑伤身；忧愁致命	《无事生非》
catch sb. upon the hip	抓住要害；制服某人；压倒某人	《威尼斯商人》
caviar to the general	阳春白雪；曲高和寡；过于高雅的事物	《哈姆莱特》
cold comfort	不起作用的安慰；于事无补	《驯悍记》《约翰王》
comb sb's noddle	给某人梳头；打；揍	《驯悍记》
Come what come may.	让任何可能会发生的事情发生吧	《麦克白》
crocodile tears	鳄鱼的眼泪；假慈悲；伪善	《奥瑟罗》
cudgel one's brains	绞尽脑汁；苦思冥想；伤脑筋	《哈姆莱特》
die in harness	在工作中死去；殉职	《麦克白》
enough to make a cat speak	连猫都会讲起话来；离奇得令人惊讶；(尤指酒)好得令人叫绝	《暴风雨》
enough to make the angels weep	即使是天使也要伤心；令人伤心；令人失望	《一报还一报》
Et tu, Brute?	吾儿，亦有汝焉？	《裘力斯・凯撒》
Every why has a wherefore.	有理由必有原因；凡事皆有因	《错误的喜剧》

（续表）

英文	中文	出处
fair play	公平的竞争	《暴风雨》
fancy-free	没有束缚的；情窦未开的；情无所钟的；任凭想象随意驰骋的	《仲夏夜之梦》
fetch and carry	打杂；跑腿	《维洛那二绅士》
find quarrel in a straw	找碴；吹毛求疵	《哈姆莱特》
for goodness' sake	行行好吧	《亨利八世》
for vain	徒劳；徒然	《一报还一报》
forever and a day	比永远还多一天；永永远远；直到永远	《皆大欢喜》
gain the cap	受人尊敬	《辛白林》
give a taste of one's quality	显示某人的本领（或才能等）	《哈姆莱特》
give an edge to	刺激；加剧；鼓舞	《哈姆莱特》
give no words but mum	保守秘密；什么都不要说；不要告诉任何人	《亨利六世》（中篇）
give pause to	使……踌躇；使……停顿	《哈姆莱特》
give tongue	（犬）吠；开口；说话；大声说出；明确表示	《哈姆莱特》
golden opinions	高度的评价；无上的美誉	《麦克白》
Good riddance.	终于解脱；终于摆脱了（包袱）	《特洛伊罗斯与克瑞西达》
green-eyed monster	绿眼怪；绿眼妖魔；妒忌；嫉妒；羡慕嫉妒恨	《奥瑟罗》
hairbreadth escape	九死一生；死里逃生；幸免于难	《奥瑟罗》
have a heart of gold	拥有一颗金子般的心；心地非常善良	《亨利五世》
head and front	本质；要点	《奥瑟罗》
heart's content	尽情；心满意足	《威尼斯商人》
high time	该做某事的时间；是……的时候了；正是时候；快乐时光	《错误的喜剧》
I bear a charmed life.	我有护身符；我是有魔法保护的；我有刀枪不入的能耐	《麦克白》

（续表）

英文	中文	出处
I must be cruel, only to be kind.	要想善良，必先残忍；我的残酷是为了你好；忠言逆耳利于行	《哈姆莱特》
I'll send him packing.	让他收拾东西走人	《亨利四世》(上篇)
If music be the food of love, play on.	若音乐是爱情的美食，请继续演奏下去	《第十二夜》
if truth were known	真相大白	《冬天的故事》
in a pickle	处境困难；处境窘迫	《暴风雨》
infinite variety	千姿百态	《安东尼与克莉奥佩特拉》
in one fell swoop	突然间；一下子	《麦克白》
in one's heart of hearts	在心灵深处；秘密地	《哈姆莱特》
in the dumps	神情沮丧；郁郁寡欢	《驯悍记》
in the twinkling of an eye	立刻；一下子；转眼之间	《威尼斯商人》
It's Greek to me.	一窍不通；完全不懂；完全无法理解	《裘力斯·凯撒》
kill sb. with kindness	把某人宠坏；好得让人受不了	《驯悍记》
know one's distance	知分寸；守本分；避免过度亲近	《终成眷属》
lie in one's throat	胡扯；胡说八道；撒弥天大谎	《第十二夜》
lie low	潜伏；韬晦	《裘力斯·凯撒》
lily-livered	胆小如鼠	《麦克白》
look for a needle in a bottle of hay	在草堆里找针；大海捞针；做徒劳无益之事	《仲夏夜之梦》
Love is blind.	爱情是盲目的	《威尼斯商人》
make assurance double sure	慎之又慎；加倍小心	《麦克白》
make night hideous	使黑夜变得恐怖；夜里吵得令人无法入睡	《哈姆莱特》
make one's hair stand on end	使某人毛骨悚然；使某人极度震惊	《哈姆莱特》
man and boy	从少年时代起；一辈子；从小到大	《哈姆莱特》
measure swords	(决斗前)比量剑长；决斗；较量	《皆大欢喜》
midsummer madness	仲夏疯；愚蠢或极端的行为；十足的疯狂	《第十二夜》

（续表）

英文	中文	出处
mooncalf	妖怪；白痴	《暴风雨》
needs must when the devil drives	形势所迫，只好如此；人在屋檐下，不得不低头	《终成眷属》
not budge an inch	一动也不动；一点也不愿妥协；毫不改变主意	《驯悍记》
observed of all observers	被大家注视的人；众人瞩目的中心	《哈姆莱特》
Off with his head.	砍掉他的头	《理查三世》
on the rack	受酷刑；（身心）受到极大折磨；极度焦虑不安	《威尼斯商人》
out of joint	脱节；乱套；不正常	《哈姆莱特》
out of the jaws of death	脱离危险	《第十二夜》
paint the lily	给百合花涂上色彩；画蛇添足；多此一举	《约翰王》
patience on a monument	碑上刻着的忍耐；极有耐心	《第十二夜》
pigeon-livered	鸽子般温和的；温顺的；胆怯的	《哈姆莱特》
pride of place	头等重要的地位；高位；傲慢；最高荣誉	《麦克白》
pure as the driven snow	纯洁无瑕	《冬天的故事》
put out one's light	熄灭某人的生命火花；杀死某人；送某人上西天	《奥瑟罗》
put the finger in one's eye	哭泣；掩面而泣	《错误的喜剧》
salad days	少不更事	《安东尼与克莉奥佩特拉》
sea change	巨变；彻底转变	《暴风雨》
set one's eyes at flow	痛哭流涕	《雅典的泰门》
set one's heart at rest (ease)	使某人放心	《仲夏夜之梦》
shift one's ground	换地方；改变立场；改变主意	《哈姆莱特》
set one's teeth on edge	使人牙根发酸；使感到不舒服	《亨利四世》（上篇）
shuffle off this mortal coil	摆脱人间的纷扰；离开尘世；斩断尘缘；死亡	《哈姆莱特》
Smooth waters run deep.	静水流深；沉默者深谋；真人不露相	《亨利六世》（中篇）

（续表）

英文	中文	出处
speak by the card	说话精确；措辞严密	《哈姆莱特》
spotless reputation	清白的名声	《理查二世》
stand on ceremony	客气；客套	《麦克白》
star-crossed lovers	不幸的恋人	《罗密欧与朱丽叶》
stick in one's throat	难以启齿，说不出口；难以接受，无法接受	《麦克白》
strange bedfellows	同床异梦的人	《暴风雨》
Such stuff as dreams are made.	人生如梦	《暴风雨》
suit the action to the word	言行一致；说到做到	《哈姆莱特》
take eggs for money	使自己上当；让自己受骗	《冬天的故事》
the be-all and end-all	一切的一切；根本	《麦克白》
The course of true love never did run smooth.	真爱无坦途	《仲夏夜之梦》
the melting mood	感伤的心情；温柔同情之心	《奥瑟罗》
the milk of human kindness	人的善良天性；对别人的同情、关心；恻隐之心	《麦克白》
the pricking of one's thumbs	拇指跳动；凶兆；预感；直觉	《麦克白》
The quality of mercy is not strained.	慈悲并非出于勉强	《威尼斯商人》
the Queen's English	标准英语	《温莎的风流娘儿们》
the world's end	世界尽头；天涯海角	《无事生非》
The world is my oyster.	世界是我的牡蛎；世界掌握在我手中；我随心所欲得心应手	《温莎的风流娘儿们》
There's the rub.	这就是困难所在；问题就在这里	《哈姆莱特》
the long and (the) short of it	总而言之；总的情况	《温莎的风流娘儿们》
Though this be madness, yet there is method in 't.	看似疯狂，实则有因	《哈姆莱特》
to be or not to be	生存还是毁灭	《哈姆莱特》
to one's account	面对上帝的审判；死亡	《哈姆莱特》
to the top of one's bent	尽情地；尽量地；尽最大努力地	《哈姆莱特》

（续表）

英文	中文	出处
too much of a good thing	好事过头反成坏事；好事不宜做得过火；过火举动；过分的事	《皆大欢喜》
Too swift arrives as tardy as too slow.	太快和太慢，结果都不会美满	《罗密欧与朱丽叶》
trip up one's heels	绊倒某人；把某人打翻在地；使某人计划落空	《皆大欢喜》
true penny	诚实的人；信得过的人	《哈姆莱特》
Truth will out.	真相始终会大白	《威尼斯商人》
vanish into air/melt into thin air	不知去向；消失得无影无踪	《奥瑟罗》《暴风雨》
venture all in one bottom	把成败寄托在一艘船上；孤注一掷	《威尼斯商人》
We have seen better days.	我们曾经历过好日子；今非昔比	《雅典的泰门》
wear one's heart upon one's sleeve	十分坦率；公开表露感情；把心事挂在脸上	《奥瑟罗》
What's done is done.	无可挽回的；木已成舟	《麦克白》
What's in a name?	名字有什么要紧？/名称有什么关系？	《罗密欧与朱丽叶》
Wherefore art thou Romeo?	为什么你是罗密欧？	《罗密欧与朱丽叶》
white as snow	纯白的；洁白的	《哈姆莱特》
white-livered	肝呈白色的；怯懦的；胆小的	《威尼斯商人》
Woe is me!	我好苦啊；哀哉	《哈姆莱特》

人物典故

英文	中文	出处
Alonso	阿隆佐；贪婪；贪得无厌	《暴风雨》
Cordelia	考狄利娅；诚实坦率的人	《李尔王》
Hamlet	哈姆莱特；优柔寡断的人	《哈姆莱特》
Iago	伊阿古；恶棍	《奥瑟罗》
Puck	迫克；爱恶作剧的妖怪	《仲夏夜之梦》
Romeo	罗密欧；热恋中的风流男子；任何男性情人；情夫	《罗密欧与朱丽叶》
Shylock	夏洛克；冷酷无情的高利贷者	《威尼斯商人》

莎士比亚词汇(节选)

英文	中文	出处
abstemious *adj*.	饮食有度的;有节制的	《暴风雨》
accused *adj*.	被告的	《理查二世》
addiction *n*.	倾向;喜好;嗜好	《奥瑟罗》
advertising *adj*. (= attentive)	专注的;注意的	《一报还一报》
aerial *adj*.	空中的;空气中的	《奥瑟罗》
alligator *n*.	短吻鳄	《罗密欧与朱丽叶》
amazement *n*.	惊奇;惊愕;惊诧;不知所措	《约翰王》
amazing *adj*. (=astounding)	令人惊异的	《理查二世》
assassination *n*.	暗杀;行刺	《麦克白》
backing *n*.	支持;援助	《亨利四世》(上篇)
baseless *adj*.	无根据的;无缘无故的	《暴风雨》
beached *adj*.	沙滩的	《仲夏夜之梦》
bedazzle *v*. (= to dazzle so as to blind or confuse)	使目眩;使困惑	《驯悍记》
beetle *v*. (beetle-brows: prominent brows)	突出;伸出	《哈姆莱特》
belly-pinched *adj*.	挨饿的;紧缩身子的	《李尔王》
besmirch *v*.	弄脏;诋毁	《哈姆莱特》
bet *v*.	下赌注;打赌	《亨利四世》(下篇)
blanket *v*.	覆盖;用毯子或类似毯子的东西掩盖	《李尔王》
buzzer *n*.	发出嗡嗡声的东西;传播谣言的人;蜂鸣器	《哈姆莱特》
cake *v*.	变硬;变实;形成硬壳	《雅典的泰门》
cater *v*.	提供食物;提供必需品	《皆大欢喜》
champion *v*.	挑战;公然不顾;拥护;支持;捍卫	《麦克白》

（续表）

英文	中文	出处
co-mart *n*.（= joint bargains; covenant; compact made together）	联合交易；协议；协定	《哈姆莱特》
co-mate *n*.	同伴；伴侣	《皆大欢喜》
cold-blooded *adj*.	冷酷的；残酷的；无情的；冷血的	《约翰王》
compromise *v*.	相互承诺；达成一致；妥协	《威尼斯商人》
courtship *n*.	奉承；讨好；献殷勤；追求	《爱的徒劳》
cow *v*.	威吓；恐吓；吓唬；胁迫；威胁	《麦克白》
credent *adj*.	信任的；容易相信的；轻信的	《一报还一报》《冬天的故事》《哈姆莱特》
dauntless *adj*.	无所畏惧的；吓不倒的；勇敢的	《麦克白》
dawn *n*.	黎明；破晓	《一报还一报》
deafening *adj*.	震耳欲聋的；极喧闹的	《泰尔亲王配力克里斯》
denote *v*.	标志；预示；象征；表示；意指	《奥瑟罗》
design *n*.	规划；设计；目的	《爱的徒劳》
discontent *n*.	不满意；不满足；不满；不悦	《理查三世》
disgraceful *adj*.	不光彩的；可耻的；丢脸的	《亨利六世》(上篇)
dislocate *v*.	使移位；使脱臼	《李尔王》
divest *v*.	使(某人)脱去(衣服)；剥夺	《李尔王》
downstairs *adv*.	楼下；在楼下	《亨利四世》(上篇)
droplet *n*.	小滴；微滴	《雅典的泰门》
drug *v*.	在(食物或饮料中)投放麻醉药；下麻醉药	《麦克白》
dwindle *v*.	(逐渐)减少；变小；缩小	《麦克白》
elbow *v*.	用肘推；用肘挤	《李尔王》
embrace *n*.	拥抱；怀抱	《罗密欧与朱丽叶》
employer *n*.	雇用者；使用者	《无事生非》
engagement *n*.	安排；约定；婚约	《裘力斯·凯撒》
enmesh *v*.	缠住；使陷入(困境等)	《奥瑟罗》

（续表）

英文	中文	出处
equivocal *adj*.	模棱两可的；意义双关的；含糊其辞的；难以理解的；难以解释清楚的	《奥瑟罗》
eventful *adj*.	充满大事的；重大的；有重要意义的	《皆大欢喜》
excitement *n*.	激动；兴奋；刺激；令人激动（或兴奋）的事	《哈姆莱特》
exposure *n*.	暴露	《麦克白》
eyeball *n*.	眼球；眼珠	《暴风雨》
faint-hearted *adj*.	懦弱的；胆怯的；畏怯的	《亨利六世》（上篇）
fashionable *adj*.	流行的；时兴的；时髦的	《雅典的泰门》
film *v*.	在表面覆以薄膜	《哈姆莱特》
fishify *v*.	鱼化；变成鱼	《罗密欧与朱丽叶》
flawed *adj*.	有错误的；有缺点的；有瑕疵的	《李尔王》
force *v*.（=reinforce; provide with forces）	加强；充实；提供力量	《麦克白》
fortune-teller *n*.	先知；预言家；给人算命的人；算命先生	《错误的喜剧》
friended *adj*.（= befriended）	做朋友的；成为朋友的；友善对待的	《一报还一报》
friending *n*.（=friendly feeling）	情谊；友谊感；恩情；友好的感觉	《哈姆莱特》
full-grown *adj*.	长成的；成熟的	《泰尔亲王配力克里斯》
futurity *n*.	将来；未来	《奥瑟罗》
generous *adj*.	出身高贵的；出身名门的；慷慨大方的；宽宏大量的	《爱的徒劳》
gloomy *adj*.	黑暗的；阴暗的；幽暗的；忧郁的	《亨利六世》（上篇）
glow *n*.	满面红光；红色；暗淡的光	《皆大欢喜》
gnarled *adj*.	扭曲的；疙疙瘩瘩的	《一报还一报》
go-between *n*.	调解者；中间人	《温莎的风流娘儿们》

（续表）

英文	中文	出处
gossip *v*.	闲聊；说三道四；说长道短；传播流言蜚语	《仲夏夜之梦》
green-eyed *adj*.	绿(碧)眼的；嫉妒的；不信任的	《奥瑟罗》
gust *n*.	一阵强风；(感情的)迸发	《泰特斯·安德洛尼克斯》
heartburning *adj*.	嫉妒的；不满的	《爱的徒劳》
hint *n*.	时机；机会；暗示；提示	《奥瑟罗》
hurry *v*.	赶快；匆忙；急忙；迅速移动；催促	《错误的喜剧》
hush *adj*.	安静的；肃静的；不对外泄密的	《哈姆莱特》
impede *v*.	阻碍；阻止	《麦克白》
inaudible *adj*.	听不见的	《终成眷属》
instinctively *adv*.	本能地；凭直觉；自然而然地；不由自主地	《暴风雨》
investment *n*.	衣物；捐赠的钱物；以金钱回报为目的的货币支出；投资(物)	《哈姆莱特》
invulnerable *adj*.	不会受伤害的；打不败的；安全的	《哈姆莱特》
juiced *adj*.	有汁的	《罗密欧与朱丽叶》
kissing *adj*.	接吻的；亲密的	《仲夏夜之梦》
label *v*.	贴标签于；用标签标明	《第十二夜》
lackluster *adj*.	无光泽的；无生气的	《皆大欢喜》
land-damn *v*.	处死；埋葬	《冬天的故事》
lapse *v*. (= catch or cease; slip or fall into error)	抓住或终止；失误；衰退	《第十二夜》
laughable *adj*. (= funny; humorous; ridiculous)	有趣的；滑稽的；荒唐可笑的；荒谬的	《威尼斯商人》
manager *n*.	管家；管理者；经理	《仲夏夜之梦》
misgiving *n*. (= doubt; apprehension)	疑虑；担忧；害怕	《裘力斯·凯撒》
mistempered *adj*.	脾气暴躁的；错误锻造的；不良的	《罗密欧与朱丽叶》
negotiate *v*.	磋商；商议；谈判	《无事生非》

（续表）

英文	中文	出处
nervy *adj*. (= sinewy or strong; courageous; nervous)	健壮有力的；有胆量的；紧张的	《科利奥兰纳斯》
never-ending *adj*.	无止境的；无限的	《鲁克丽丝受辱记》
pageantry *n*.	盛典；壮观；华丽；炫耀；虚饰	《泰尔亲王配力克里斯》
plantage *n*. (= vegetation; all that is planted)	草木；种植物	《特洛伊罗斯与克瑞西达》
primy *adj*. (= spring-timed; early-blooming)	初春的；早开的	《哈姆莱特》
proud *n*./*v*.	荣耀；炫耀	《罗密欧与朱丽叶》
relume *v*. (= relight; light again)	再点亮；再点燃	《奥瑟罗》
rubious *adj*. (= ruddy; ruby red)	红润的	《第十二夜》
skim milk	脱脂牛奶	《亨利四世》(上篇)
smilet *n*. (= attempted smile; half smile)	小小的微笑	《李尔王》
suppliance *n*. (= that which is supplied)	提供(物)；供给	《哈姆莱特》
supplyment *n*. (= continued supply)	持续的供给	《辛白林》
uncomfortable *adj*.	不舒服的；不自在的	《罗密欧与朱丽叶》
well-bred *adj*. (=well brought up; properly trained and educated)	有教养的	《亨利四世》(下篇)

古今英语对照

古体词和现代词拼写对照

中古英语		现代英语	用　法
thou	[ðaʊ]	you	第二人称单数的主格"你,汝,尔"
thee	[ðiː]	you	第二人称单数的宾格"你,汝,尔"
thy	[ðaɪ]	your	第二人称单数所有格"你的"
thine	[ðaɪn]	yours	第二人称单数物主代词"你的……"第二人称单数所有格用于元音或 h 前"你的"
art	[ɑːt]	are	be 的第二人称单数现在式
wast	[wɒst, wəst]	were	be 的第二人称单数过去式
doth	[dʌθ]	does	do 的第三人称单数现在式
dost	[dʌst]	do	do 的第二人称单数现在式
hath	[hæθ]	has	have 的第三人称单数现在式
hast	[hæst]	have	have 的第二人称单数现在式
hadst	[hædst]	had	have 的第二人称单数过去式
canst	[kænst]	can	can 的第二人称单数现在式
durst	[dɜːst]	dared	dare 的过去式及过去分词
wilt	[wɪlt]	will	will 的第二人称单数现在式
seemeth	[siːmθ]	seems	seem 的第三人称单数现在式
whatsoever	[ˌwɒtsəʊˈevə(r)]	whatever	"无论什么"
whichsoever	[ˌwɪtʃsəʊˈevə(r)]	whichever	"无论哪个"
howsoever	[ˌhaʊsəʊˈevə(r)]	however	"无论如何"
hither	[ˈhɪðə(r)]	here; to this place	"到此处,向此地"
thither	[ˈðɪðə(r)]	there; to that place	"到那里,向那里"
whither	[ˈwɪðə(r)]	where; to which	"哪里,何处,到何处"
hence	[hens]	from this place	"从这里"
thence	[ðens]	from that place	"从那里"
whence	[wens]	from where	"从何处,从哪里"

常见词汇古今义对照

词汇	中古常用义	现代常用义
abroad	在室外;到户外	在国外;到国外
affect	喜欢;假装,佯装	影响;深深打动
become	适合	成为
brave	崭新的;华丽的	勇敢的
courtesy	行屈膝礼	礼貌
fell	= cruel 残忍的	fall 的过去式
fond	= foolish 愚蠢的	喜欢的
gay	艳丽的;快乐的	同性恋的;同性恋者
habit	衣服;长袍	习惯
hasty	易怒的	匆忙的;草率的
inmate	同住者	居住者
learn	教导(某人)	学习;得知
meet	合适的,恰当的	见面,碰头;集合,开会
naughty	邪恶的	顽皮的,淘气的
prefer	提拔	更喜爱,宁可
proper	= handsome 英俊的	适当的;正确的
queer	略感不适的	奇怪的;反常的
reverence	鞠躬	尊敬,崇敬
still	= always 一直;总是	还,依旧;仍然,还是
softly	= wait 等一等	轻轻地;轻柔地;温和地
suffer	容许,允许	受苦,受折磨;经受,遭受
want	缺乏,缺少	想要,希望;需要
without	在外面,在外部	没有,缺乏